W9-BLZ-142

NEWFOUNDLAND AREA PUBLIC LIBRARY
Newfoundland, Penna. 18445

Rebels in Blue

REBELS IN BLUE

The Story of Keith and Malinda Blalock

Peter F. Stevens

TAYLOR PUBLISHING COMPANY

DALLAS, TEXAS

Copyright © 2000 by Peter F. Stevens

All rights reserved

No part of this book may be reproduced in any form or by any means—including
photocopying and electronic reproduction—without written permission from the publisher.

Published by
Taylor Publishing Company
1550 West Mockingbird Lane
Dallas, Texas 75235

Library of Congress Cataloging-in-Publication Data

Stevens, Peter F.
    Rebels in blue: the story of Keith and Malinda Blalock / by Peter F. Stevens.
      p. cm.
    Includes bibliographical references and index.
    ISBN 0-87833-166-2
    1. Blalock, Keith, 1837–1913. 2. Blalock, Malinda, 1842–1903. 3. United
States—History—Civil War, 1861–1865—Social aspects. 4. North Carolina—
History—Civil War, 1861–1865—Social aspects. 5. Unionists (United States
Civil War)—Confederate States of America—Biography. 6 Married people—
Blue Ridge Mountains—Biography. 7. Soldiers—Blue Ridge Mountains—
Biography. 8. Blue Ridge Mountains—Biography. 9. Blalock family. 10.
Pritchard family. I. Title.

E468.9 .S88 2000
973.'092'2—dc21
[B]
                                                     99-056772

Designed by Barbara Werden

10   9   8   7   6   5   4   3   2   1

Printed in the United States of America

CONTENTS

Part Four
A Grim Cycle

Part Five
Hospitable and Highly Regarded or
The Terror of This Town

PREFACE AND ACKNOWLEDGMENTS

MY introduction to the Civil War story of William McKesson "Keith" Blalock and his wife, Malinda Pritchard Blalock, came during my research for an article about a daring and notorious Union army officer and guerrilla leader, George W. Kirk. In several accounts of Kirk's raids throughout the Blue Ridge and Great Smoky Mountains of western North Carolina and east Tennessee, there appeared references to a husband-and-wife team of Union guerrillas named Blalock. Intrigued, I began to research the North Carolina couple, whose Civil War experiences proved, I felt, nothing short of remarkable.

For starters, Keith and Malinda Blalock served the Confederacy at the conflict's start, but were feared Union raiders by its end. Their saga is how they got there—from Confederate infantrymen in the 26th North Carolina Regiment; to federal partisans at the head of their own guerrilla band; to scouts, or "pilots," guiding recruits to Union regiments in Kentucky and Tennessee and escaped Union prisoners of war to safety across the Blue Ridge Mountains; to raiders with George Kirk's mounted infantry regiments in actions throughout the mountains; and, finally, as scouts and raiders in the 10th Michigan Cavalry Regiment with Union General George Stoneman's federal riders, his "Cossacks," as they rampaged across the Blalocks' own county and much of North Carolina in the war's last campaign.

Along the couple's savage trail, Malinda Blalock became the only known woman to have borne arms for both the Confederacy and the Union. The Blalocks are the only known husband and wife to have served together on both sides—Confederate and Union.

From the war's very beginning, Keith Blalock was, in his own words, "a Lincolnite" in a region split by factions of both sides and every possible permutation between them. The full story of how Keith and Malinda Blalock began, conducted, and finished their brutal and bloody "adventure" together is a forgotten chapter in a too-long neglected Civil War theater of operations—the mountain warfare of the Blue Ridge and Great Smoky Mountains. In that region, one whose scenic splendor is breathtaking by any visual yardstick, was waged a war whose savagery unnerved even hard-boiled Union General William Tecumseh Sherman.

The mountain war was fought by men, women, and even children who were all fiercely independent, as brutal and unwavering as any Old Testament judge when it came to loyalties and feuds, and split within their own families on the issues of slavery, states' rights, secession, the Union, and every other aspect of the war itself. In the mountains, the war truly became personal—men literally looked into the eyes of kin, former friends, and lifelong enemies before pulling the trigger. Grueling treks, bloody raids, executions, depredations of every sort, narrow escapes, shoot-outs, ambushes—"bushwhacking"—inflicted and suffered —all were cruel part and parcel of the mountain war as a whole and of the Blalocks' experience from the conflict's early days to its end.

In the Blue Ridge counties of North Carolina, the Blalocks were lauded as tough-minded soldiers by unionists, as murderous bushwhackers and thieves by Confederates, and as both by mountain families who espoused neither cause and suffered at the hands of rebels and Yankees alike. Today, descendants of the Blalocks' rebel enemies still revile them as traitors to their county and to the Confederacy. Conversely, many locals who count federal soldiers and families among their ancestors view Keith and Malinda Blalock as harsh but loyal Union figures. Of the couple's devotion to each other, no dispute exists.

⁂

In researching and writing this book, I am indebted to many. I found a treasure trove of letters, documents, military-service histories, medical files, legal archives, veterans' pension files, and other firsthand material at the National Archives in Washington, D.C., during long sessions amid the institution's Civil War records. In all of this, I owe much to Michael Anderson, whose knowledge of the Civil War and the archives is truly special.

The William Eury Collection of Appalachian History at Appalachian State University in Boone, North Carolina, gave me access to letters, journals, diaries, and other material relating to the Blalocks, George W. Kirk, and the Civil War in western North Carolina. My thanks to Dean Williams.

At the extensive Southern Historical and Civil War Collections at the University of North Carolina, Chapel Hill, I took full advantage of similarly invaluable sources.

Of all the research for the book, I found my interviews and conversations with descendants of the Blalocks and several of the story's other figures the most illuminating in many ways. I easily can recall how I nearly dropped the phone when Steve Sudderth, a Blowing Rock, North Carolina, historian and author, asked me if I would like to speak with Murray Coffey, a remarkable man who, as a boy, had actually known Keith Blalock well. Steve Sudderth, incidentally, is the great, great, great-grandson of one of Keith and Malinda Blalock's sworn enemies.

My gratitude also goes out to Jessie Blalock and Paul Henley, whose great, great, great-grandfather battled the Blalocks throughout the Blue Ridge, for their generosity and their help.

For anyone researching the Civil War in the North Carolina mountains, Phillip Shaw Paludan's book *Victims: A True Story of the Civil War* is, in my opinion, an essential precursor to one's own journey to the mountain trails upon which the Blalocks and their contemporaries fought such a pitiless and, ironically given the region's majestic aspect, dirty war. John P. Arthur's *A History of Western North Carolina* and *The History of Watauga County*, the Blalocks' old home, are also invaluable, particularly because the author interviewed the Blalocks and most of their surviving wartime allies and foes extensively. Arthur's collected papers at Appalachian State provide material about the Blalocks and the war far beyond what he used in his two volumes.

This book would not have been possible without the support and the skill of my literary agent, Frank Weimann. And while I would love to take credit for the book's title, that kudo goes to Jim Hornfischer, of The Literary Group International.

Special thanks also to the project's editor, Fred Francis, for his knowledge as well as his forbearance.

As always, my deep and appreciative thanks to Peg Stevens, Karen Stevens, Valerie Doran, the Marshes—Pat, Jim, John, Patrick, Atsumi, Milt, and Joanna—and the Bidwell clan—Theresa, Mike, and the boys.

Finally, without the ongoing encouragement of Paula Stevens and Joe Axelrod, none of this would have been possible.

PART ONE

Enlist or Face the Consequences

Chapter One

A Young Giant

❧

ALONG the pine-shrouded Morganton Road, oxcarts, buckboards, and a handful of costly two-horse phaetons stretched nearly a mile east and west of the Presbyterian church in Coffey's Gap. From every corner of Watauga, Caldwell, and Mitchell Counties, members of the Blalocks, Pritchards, Coffeys, Carrolls, Moores, Boyds, and other local clans were gathering in early April 1861 for the wedding of Keith Blalock and Malinda Pritchard.

As the guests streamed up a hill and into the trim, white-planked church, the scene offered nothing unusual. April, when breezes carried the scents of mountain wildflowers and sunshine proved frequent, was traditionally a favorite time for Blue Ridge marriages.

The weather for the wedding was typical for the season, but the marriage itself was anything but common for Watauga County. Unions between the Pritchards and the Blalocks, who had fought each other for more than 150 years over mountain acreage, insults real or imagined, and politics, had proven rare.

The earliest Pritchards under Grandfather Mountain had arrived in the mid-1700s, Scottish immigrants who had fled the Jacobite Wars or had been captured in battle against the English and sent in chains to North Carolina's tobacco plantations along Albermarle Sound. Hailing from the crags of Wales to north of Inverness, several Pritchard men and women escaped from the coast and fled westward toward the Blue Ridge Mountains. With a steady stream of indentured servants and African slaves to draw upon, few plantation owners chose to pursue the handful of runaway Scots and Welsh.

Thirty-one-year-old Robert Pritchard, one of the rebels shipped to North Carolina in shackles, was one of the first recorded Pritchards in the region of Grandfather Mountain, and by 1775, several branches of the family were farming, hunting, and operating water-powered grist mills throughout the mountains and valleys of the future Watauga County. With the family's hatred of the English passed from generation to generation, Pritchards served and died in the American Revolution and the War of 1812.

Keith Blalock's ancestors had followed virtually the same route as the Pritchards to the lands beneath the Grandfather. In the border counties of

Scotland, the Blalocks had farmed and herded cattle and sheep in the hills to the northeast of the Pritchards' lands. The two families had clashed over boundaries for centuries in clan warfare, ambushes, murders, and the occasional pitched battles, the legacies that both clans carried to North Carolina. The Blalocks and Pritchards had declared tacit truces only at the chance to fight the English.

Along with the feuds that the families brought from the Old World to the Blue Ridge country, the Blalocks' and Pritchards' many branches in western North Carolina fought among themselves over everything from land deeds to local politics and—after independence from Britain—national politics, not to mention the petty squabbles typical of all families. Although not with as much frequency as in Europe, a Pritchard or a Blalock man was occasionally shot or knifed on a Watauga trail or mountain. Revenge by the aggrieved clan was a given.

During the Mexican-American War, 1846–48, which pitted slave-owning Southerners against abolitionists for control of the conquered new territories from the Rio Grande to the Pacific, North Carolinians split on the issue of slavery. In the state's eastern half, affluent coastal and riverside plantation owners espoused the expansion of slavery. But in the western mountains, where there were no plantations and relatively few slaveholders, many of the Scottish settlers' descendants, mindful that their own ancestors had arrived in the thirteen colonies in bondage, loathed slavery even though they still viewed blacks as inferior to whites. In Keith Blalock's county of Watauga, slaves numbered only 2 percent of the population. Taken as a whole, the mountain counties' collective figure of 4.5 slaves per square mile was less than half of the rest of North Carolina's 9.5 per square mile.

Still, slavery was entrenched in several mountain counties, most notably Caldwell, where slaves comprised nearly 20 percent of the population and where several Pritchards who farmed large tracts were among the locals who did own slaves. Even many Pritchards who had never bought a slave believed in their right to do so and would fight for it.

"Slave labor in the North Carolina mountains was far less crucial to the Appalachian economy than was the case in most areas of the South," asserts historian John C. Inscoe. "Yet the future of the system was as much at the forefront of the Secessionist crisis there as elsewhere. Enough Western North Carolinians, particularly those in positions of leadership and influence, had sufficient vested interests in slavery to make it a predominant consideration in the decision to leave or to remain with the Union early in 1861."[1]

Slavery's role notwithstanding, of far more importance to most Blue Ridge clans was the question over states' rights versus preservation of the Union. Believing that Southerners could govern themselves better than Yankee politicians in Washington, D.C., could, most of the Coffeys and the Pritchards vehemently endorsed secession from the Union. Yet only a few of Malinda Pritchard's male relatives, cousins from Tennessee, would fight in the rebel army.

Like the Pritchards, the Blalocks throughout the Blue Ridge counties were torn over the question of secession. As war loomed closer at the end of 1860, several of Keith Blalock's cousins crossed the mountains into Tennessee and made their way to the homes of relatives in Kentucky and Michigan. If war came, these Blalocks intended to enlist in the Union army; among them was William Blalock, Keith's first cousin. The pair had fished and hunted together since their childhood, and, as William wrote, were as close as any brothers. William had tried to convince Keith to join him on the trip north, away from the secessionist militias that would drag Watauga County for recruits. But Keith was engaged to Malinda by 1860. For the moment, his upcoming marriage and Malinda's pro-Southern beliefs ruled out any chance that he might convince her to flee to Michigan. He chose to stay in Coffey's Gap.

Keith Blalock was born on the lower slopes of Grandfather Mountain on November 21, 1837, the first of William and Mary (McKesson) Blalock's two children. Thirty-eight-year-old William Blalock, who at sixteen had run away to fight in the War of 1812, married later than most men of the region. Owner of several acres of farmland, he spent just enough hours in his fields to bring in subsistence crops and the bulk of his time in the dense woodlands flanking the mountain. He hunted deer and trapped and fished in the up-country streams. A neighbor remembered him as a man who preferred the company of his hunting dogs to people, so when he married twenty-year-old Mary McKesson, a beautiful, black-haired young woman from Caldwell County, he surprised locals.

Christened William McKesson Blalock, Keith, as he was later nicknamed, was joined by a sister in 1838. Shortly after Jane Blalock's birth, William Blalock headed into the mountains to hunt deer; two months later, relatives found his decomposed body near a stream. No one could determine whether he had been surprised by a black bear or by a mountain lion or whether he had been ambushed—"bushwhacked" in the local vernacular. Raising family suspicions was that his body was found a few hundred yards from two hunting camps, one belonging to the Pritchards, the other to the Boyds. No one could ever prove murder, according to several sources.

A widow with young children, Mary Blalock accepted the proposal of a man named Austin Coffey, who owned one of the largest farms in Watauga County and several hunting cabins across Grandfather Mountain. At forty-three years, Coffey was nearly two decades older than his wife, and a childless widower of 10 years. His ancestors had settled in and around a postal hamlet they named Coffey's Gap. Several Coffey men of the region had fought in the War of 1812.

Coffey raised Keith as his own. He taught the youth to plant wheat, corn, rye, oats, and Irish potatoes and to tend the family's apple, peach, and pear trees. While Keith learned his agrarian lessons well, he preferred a fishing pole and a hunting rifle from the moment he was introduced to them as a child. Under his stepfather's tutelage and later with cousins or alone, Keith fished the pristine mountain streams and tracked game in the yellow and white pine forests of Watauga. He not only learned to shoot well, but to shoot economically—which meant head shots that ensured that no meat was lost from a ball tearing through a deer or other quarry's fleshiest parts.

Early on, Austin Coffey also imbued his stepson in the mountains' credo, as well as that of the era's society as a whole, that in family life, "men were the masters, the favored lords of all they surveyed."[2] He sat at the dinner table with the Coffey men as the women served them. The game and fish on the family's plates came from the men's rifles and fishing poles, pork and bacon from the hogs the Coffey and Blalock males slaughtered each fall. In the Coffey household, Austin Coffey set the rules.

As in the upbringing of most mountain youths, Keith learned that weakness was to be abhorred and reviled and that courage was to be prized above everything except God Himself. Keith's mother and other Blue Ridge women of the day also embraced bravery—whether that of a man standing up to an enemy or that of a wife enduring difficult childbirth and other hardships with stoic acceptance—with religious fervor.

A mountain woman of the nineteenth century wrote words that applied to the Blalocks, the Coffeys, the Pritchards, and the other clans of antebellum Watauga and Caldwell Counties: "Courage seemed to be the keynote of our whole system of religious thought. The fatalism of this free folk is unlike anything; dark and mystical though it be through much brooding over the problems of evil, it is lighted with flashes of the spirit of the Vikings. A man born and bred in a vast wild land nearly always becomes a fatalist. He learns to see Nature not as a thing of fields and brooks, friendly to man and docile beneath his hand, but as a world of depths and heights and distances illimitable, of which he is but a tiny part. He feels himself carried in a sweep of forces too vast for comprehension, forces variously at war, out of which are the issues of life and earth, but in which the Order, the Right, must ultimately prevail. This is the beginning of his faith; from thence is his courage and independence. Inevitably he comes to feel with a sort of proud humility that he has no part or lot in the control of the universe save as he allies himself, by prayer and obedience, with the Order that rules."[3]

In the beautiful but harsh valleys and peaks of the Blue Ridge, a fatalistic view of life, in which anyone who reached the age of forty earned the appellation "old," served as a fire wall against constant fear. Hard conditions bred hard men in the Blue Ridge, and by the time Keith Blalock reached his teens, he had been toughened by his parents and by his environment for burdens and battles that would inevitably face him.

To further prepare Keith and every other local boy and girl for life's difficulties, parents, grandparents, and virtually every adult member of a Blue Ridge family filled the young ones with the very marrow of familial life: tradition. Mountain native Emma Miles remembered: "Every phase of the mountaineer's life connects in some way with tradition."[4]

The strict adherence of the Blalocks, the Pritchards, and other Appalachian families to the time-honored traditions and tenets of their Scottish, Scots-Irish, and English ancestors who first settled in the mountains nourished, comforted, and, to countless outsiders, isolated them from much, if not all, of the events beyond the crags, chasms, and valleys. A visitor to the region likened the mountain clans to "castaways on some unknown island . . . untroubled by the growth of civilization . . . customs and ideas unaltered from the time of their fathers." He added: "Mountain folks still live in the Eighteenth Century."[5]

Respect and love of archaic social tenets may have puzzled travelers and newcomers to Watauga, Caldwell, and the other counties of western North Carolina, but to the mountain folk, their forefathers' way of life made utter sense, offering a blueprint that was comfortable despite its harshness. Reverence for the past allowed most to approach the present in a "tried and true" manner, and for the Blalocks and Coffeys, there was comfort and kinship in it.

"Traditionalism lay back of every aspect of [the Blue Ridge's] culture," an observer noted, "sanctioning and accounting for the behavior, attitudes and valued ideals of the people."[6] Even most of the songs that Keith and Malinda knew were those of another age. Englishman Cecil Sharp, a fittingly named music scholar hunting for evidence of authentic eighteenth-century English, Scottish, Welsh, and Irish folk music in isolated regions of America, discovered to his surprise and delight that old and young alike in the Blue Ridge still fiddled ancient reels and sang tunes that the region's earliest white settlers had brought from their old homelands. Sharp forever preserved over three hundred and fifty such songs that had died away everywhere except in Keith's and Malinda's birthplace, and noted that the people of the mountains not only sang archaically worded stanzas, but also spoke "Old English, not American . . . the language of a past day."[7]

Throughout the mountains, the Coffeys had long earned acclaim as fine singers, especially of religious hymns. Keith grew up with "church songs" that radiated love of God and an encompassing fatalism. That death was always lurking and inexorably guaranteed for everyone permeated the lyrics of hymns that the Coffeys delivered in "oddly changing keys . . . endings that leave the ear in expectation of something to follow . . . quavers and falsettos

[that] become in recurrence a haunting hint of the spiritual world; neither beneficent nor maleficent, neither devil nor angel, but something—something not to be understood, yet certainly apprehended."[8]

The fatalism that would allow western North Carolina troops and guerrillas to "soldier manfully" on both sides of the Civil War shaded the refrain of one particularly popular mountain ballad: "Oh, ye young, ye gay, ye proud. You must die and wear the shroud."[9]

The Baptist and Presbyterian churches in which the Blalocks and the Coffeys sang and prayed comprised the foundation of mountain life, along with family ties. Sunday services brought people from remote locales to worship and mingle in "community with their fellows." Before and after a service, "the women especially could exchange gossip and mutual caring and the young could court and discover someone to care about."[10] The social aspects of church attracted even the handful of mountain folk who were not particularly religious, people gathering on Sundays in small log churches framed by mist-shrouded peaks and lofty forests that worshipers revered as God's handwork. Bathed in the dim, almost mystical flicker of pine torches, Blalocks, Coffeys, Pritchards, Greens, Moores, and other clans alike found their churches a source of inspiration, comfort, and "the indwelling power of the spirit."[11]

In the mountains, people felt a "personal relationship with God" but even though many men in Keith's family could recite the most arcane scripture verbatim, they never pretended they could ever fully "know" the mind of their Maker.[12] They generally accepted that God and nature were unfathomable for the most part and that God must have a reason for that fact. As a Blue Ridge preacher said, "I thank Thee, Oh, Father, because Thou has hid these things from the wise and prudent."[13]

Still, even though locals believed that God's mind might always remain hidden from them, they also accepted that spirits and omens lay all around one, if one had the presence of mind to recognize them. Keith and Malinda, as with most all mountain children, were taught that signs, portents, and even witches were everywhere. The phases of the moon revealed the proper times to plant and harvest. If one saw a wood tick on an infant and killed it with a book, the child would have the gift to "speak all kinds o' proper words"[14]; if a parent killed the wood tick with a banjo string, the baby would learn to play the instrument beautifully.

Superstitions, omens, and old wives' tales and cures played a part in rural communities' religion throughout the United States of the mid-nineteenth century, but when the savagery that would stain Blue Ridge trails, peaks, and valleys with the blood of Yankees, rebels, and neutral people alike erupted from the earliest days of the Civil War, even hard-boiled soldier General William T. Sherman would wonder how God-fearing mountaineers could fight so pitilessly and brutally against those with whom they had once shared rude pews. Generations of travelers to the mountains would ask the same question. A scholar of nineteenth-century Appalachia would explain: "The religion of the mountaineer brought him release, community, and a sense of oneness. What it seems not to have done was to affect his code of ethics significantly. That code was dependent on self-preservation intertwined with self-righteousness. This combination, nurtured by isolation, independence, and a personal religious code, often encouraged brutality rather than restrained it. Men who would feel conscience-stricken over something like breaking the Sabbath or swearing could commit murder and feel that their souls somehow remained unblemished."[15]

In Keith Blalock's experience, "an eye for an eye" would prove not just a biblical maxim, but a fact of life. If a neighbor or a stranger harmed one's kinfolk, retribution came sometimes swiftly, sometimes long after the fact. But in the world of the Blalocks and their neighbors, revenge—or vengeance, as the aggrieved family viewed it—would inevitably arrive on some mountain trail or on one's very doorstep. The bloody cycle of countless misdeeds breeding equal measures of retaliation would engulf Keith and Malinda Blalock and virtually every neighbor living under the Grandfather, in the Globe Valley, and every tract from Blowing Rock to the Great Smoky Mountains.

An old mountain tale aptly described the Civil War future of the Blalocks and most Blue Ridge families. The story describes a preacher who, as he rode down a ravine, spotted a mountain man crouching in a thicket with his hunting rifle.

"What are you doing there, my friend?" asked the cleric.

"Ride on stranger," the hunter growled. "I'm a waitin' fer Jim Johnson, and with the help of the Lawd, I'm goin' to blow his damn head off."[16]

Keith, Malinda, James Moore, John Boyd, Robert and Lott Green, the Coffey brothers, and many others—all would be "the hunter," "Jim Johnson," or both once the war turned families and neighbors against each other.

Keith Blalock was taught as a boy that success against one's foes was a sign of God's favor. A mountaineer embroiled in a bitter, long-running, and bloody feud with another clan articulated "the way of things" in Keith Blalock's similar path: "I have triumphed agin [sic], and I gets a better Christian ever' year."[17]

Once Keith Blalock and other rugged Blue Ridge men believed themselves wronged by another, they would not budge in their brutal resolve. A regional historian writes: "This capacity to judge others and find them wanting seems to have been one that many mountain killers possessed. Some folks deserved killing, and a man had the right, and maybe even the obligation, to determine who those folks might be."[18] In Blalock's future experience, the wartime line between murder and a "righteous" killing would prove nonexistent: all the men whom he cut down "had it coming," according to his code of "an eye for an eye."[19]

What the outside world deemed murder was more opaque in the mountain counties. Keith, who would stand accused of cold-blooded murder by the Civil War's end, would likely have commiserated with another mountaineer who had settled a "grievance" against a neighbor. "I tell you, sir," the accused said, "as sure as God made apples, a meaner man never broke the world's bread. The only reason he hadn't died long ago was that God didn't want him, and the devil wouldn't have him."[20]

During Keith and Malinda's childhood and teens, men inflicted retaliation upon each other, but not yet upon women and children. Men marked for retribution drew a reprieve if their enemies encountered them with their families, but only for the moment. Although women had generally remained immune, the passions unleashed by the Civil War in the mountains changed everything. The old "code" of retribution evaporated, and women and children were victimized for their husbands', brothers', fathers', and sons' rebel or Yankee stances. In wartime Watauga and Caldwell Counties, Malinda Blalock would incur nearly as much enmity as her husband, their legion of enemies hoping for the chance to gun her down on sight.

Until the war, mountain boys in their early teens were generally spared from retribution unless their alleged transgression proved monstrous. Even then, a man who killed such a youth had to offer an explanation that would condone his violation of the unwritten code of revenge. Teenaged boys, too, would become "fair game" for unionists and rebels in the mountains as the youths lied about their ages to serve in regular regiments or fought in the Confederate Home Guards. During the war, Keith and Malinda would discover just how dangerous a teenager with an accurate trigger finger could be.

Beneath Grandfather Mountain, Keith and Malinda learned that all justice was "personal." Even in the rough-and-tumble local courts in Boone, Lenoir, and Morganton, juries routinely disregarded evidence and facts to render verdicts according to which miscreants or victims the panel liked or loathed, which ones' values the jurors accepted or respected. A neighbor of the Coffeys remarked: "It doesn't make any difference what the evidence is, the case goes the way they want it to go. Then there is nothing for me to do but to accept and let them throw off on me as a coward, if I stay in the country; to leave the country and give up all that I own, and still be looked on as a coward; or to get my kinfolk and friends together and clean up on the other crowd. What would you do?"[21]

"Cleaning up on the other crowd" would provide Keith's and Malinda's response to the question throughout the looming war in the mountains. That did not make them unusual in Watauga and Caldwell, for most people there believed private justice could be fairer than that of any court in which strangers—"outsiders"—participated. If a clan and its neighbors shared a common heritage and values, the thinking went, "traditional" justice, administered personally and away from any courtroom, was fairer. As one local historian surmises, for the Blalocks and their neighbors, "the order of custom might be preferable to the rule of law."[22]

In the decade before the Civil War, officials in the mountain counties strained to place due legal process above personal bias in cases of one man's or family's retaliation against another. The law and courts, such as they were, tried to stress the importance of evidence before sentence and punishment, but the Blalocks and other mountain clans bucked the notion, imbued with the tradition that real justice was personal. In short, they believed that "those who deserved killing were the ones who got killed."[23] And when the war tore apart the region, Keith and company would have few qualms in deciding who "deserved" to die.

As mountain-born writer A. S. Merrimon wrote in the 1850s, the Blalocks and other Appalachian clans could scarcely be blamed for their belief that court justice left much to be desired. When superior circuit courts convened twice a year in Boone, Marshal, and other mountain towns, people came "to watch the show and to kick up their heels."[24] At a circuit court session in October 1853, Merrimon wrote, "What degradation! I do not know any rival for this place in regard to drunkenness, ignorance, superstition, and the most brutal debauchery. . . . As is usual for this place, drunkenness is carried on to an incredible extent . . . a wretched state of morals."[25] Of course, the same ills—alcohol, prostitution, brawling—could be readily found in the more "civilized" surroundings of the state's large cities.

City-bred observers of life in the Blue Ridge in the Civil War era often magnified common and understandable emotional scenes into episodes that the "outsiders" branded barbaric. In the winter of 1861, the war's first, a Confederate officer leading a search party that was ransacking farms and terrorizing families as the soldiers searched for unionist men expressed "shock" that the wives and mothers of the fugitives were "in some cases greatly alarmed, throwing themselves on the ground and wailing like savages." He derided the unionists as "a primitive, savage people."[26]

Genteel visitors to the mountains also found the men's conduct "primitive," especially the propensity to settle disputes with their fists. As a youth, Keith learned a savage male necessity of mountain life: self-defense. He gleaned particular expertise in "the manly arts" from Austin Coffey, for, in his youth, Coffey had been one of the best bare-knuckled boxers in the region, knocking out many larger opponents. In Keith, he found a natural fighter, a boy whose reflexes and strength developed at an early age. A local historian wrote: "The boys he played with 'double-teamed' on him sometimes because he could handle one too easily, but [they] always got thrashed. They then called him 'Old Keith.'"[27]

Keith took special pride in the sobriquet, for it referred to Burnsville,

North Carolina, pugilist Alfred Keith, a fearsome bare-knuckled brawler once regarded as the South's unofficial heavyweight champion. The nickname stuck to Blalock. Although his signature would always read W. M. Blalock, he referred to himself as Keith. In later years, several family members combining "Keith" and "McKesson," Blalock's middle name, came up with the nickname "Keese."

Nearly six feet tall by his thirteenth birthday and already more muscular than many grown men, Keith first entered boxing matches at annual county fairs in his teens and never lost a bout. At a Fourth of July celebration in 1853, he "came to square" and stepped into the ring against Zack Crowe, a cagey professional whose only loss had been to Alfred Keith's fists. Young Blalock sent Crowe sprawling in the first round. Revived several minutes later, Crowe said that not even Alfred Keith had ever punched him so hard.

By the time he reached nineteen, Keith's punching power was known throughout the mountains and valleys of the region. A local said: "He [Keith] was a young giant of a fist and skull fighter. His fists, which folks claimed were as big as hams and hard as flint, earned him a healthy respect."[28]

Two other facets of Keith's makeup—"his high intelligence and ability to lead"—added to his formidable local reputation.[29] As Malinda would say, "Men either liked or hated him, but they all noticed him."[30]

Standing six feet, two inches tall, with light-blue eyes and dense light hair framing his square-jawed features, the 220-pound young man was hard to miss.

The strapping young mountaineer had not only learned how to fight, but had also been tutored in what was most worth fighting for: one's kin, one's honor, and one's land. There was almost no way to overstate the importance of land to the clans dwelling under the Grandfather and in the Globe Valley. In that respect, the people of the Blue Ridge differed little from the over two-thirds of mid-nineteenth-century Americans who lived in largely rural regions. For the Blalocks, the Coffeys, the Pritchards, and their fellow Appalachian families, the land was not merely their home, but was their place, where their ancestors' graves lay, where the clans' past and present merged in a seemingly timeless pattern in which birth, marriage, and even death revolved in every way upon the land on which a family lived. The acres that were first cleared and plowed by one's ancestors, the same streams that they had fished, the same woods and mountains where past generations of mountaineers had hunted game—all of these bound Keith's and Malinda's families to their fields, valleys, and peaks.

The Coffeys and the other clans did not sell their land to strangers, nor did many locals offer their property as collateral for any reason. As Keith and Malinda were taught early in their lives, the parents passed their land to their children, and the children to their children. They knew everything about their own acreage and knew everyone on the surrounding lands. A visitor to the Blue Ridge recorded that locals were amazed that in New York, Boston, and Philadelphia, people did not know all of their neighbors.

During Keith Blalock's earliest years and those of the boys and girls with whom he played, the adults in their families imbued a proprietary pride in the ancestral land. Their first introduction to it, as a traveler to the mountains wrote, often came when a mother "put the child down on the ground and gently fondled him [or her], and moved him a bit with her feet, which purposely were not at the moment covered with shoes or socks. The child did not cry. The mother seemed to have almost exquisite control of her toes. It all seemed very nice, but I really had no idea what [the mother] really had in mind until she leaned over and spoke gravely to her child: 'This is your land, and it's time you started getting to know it.'"[31] Keith and Malinda would learn every inch of their own land and the mountains jutting from it.

As children became old enough to explore the forests and mountain trails with their brothers, sisters, cousins, and friends, their love for the natural splendor everywhere around them grew. A neighbor would write that the love that Keith, Malinda, their kin, and their enemies bore for the land evolved "from a babyhood when the thrill of clean wet sand was good to little feet; when 'froghouses' were built, and little tracks were printed in rows all over the shore of the creek; when the beginnings of aesthetic feeling found expression in necklaces of scarlet haws and headdresses pinned and braided together of oak leaves, cardinal flowers and fern; when beargrass in spring and berries in summer and muscadines in autumn were first sought after and prized most for the 'wild flavor,' the peculiar tang of the woods which they contain."[32] Keith and Malinda took to heart an axiom that their mothers and those of their friends preached: "Remember, it's the land that's seen you trying and that's tried back, tried to give you all it could."[33]

In the Blalocks' reverence for the woods, mountains, and valleys, the bloodlines of their land-hungry, land-worshipping Scottish, English, and so-called Scots-Irish ancestors flowed in a real sense through the centuries, the fierce agrarian love of former tenant farmers or farmers run off their plots in the Old World and determined in the new one to hold on to their hard-won turf at any price. Their descendants believed that they did not just own the land, but were as much a part of it as anything that grew there. The women's traditional attachment lay in and around their houses or cabins, whether new ones or, more likely, ones in which generations of their kinfolk had dwelled. But the men and the boys of the Blue Ridge claimed any stretch of unsettled forest, any ancient Indian or more recently fashioned paths and trails, and the very mountains as their own.

In the home, young Keith, the Coffeys, and their male neighbors would "eat and sleep, but their life is outdoors, foot-loose in the new forest or on the farm that renews itself crop by crop," a local woman remembered.[34] She described Keith Blalock: "His is the high daring and merciless recklessness of youth and the characteristic grim humor of the American, even though he live to be a hundred. Heartily then he conquers his chosen bit of wilderness and heartily begets and rules his tribe, fighting and praying alike fearlessly and exultantly. . . . For him it is the excitement of fighting and journeying, trading, drinking and hunting, of wild rides and nights of danger."[35]

Keith, from boyhood, claimed the Grandfather as "his chosen bit of wilderness."[36] "High daring," "the excitement of fighting," "wild rides and nights of danger"—all of these awaited Keith Blalock. Few who knew him would have wagered a penny that he would "live to be a hundred."[37] Fewer still would have bet that a woman would seek and experience all of the same adventures. Malinda Pritchard, however, was not the usual woman of the region.

Malinda Pritchard, whose family lived five miles south of Keith's home, was born in 1842 in Caldwell County and within sight of Grandfather Mountain, the sixth of John and Elizabeth Pritchard's nine children. Malinda learned early in her life the traditional role and duties of women in the Blue Ridge. At an early age, girls were expected to help with the lighter household chores: sweeping, dusting, picking and cleaning vegetables, drying dishes and pans, gathering eggs from chicken coops, and other such tasks.

By her early teens, Malinda helped out as expected with all of the other domestic duties—sewing, quilting, scrubbing floors, tending vegetable gardens, cooking, baking, and taking on myriad other chores. She was fortunate that her family was better off than most in the region, where, as Emma Miles pointed out, women belonged "to the old people"—in other words, life's privations and ceaseless labor made them old far beyond their years.[38] Malinda, as well as Keith's mother, escaped the worst physical ravages of many mountain women who were worn down by "toil, sorrow, childbearing, loneliness, and pitiful want."[39]

Malinda and the girls she grew up with lived, whether destitute or comfortable, in old family homes that were "thronged with the memories of other lives."[40] Parents, grandparents, or ancestors long deceased had built and expanded every inch of the home, had sewn every curtain, had hooked rugs, had cleared and planted acreage, and groomed orchards. Every household item and every floorboard had its story, one associated with kin living or dead, and the girls learned every one of those tales, their families' heritage. Mothers and grandmothers taught each girl that "nothing can happen which has not happened before; that whatever she may be called upon to endure, others have undergone its like over and over again."[41] In that regard, Malinda's upcoming experiences would both mirror and contradict the axiom, for she would endure many ordeals and adventures that no woman in her family had ever experienced.

Although men were the providers and ruled the proverbial roost, Blue Ridge women were generally neither meek nor utterly subservient. Males of any age, so long as they lived in their parents' home, were expected to obey their mother as well as their father. Keith accorded his mother the same respect as he did his stepfather, and Keith and Malinda both learned that "for all their differences, [Blue Ridge] men and women were alike in sharing the traditions and necessities of the place. And they were alike in a profound individualism, a quality inescapable, given the valley's isolation, but one that could produce a narrow-mindedness."[42]

Keith and Malinda embodied the self-confidence of many young men and women of the region. The patterns of their prewar lives radiated in regular routines—planting; harvesting; hunting; fishing; domestic tasks performed at the same times on the same days, weeks, and months; Sunday services; and nights spent with one's kin. Several generations of families either lived in the same home or in lodges and cabins literally within view of each other. Cousins were as close as brothers and sisters, and children's grandparents served as much as parents as the boys' and girls' actual mothers and fathers. The death of any relative was mourned as the entire clan's loss, death having robbed the clan of "someone who had been cared for by older brothers and cousins and uncles, as well as parents."[43] And when the death was the result of a feud, the grieving family believed themselves honor-bound to seek retaliation. Boys and girls alike accepted the harsh tenet from their earliest memories. Certain of their families' traditions and routines, Blue Ridge families possessed an ironclad confidence that the way that they lived was the only proper way they should conduct their lives. Among the mountain clans, that confidence bred a sense of self-assurance that their decisions were right simply because they thought so.

Outsiders, including Union and Confederate soldiers, would find the mountaineers' mix of self-confidence and self-righteousness frightening. Keith and Malinda carried both from their earliest years. Like their peers in the Blue Ridge, the Blalocks could always find "justification" for brutal acts against any neighbor or stranger who harmed their kinfolk and accepted that other families did the same.

Malinda's mother and the other Pritchard women instructed Malinda in the clan's traditional methods of raising boys to become the kind of men who would protect their kin and kill for them as the occasions arose. Long before girls were capable of birth themselves, they spent countless hours "minding" their younger brothers and watching how their mothers, grandmothers, and aunts pushed boys to emulate the men at as early an age as possible. Both the Pritchards and the Blalocks raised their boys in the manner of typical mountain women, as described by a neighbor. The mother was tending her seven-year-old son, who gamely attempted to mimic his father's manner, but "lapsed" at times into childish behavior.

"Does he ever want you to rock him to sleep?" the mother was asked.

"Oh," the woman replied, "when he's sick or tired, he's right glad to be my little boy for awhile. But he's always a growed man 'in he wakes up in the morning."[44]

Keith Blalock and Malinda's brothers grew up fast because they were raised that way and because life in the mountains dictated it.

Malinda likely met Keith inside the village's schoolhouse. Typical of the era, the one-room structure contained two rows of benches on which children aged six to sixteen sat, girls on one side, boys on the other. She was eight, Keith twelve, and the first time he really noticed her, he would tell a friend, was in an impromptu race in which she had beaten all the boys, including himself.

By the time Malinda was thirteen and Keith was seventeen, he had carved their initials on a huge pine spreading across both Blalock and Pritchard land. Around that time, he had also come to her defense for the first time, against Harmon Greene, the local schoolmaster. Greene had struck Malinda's right palm with a switch because she had talked with another girl during a lesson. Keith confronted the teacher, lifted him off the floor, and warned him never to strike Malinda again.

That same day, Greene demanded that Austin Coffey punish the youth, but Blalock's stepfather merely made the boy apologize to the teacher and removed Keith from school. Over the ensuing years, Coffey took over the boy's education, focusing on history and politics.

The youth regarded his stepfather with a mix of love and awe and always obeyed him. With the future exception of army officers, Austin Coffey was the only man to whom Blalock deferred, and as he approached adulthood, he fiercely embraced his stepfather's staunch support of the Union and his opposition to slavery.

Throughout their teens, Keith and Malinda spent countless hours together near the summit of Grandfather Mountain. "They'd sit up there holding hands and watching the eagles," Malinda's friend Sarah Robertson said. The couple would look down at acreage that Austin Coffey had promised his stepson as a wedding gift.[45]

Keith was far from the only young man—as well as several older ones—enamored with pretty, dark-haired Malinda Pritchard. Suitors from several counties courted the five-foot-four-inch, 110-pound young woman, but she spurned everyone except Keith. One admirer, John Green, a twenty-year-old Watauga man whose gangly frame somewhat masked his quick fists and strength, continued to visit Malinda despite her polite discouragement. He did so even after Keith proposed to her at Grandfather Mountain's summit on a Sunday in July 1860 and she accepted. When Keith asked Green to give up on Malinda, Green challenged him to a fight.

In front of several dozen locals just outside Coffey's Gap, Green emerged from the bout with a shattered nose, several cracked ribs, and a broken jaw that would never set properly and would cause him pain throughout his life. He would grow a beard to conceal the slight sag Blalock's right hand had left near the chin.

Notwithstanding the beating, Green gained the respect of his neighbors and of Blalock. Blalock had made a lifelong enemy of Green and his family, the bad blood soon to erupt over personal and political enmity alike.

Now, in April 1861, Reverend Isaac Muir married Keith Blalock and Malinda Pritchard, the groom wearing his Sunday suit—a white, starched linen shirt and a heavy woolen frock coat—the bride in a demure, ivy-hued bodice and ankle-length white skirt. In Malinda's dark upswept hair, she had pinned tiny dark-blue flowers from Grandfather Mountain, maid-of-honor Sarah Robertson wrote, picking the color because it matched Malinda's eyes.[46]

Bob Pritchard, Malinda's oldest brother, who had the same dark hair and blue eyes as his sister, gave the bride away in place of John Pritchard, who had died of a winter fever three months earlier. According to Robertson, the very sight of Malinda marrying a Blalock might have killed a healthy John Pritchard anyway.

After the couple's short, formal vows, Austin Coffey delivered a testimonial. Still vigorous at sixty-six years, he spoke of his hopes that the couple's union would smooth old feuds between the families and lamented that Keith's grandmother, who had died of a summer fever in 1843, and his half-brother Samuel, Coffey and Aileen's child, could not be there. An infant at the time of the summer fever epidemic, Samuel had been sent off to Coffey's childless relatives in western Tennessee to spare him from the malady. Neither Coffey nor Keith had seen the boy since, only his occasional letters serving to let them know that he was healthy and wished to remain with his adoptive family. Though the youth's choice pained his father, he acceded.

In one of the pews in front of Coffey was John Boyd, attending only because Keith's sister, Jane, had married a Boyd. John Boyd loathed Keith's Unionism, which would soon pit the two men against each other, and a guest caught him glaring several times at the couple.

Shortly afterward, at the churchyard reception, scenes typical of any Blue Ridge wedding followed. Malinda and Sarah Robertson would record how men in dark frock coats and top hats or brimmed farmer's caps, and women in calico jackets, plaid or dark skirts, and bonnets festooned with flowers congratulated the couple. James Marlow, a handsome friend of the couple and the future husband of Malinda's sister Jean, would joke that the congratulatory kiss he placed upon Malinda's cheek was the first and only time he dared to kiss Keith Blalock's wife.

Other familiar sights unfolded across the churchyard. Around long pine tables piled with ham, chicken, cornbread, vegetables, and pastries milled Blalocks, Pritchards, Coffeys, Carrolls, Moores, Boyds, and other clans. Eventually, as they always did, the men and women congregated in separate groups, and the men passed around earthenware jugs and silver flasks of corn whiskey.

Fiddlers regaled the guests with many of the same reels and jigs their ancestors had listened and danced to in the Highlands of Scotland. But, according to James Marlow, at Keith and Malinda's wedding, the notes that usually filled dance-squares attracted only a few young women and children. The adults were more concerned with talk about the prospects of war, and whenever the fiddlers took a break, a bagpiper played ancient Scottish battle songs.

The martial music fit the conversation of the guests, for, despite Reverend Muir's earlier prayer that the Blalocks' marriage would be blessed by children and by years of peace, talk of war was everywhere in Watauga County. Austin Coffey's brothers—McCaleb, Reuben, and William, all supporters of secession—were at the wedding, but barely speaking to their pro-Union brother. Bob Pritchard, James Marlow, and Keith's first cousin and friend Micah Blalock, a short, rugged young man, were eager for war against the North and had asked Keith over the previous month whether he would join them or his cousins who had fled to Michigan. "I told them," Keith later said, "that if it came to a fight, I'd be in it. I just didn't say which side yet."[47]

One reported wedding guest whose loyalties were also in question was a broad-shouldered, six-foot, 230-pound man in a well-cut suit. Thirty-one-year-old Zebulon "Zeb" Vance, a Whig representative in the U.S. Congress, had not shown up at the wedding to cull votes: the House and Senate had effectively disbanded following Abraham Lincoln's inauguration. Vance, who knew and liked both Blalock and his stepfather, had been traveling to weddings, town meetings, and assorted rallies through the mountain districts, urging men not to follow South Carolinians into secession.

Brilliant and ambitious, a future military hero and governor of North Carolina, Vance talked to Union men and secessionists alike of the need for reason above rancor. They listened to him because he was not some lowland aristocrat, but one of them. Born and raised in the rugged mountains flanking Asheville, married to Hattie Espy, a pretty red-haired local girl, he knew and understood the Blalocks and their guests. He knew how far removed the lives of Watauga, Caldwell, Bunscombe, and Mitchell Counties' farmers, millers, woodsmen, and merchants were from genteel plantation society. Vance had stated that even if a man was against the Union, no western North Carolinian had a genuine stake in supporting slavery. However, as his critics noted, Vance owned six slaves himself. On the political stump, his view that neither the preservation of slavery nor secession was worth fighting for galled many locals.

A year before the wedding, Vance had first met Austin Coffey and Keith after the congressman had given an open-air speech at Coffey's Gap. Vance, who had heard of Keith Blalock's boxing skills, wrote that he had been impressed by Blalock's intelligence and knowledge of politics. Blalock, in turn, admired Vance, whose opposition to secession and to a war mirrored Blalock's own beliefs. "Vance was a man," Blalock said. "He wasn't afraid of anybody."[48]

Many of the guests opposed Vance's views on slavery and the Union, but the *Asheville Recorder* had proclaimed its certainty that he would fight for his home state against the Union. It reminded readers in the western counties of a noteworthy incident highlighted by Vance's support for a project to dredge North Carolina's French Broad River so that locals could move their goods more easily to the lowland ports. When a Rhode Island congressman had dismissed Vance's constituents as insignificant, Vance retorted: "The gentleman who makes that remark comes from the puny little state of Rhode Island. Why, I could stand on one border of Rhode Island and piss clear across the state."[49]

"That was one of Keith's favorite stories," a relative would say.[50]

Robertson also recalled that even at the wedding, neighbors including Bob Pritchard and Micah Blalock asked Keith and Vance on which side they would fight. Both reiterated their hope that there would be no war.

Late into the reception, John Boyd was drunk, Robertson wrote, and about to challenge Blalock's loyalty to his home state. Boyd's friends hauled him from the churchyard before he could provoke the groom.

"I heard Malinda's brother Bob say, 'Don't let Keith talk you into running north,'" Sarah Robertson wrote. "He said, 'Remember that you're a Pritchard before a Blalock.' Malinda said back, 'Have you ever known anyone else to speak for me?'"[51]

As the wedding broke up near dusk, Vance invited guests to an antisecession speech he would give in Asheville on April 13, 1861.

CHAPTER TWO
Madness Rules the Hour

O VER the next ten days, Keith and Malinda began their marriage on the land Austin Coffey had given them. He and Keith had cleared several acres near one of Coffey's hunting cabins, a three-room, slope-roofed pine dwelling nestled near a crystalline stream two thousand feet above Coffey's Gap and the Globe Valley. When Keith went hunting in the vast pine and spruce forests for three days, Malinda, a good shot, joined him.

Although the newlyweds began their life together in better straits than many mountain couples—the Pritchards were better heeled than most locals and Austin Coffey was a modestly successful man—the couple was a traditional one. Keith took on the customary role of provider, clearing enough land for subsistence crops and using his skills as a "stalker" in the woods and mountains. As a trapper and a hunter, Keith knew the region like the proverbial back of his hand.

Malinda was expected to take on traditional women's work, tending to the cabins, the stove, and her vegetable plot and to the children when they came—"the same harsh, toilsome grooves already worn by her predecessors."[1] She would not shirk these time-honored mountain duties, but was not willing to bind herself to domestic tasks only. She viewed herself as much a *partner* to Keith as a wife and helpmate. Having roamed the trails and woods of the county since her childhood with her brothers and able to shoot as well, if not better, than most men, she had no intention of being left behind when her "vigorous young husband" went hunting for weeks at a time.[3] Many men of the mountains would never have tolerated such behavior from their wives, but Keith was different. He did not like being away from Malinda for long and knew that the local men, always wary of "the young giant's"[3] prowess as "a fist and skull fighter,"[4] would not risk accusing him of being "biddy-pecked" by Malinda.[5] Theirs was a union of shared love.

Still, no matter how high above the fertile Globe Valley Keith and Malinda climbed in the spring of 1861, they could not escape the political and civil turmoil engulfing the mountain counties. Although the nearest railway line, the Western Carolina, and telegraph reached no further than Morganton, newspapers, travelers, and river men spread the latest news with surprising speed and efficiency throughout the region. War was coming, and the locals grasped that it would sweep across the entire state. Keith would say, "When the Civil War came, I knew that I would have to get in it."[6]

The victory of Abraham Lincoln in the 1860 presidential election ensured that Keith and the other young men of Watauga and the northwestern counties would soon have to declare as "Secessionist or Unionist." Keith and his stepfather, Austin Coffey, would have agreed with local preacher Reverend J. Buston, who lamented that "the disunion mania is a practical blindness and a scheme against God and man."[7]

Throughout the weeks leading to the election, Keith declared himself "a Lincoln and Union man now and always."[8] He would tell a relative that "slavery meant nothing to me, and secession was treason."[9] Slave owners and secessionists were already branding Coffey and Blalock "Southern Yankees."[10] As a local historian notes: "To defend slavery or the rights of the planter aristocracy, not one mountain man in a hundred would have shouldered a musket for the Confederacy."[11]

Men like Keith who "didn't give a hoot-owl's damn whether people in Kansas owned slaves or not" did often differ on the prospect of the federal government's preserving the Union by force of arms.[12] Many of Keith's friends, family, and acquaintances professed their determination to fight against any Union troops on North Carolina soil.

Up on the Grandfather, Keith wrote, he and Malinda's family, vociferous in their denunciations of Lincoln and in their support of secession, had little notion that Malinda, who did not yet share Keith's "intense degree of personal, militant zeal" for support of the Union, was still willing to turn her back on her family's political tenets and to support her new husband's stance.[13] As Malinda told a relative, love made her choice a clear-cut one: "Mountain women are plumb foolish about their menfolk. While they may biddy-peck and fault their yoke-mate behind the door, they'll go through thick and thin for him without asking why."[14]

Her husband and Austin Coffey had cast votes for Lincoln in November 1860 at the Watauga County Courthouse and had voted there again in February 1861 in the statewide plebiscite on whether to hold a secession convention. There was no mystery regarding Keith and Coffey's vote, and on their home turf, the ten counties west of the Blue Ridge, only three favored the secessionists. East of the mountains, coastal and Piedmont slave owners won five counties, but still lost six. A state delegate from Watauga mirrored Keith Blalock's own sentiments: "Let South Carolina nullify, revolute, secess, and be damned! North Carolina don't need to follow her lead!"[15]

Despite those words, Keith Blalock and other mountain men supportive of Washington's right to quell secession by force of arms faced a groundswell of unionists who opposed federal intervention. Less than two weeks after Keith had done his part to vote down a secession convention, even a pro-Union

Salisbury, North Carolina, newspaper opined: "Another point, that of coercion of the seceding states, as a means of bringing them back into the Union. The triumph of Union men here [the February plebiscite], if they have triumphed, does not affect this question, but believing there is no constitutional power in the government for such a measure and that it would be mischievous in its effects for reasons independent of its unauthorized character, the Union men of North Carolina are not less opposed to this doctrine because they have condemned the actions of the seceding states."[16]

The editorial writer was dead wrong in his contention that all Union men in the state were opposed to quelling secession by force. Keith Blalock said, "The Union. No other way."[17]

On April 13, 1862, Keith and Malinda, accompanied by Austin Coffey, drove a small, flat-back oxcart into Asheville in an annual spring trek to stock up on seed, powder and ammunition, coffee, and other staples. They also arrived to hear Zeb Vance's speech, at 7 P.M. Several thousand people, many of the men brandishing pistols and shotguns, gathered throughout the day on the lawn of the county courthouse and spilled into the main street. Early arrivals, the Blalocks and Coffey stood near the courthouse steps. By late afternoon, people also jammed the windows and balconies of the courthouse and the windows and roofs of nearby homes.

At 7 P.M., Vance took the podium to both cheers and boos. Placards emblazoned with pro- and anti-secession slogans alike, and pine torches bobbed above the crowd. Standing between two white pillars, placing his hands on his hips in his customary stance, Vance began his speech by reminding the crowd that in February 1862, North Carolinians had voted against secession by a 2 to 1 margin. Then he launched into rhetoric that Keith and his stepfather endorsed. "I was canvassing for the Union in that speech with all my strength," Vance would write, "and literally had my hand extended upward in pleading for peace and the Union of our fathers, when the telegraphic news was announced of the firing on Sumter and President Lincoln's call for 75,000 volunteers."[18]

The crowd grew silent at the news, waiting to hear on which side Vance would fight. A reporter carried away by the moment wrote: "As Vance stood there, the courthouse's very bricks appeared to turn from pink to bloody red."[19]

"My hand fell slowly and sadly by the side of a Secessionist," Vance recalled. "I immediately, with altered voice and manner, called upon the assembled multitude not to fight against, but for South Carolina.[20]

"If we had to shed blood, I preferred to shed northern rather than southern blood. I would raise a company of militia."[21]

When Vance waded into the crowd, he spotted Keith Blalock and asked if he would fight alongside him for North Carolina.

Malinda would say: "That was the start of our great adventure."[22]

For Keith Blalock, the attack on and surrender of Fort Sumter was the worst possible development. "Not only had [I] just acquired a new bride," he would write, "I knew what was coming."[23]

"What was coming" proved an almost instantaneous conversion of many Watauga men from unionists into defenders of their state from an imminent invasion by Yankees. On April 23, 1861, Keith and Austin Coffey encountered the shifting local viewpoint on the front page of *The Carolina Watchman:* "Old lifelong conservative men, who throughout had labored and prayed for a peaceful solution to the national troubles and have never once given up all hope, yielded with anguish of the heart when they could hold out no longer. The miserable duplicity of Abraham Lincoln stung them to the quick, one and all are freely bringing their sons and their treasures to offer on the altar of liberty. . . . Who would measure the deep damnation due to those, North and South, who have, through years of ceaseless agitation, brought this terrible calamity upon us? As there is a just God in heaven, they will get their reward."[24]

For the western counties' most ardent unionists, Lincoln's call in April 1861 for 75,000 troops to suppress "the Southern insurrection" pitted their collective conscience against their loyalty to their state.[25] A Watauga man would say: "When the war showed up, it made a man feel all of a sudden Southern."[26]

No matter where a North Carolinian stood on slavery and secession, B. F. Moore, of Raleigh, aptly surmised: "Civil War can be glorious news to none but demons or thoughtless fools, or maddened men."[27]

From the craggy face of Grandfather Mountain to the lush coastal plantations, the words of William A. Graham, of Greensboro, proved prophetic: "Truly indeed, may it be said that madness rules the hour."[28]

✺

Within days of Lincoln's appeal for volunteers, men Keith had grown up with joined the first volunteer rebel outfits from Watauga and other western counties. Neighboring men in Caldwell County signed and circulated, on April 30, 1861, an oath of loyalty to the state against federal invaders: "The undersigned citizens of Caldwell County, North Carolina, in view of the distracted condition of the Country do pledge ourselves, in the formation of a Volunteer Company and do hold ourselves in readiness at any and all times when called upon by the proper authorities of this state, to march in defense of the rights and honours of the South against the aggressions of the North."[29] Several Coffeys signed the pledge.

In May of 1861, a statewide election to send delegates to the secession convention in Raleigh further ripped open divisions among rebels, unionists, and those equally opposed to secession and the prospect of a federal invasion. The elections in the mountain counties unfolded amid an atmosphere of imminent threat and violence. Union men like Keith Blalock and secessionists like Carroll Moore and Robert Green showed up at the ballot booths or boxes with side arms and even rifles. In some mountain towns, clerks bellowed the names of men who cast votes for "the Lincoln candidate," inciting fisticuffs, arrests, and, in one case, the murder of a unionist by a sheriff espousing secession.[30] At the least, shouts of "traitor" followed Keith Blalock and fellow "Union men." So effective were the bullying tactics of rebels statewide that in the mountain counties alone, the total votes cast were more than forty-six thousand less than the February plebiscite.

Unionists Keith Blalock and Austin Coffey and secessionists Carroll Moore, John Boyd, and Robert Green cast their votes as much along class lines as on slavery and states' rights. Alexander Jones, a "Lincoln congressman" from Henderson County, North Carolina, contended that men who favored the Union were "the mountain boys—the wood choppers—the rail splitters—in fact the bone and sinew of the county . . . entirely irrespective of party."[31]

Keith and Austin Coffey admired the rhetoric of Jones, who painted the secessionists as "monarchists" riding roughshod over the "industrious, frugal . . . independent, but harmless and powerless."[32] Despite Jones's view, Keith Blalock proved neither "harmless nor powerless." But another of Jones's diatribes was one that Keith wholeheartedly espoused: "They [the Confederates] will never take us out of the Union, or make us a land of slaves—no, never. We intend to stand as firm, as adamant, and as unyielding as our own majestic mountains."[33] Keith and many of "the hardy mountaineers" stood ready to oppose disunion at any cost.

Although the Blalocks and the Coffeys were far more comfortable than most of their neighbors, Keith nonetheless had to help provide—farm, hunt, and fish—for the family's survival. He readily accepted Jones's assertion that the secessionists were "slavocrats who look upon a white man who has to labor for an honest living as no better than one of their negroes . . . these bombastic, high falutin, aristocratic fools have been in the habit of driving negroes and poor helpless white people until they think that they can control the world of mankind."[34]

In the *Knoxville Whig,* a paper that made its way through traveling peddlers to the mountains of western North Carolina, editor William Brownlow charged that the chief distinction between unionists such as Keith and "disunion men" was that "Unionists do not think it *degrading* to a man to labor, as do most of the Southern Disunionists."[35]

It would be inaccurate to state that all of the mountains' better-heeled men

backed the Confederacy, but, by and large, affluence often meant slave owners, translating into fervent support for the Confederacy. Equally inaccurate
was any blanket statement that all mountain unionists were of poor or mid-
dling means and that every such man loved "the Lincolnites." Sidney Andrews, who traveled Civil War North Carolina, opined: "The Unionism of
Western North Carolina of which we heard so much during the war . . . was
less a love for the Union than a personal hatred of those who went into the
Rebellion. It was not so much an uprising for the government as against a
certain ruling class."[36] Keith Blalock was somewhat unusual in that while he
did loathe local secessionist figures, he did boast: "I am a Lincolnite, no mistake about that."[37]

Although the motives behind loyalty to either side were not always so con-
crete, most of the rebels in the Blue Ridge and the Great Smokies did tend,
as Frederick Law Olmsted pointed out, to number the wealthier men—
"chiefly professional men, shopkeepers, and men in office, who are also land
owners and give a divided attention to farming" and who either owned a few
slaves or supported a man's right to do so.[38]

Keith Blalock's family owned their land, but never a slave, and the young
mountaineer had no intention of dying for neighbors and outsiders who did.

Though Keith remained recalcitrant against pressure from local rebels but determined to remain on his land, over four thousand volunteers from the
mountains joined the Confederate service in those turbulent weeks of April
and May 1861, the tally nearly one-sixteenth of all military-age men in the
Blue Ridge counties. And the numbers would swell to almost one-third of the
entire male population—68,000—of western North Carolina by the end of
the war. As events would soon show, however, the Confederate sympathies
of thousands of the volunteers ran from lukewarm to nonexistent.

North Carolina Adjutant General John Hoke had called upon the state's
counties to produce thirty thousand recruits for the rebel regiments. In the
mountain counties of Caldwell, Watauga, Ashe, and Wilkes, recruiters
printed patriotic notices in the handful of newspapers, passed out printed
broadsides and leaflets to any able-bodied man they spied, and eventually
rode up into the foothills and mountains of the Blue Ridge. Up in the tangled
laurel thickets, Keith and Malinda would see the recruiters—and remain hidden as they rode past.

Full-fledged secessionists and men whose unionist leanings fell away at the
prospect of "Yankee troops on our home soil" canvassed the towns and the
remote glens of Watauga and Caldwell Counties to raise companies for the
Confederate forces.[39] Hampered not only by the region's sparse population

in comparison to the counties of the Piedmont, but also by the fierce Union sentiments of some of the locals, rebel recruiters nonetheless had raised one company by June 1861 and stepped up their efforts to add another. Whenever such "smooth-talking rebs" as local planter, merchant, and state legislator Samuel F. Patterson stumped for the Confederacy anywhere near the Grandfather or the Globe Valley, Keith Blalock would be nowhere in sight.[40] Still, Patterson, a wealthy man whose closest exposure to the front would be loud wartime debates in Raleigh, persuaded dozens of men from the mountain counties to walk off the mountains and down to Lenoir, in Caldwell County, to affix their signatures or their "marks" to the Confederate enlistment paper.

Keith made it a point to avoid Lenoir as long as possible, stocking up on supplies as best he could in Boone or Morganton. With the steady trickle, if not stream, of volunteers turning up in the Caldwell County town and with recruits drilling on the town common every Saturday that spring and summer, a strong young man like Keith Blalock would be hard-pressed to offer a viable explanation to strangers and acquaintances alike about his lack of patriotism or, at the least, his apparent unwillingness to "defend" his home turf.

Keith and everyone else under the Grandfather learned in June 1861 that the region's first rebel company had reached its required minimum complement of sixty-four privates and "an appropriate number of noncommissioned officers, a surgeon, and officers."[41] Several distant relatives of Austin Coffey stood in Company A's ranks on June 3, 1861, as "a ceremony was held on the square in honor of [their] departure."[42] According to *The Lenoir News,* "outstanding men of the county, Samuel F. Patterson, W. F. Jones, W. W. Lenoir, and S. P. Dula gave fitting addresses" in front of "nearly the entire county," and "the ceremonies became so touching that many eyes were moist."[43]

Some observers were as moved by the pomp as much as the Lenoir correspondent, but for different reasons. A local woman wrote: "The Union is gone, and all these things follow it, as the shadow steals after a great strong man who goes out from your door forever! How quietly we drift out into such an awful night into the darkness, the lowering clouds, the howling winds, and the ghostly light of our former glory going with us, to make the gloom visible with its pale glare."[44]

Keith, "a strong and fearless young man," was caught up in that "gloom," agonizing that his neighbors, his friends, and his cousins fully expected him to rein in his unionist sympathies and fight the Yankees.[45] A Blalock relative wrote: "Keith wasn't one to run from a fight, no matter the odds. He'd get into it, and he'd lead the others, like always. But no one knew which way he'd go."[46]

With each day that passed after Lincoln's call for volunteers, Keith "felt the pressure to declare my intent. I did not want to fight for the rebels, but that was trouble in Watauga."[47] Recruiters were relentlessly riding up to homesteads throughout the county, and Keith and Malinda realized that it was only a matter of time before Confederates materialized at the cabin perched on the Grandfather.

Keith's cousin Julius had already enlisted in the Independent Guards at Cartersville, in Chatham County. Malinda's brothers, having remained home just long enough to finish the spring planting, had set out to neighboring Caldwell County to join Zeb Vance's Rough and Ready Guards. They expected Keith to "come off Grandfather Mountain and do his part as soon as he had brought in enough game to last Malinda the season."[48]

Making certain that Malinda would have supplies enough to last her through the season was a legitimate concern for Keith, and one that even local rebels suspicious of his motives could understand, as it was one weighing on their own thoughts. By late spring of 1861, wartime inflation and shortages were already being felt in the region's general stores. The Blalocks and their neighbors had to shell out ever-escalating prices for staples: "Groceries high and scarce. Coffee 37 1/2 to 40c [cents] a lb., brown sugar—none in Lenoir, bacon 15 1/2 c, salt 4.50 per bu [bundle], powder $1.00 a pound, lead 15c lb., sole [shoe] leather 10 to 45c."[49]

The scarcity of salt posed an especially frightening problem for Watauga and Caldwell Counties. The substance was the only means people had of curing and preserving meat, and with the "fall hog-killing season" looming, locals who depended upon preserved pork and bacon to carry them through the winter had reason to worry that they would not be able to afford the necessary amount of salt.[50] With the Confederate army's ceaseless demand for salt the Quartermaster General's top priority, civilians would suffer. For many North Carolina soldiers, including those wholeheartedly devoted to secession, fears for their families' subsistence gnawed at them, and many were already mulling "going over the hill" to return to their loved ones.

Despite the growing concerns of family men throughout the mountain counties, new recruits joined the Confederate companies in Caldwell County, people from the Grandfather to the Globe "in a state of feverish excitement."[51] The pressure on Keith "to declare" for the rebels soared.[52]

Eighteen of Keith's Coffey cousins would stride into Lenoir in June and July 1861 to sign the twelve-month enlistment paper of the mustering Hibriten Guards, and while visiting his stepfather in early May 1861, Keith was confronted by Austin Coffey's brother William, a vociferous secessionist. When the step-uncle shouted that Keith was either a shirker or a traitor, only his stepfather's demand that his brother leave halted the enraged Keith from throttling the man despite his advanced years. As William Coffey stomped away to his home, within eyeshot of his brother's, a feud began, one whose savagery would traumatize both families.

Flocking to fight for "the Cause" along with the sons of William, Reuben, and McCaleb Coffey were James Marlow, Boyds, Moores, Greens, and scores of other young men whom Keith had hunted and fished with throughout his youth, those whom he had pummeled when they had double-teamed him. "We were all waiting on Old Keith," Levi Coffey recalled.[53]

Keith, too, was waiting and watching. Murray Coffey remembered, "Keith told us every night [during] that spring [1861], men making their way to Kentucky to join the Yankees passed by his cabin up on the Grandfather. He and Malinda always gave them food, and Keith wanted to go with them, but couldn't on account he couldn't bear to leave Malinda behind."[54]

Keith would state that he had three choices—"all three of them bad."[55] The first was to join the growing flow of mountain unionists risking the rough trek and the rebel patrols en route to Kentucky.

Equally unpalatable was the option of going into hiding in the caves and chasms of the Grandfather. To Murray Coffey, Keith said, "I figured that she [Malinda] would want to share that exile, and didn't want it for her."[56]

The third choice distressed Keith the most. The very notion of donning a Confederate uniform meant that he must fight for a cause he loathed.

❧

In mid-June 1861, the hoofbeats of two riders awakened Keith and Malinda. As he stepped from their bed and onto the cabin's porch, the recruiters cantered up to him. They delivered a simple message: "Either enlist, or face the consequences."[57]

As they turned their horses to gallop off, one of the rebels shouted, "We'll be back in a few days."[58]

"That night," Keith would recount, "we discussed our situation . . . and we both anguished over the possibility of our being separated. I made a decision."[59]

Keith had no way to know that Malinda had also made a decision.

CHAPTER THREE
I'm Going to Fight with You

❧

IN mid-June 1861, Keith Blalock, accompanied by James D. Moore, rode from Blowing Rock and down to the Globe Valley, in Caldwell County. Keith turned up in Lenoir to sign the twelve-month enlistment paper of Company F, the Hibriten Guards, of the 26th North Carolina Infantry Regiment, which was commanded by Zeb Vance. As with several other Watauga recruits, Keith was allowed to delay his actual muster date until November 15 so that he could harvest his crops. But if he failed to report, a detachment of the regiment would come looking for him.

Keith had made his decision to wear a Confederate uniform, but only long enough to get to the front and desert to the Union lines at the first opportunity. He had sworn his loyalty to the Confederacy, as a local saying went, "from the teeth out."[1] It ended there, for Keith, in his view, was a mountain unionist "coerced" in subtle or not so subtle ways to don the gray, but "looking confidently for the re-establishment of the federal authority in the South with as much confidence as the Jews look for the coming of the Messiah . . . no event or circumstance could change or modify his hopes."[2] However, his confidence would soon face several severe tests.

When November 1861 came, he and Malinda headed to Lenoir, and within a few days, he was trudging in a rainstorm with twenty-one other recruits, miserable in his gray wool shell jacket, trousers of the same color and material, a kepi, new brogans blistering his feet, a haversack, a cartridge box and sling, and his bayonet and scabbard. An 1853 Enfield, with a rifled barrel for a .58 caliber ball, pressed against his right shoulder.

As Keith and the other men splashed out of Lenoir, only a handful of people waved their good-byes, the paltry number a far cry from the farewells lavished upon Company F's first Watauga and Caldwell recruits, who had marched off on Wednesday, July 31, 1861. Miss Lina Caison, a young Lenoir woman, wrote: "I recall a day in the summer of '61 when a flag was unfurled. It was the coat of arms of North Carolina on a blue background and was made of a dress of Miss Annie Rankin's [daughter of company commander Captain Nathan P. Rankin], then a child . . . and the coat of arms was painted by her sister. The flag was made for the second Company of volunteers leaving the county, the Hibriten Guards.

"This Company before starting on its march to Hickory was drawn up on the square, and on either end of the long veranda, while in the center of the veranda stood Miss Laura L. Norwood and twelve little girls in white dresses and blue ribbons representing the 13 Confederate States. With few words fitly spoken, Miss Norwood presented the flag, which was received by Captain Rankin in behalf of the Company. The Company marched away, for this was the famous Company F, 26th N.C. troops. . . . I was one of those little girls in white and blue."[3]

No little girls in blue or pretty local belles gathered to see Keith Blalock and the other new enlistees march away for the front in eastern North Carolina. And no man filing out in the rain had less desire to fire even one shot in defense of the Company F's blue flag or any other Confederate banner.

Compounding Keith Blalock's misery, the men with whom he slogged down the road to the depot at Newton, where they would board a train for Camp Carolina, had elected him sergeant. He was about to "see the elephant," battle, for the first time. Back home, beneath the crags of Grandfather Mountain, Malinda might also face the prospect of war, in the form of pro-Union guerrillas already launching raids from east Tennessee into Watauga County.

Out of his love for Malinda, Keith had chosen to wear the gray rather than place her at risk from rebel neighbors who might retaliate against the wife of a turncoat. Keith had made certain that his neighbors around the Grandfather and in the Globe Valley had seen him leave to report to the 26th. When he had said good-bye to his wife in Lenoir, Malinda, according to her friend and neighbor Sarah Robertson, had told Keith that they would see each other "sooner than you think."[4]

Malinda had set her own plan into motion. Along the road to Newton, Keith noticed a short, slight soldier alongside him. He took a closer look and gaped at the person, whom he recognized as Malinda. Her once waist-length hair was cropped beneath a forage cap, Keith's own hunting rifle hefted on her shoulder. She wore baggy trousers and an oversized, untucked shirt that concealed her breasts.

Malinda would recall what she said to her husband: "I'm going to fight with you."[5]

James Moore always contended that Keith had not really been surprised, "that they [the Blalocks] resolved to enlist together and seek their first opportunity of deserting and getting over to the federal lines."[6] According to Moore, Keith had vowed never to enlist in the Confederate army unless his wife be allowed to join with him. But Malinda vigorously denied the allegation, contending that Moore was not even aware that she had sneaked into the ranks of the 26th until she and Keith later reached Kinston, North Carolina. She further asserted that even though Moore agreed to keep her secret, which, in all likelihood, was a decision rooted in a healthy fear of Keith's fists and an initial belief that the Blalocks would "do their duty" for the Confederacy, neither Moore nor Keith had known of her ruse until the moment that they first saw "Sam."[7]

In Lenoir, Malinda had signed the enlistment paper as "Keith's brother."[8] "I gave my name in as S.M. [Sam] Blalock, 20 years old, and passed as a man," she wrote.[9] Whether Keith deserted or stayed with the rebels, she was determined to go with him: "I was going where he went. And my boy's hair fooled them all."[10]

According to James Moore, Malinda and Keith were going to the rebel ranks with one hundred dollars in their collective pockets: "Little Sammy Blalock and Keith each had the [enlistment] bounty of fifty dollars."[11]

Malinda had encountered little trouble in passing Company F's "physical": "Now in those days, about the only medical requirement for entering service was that you had to have at least one tooth above and in the lower jaw that met each other. This was necessary in order to bite the top out of the paper cartridges when loading one's weapon. May sound funny to you, but, back then, this simple requirement was serious. Dead serious. So with a quick gander at a boy's mouth, [we] were issued our gray fatigues."[12]

The company that now listed new recruits "L.M. [*sic*] and S.M. Blaylock [*sic*]" on the unit rolls was one of the 26th's ten companies, the standard complement of most Confederate regiments.[13] Including Company F, four of the 26th's companies had been raised in the Appalachian mountain and foothill counties of Caldwell, Ashe, and Wilkes, the other six from the Piedmont counties of Anson, Chatham, Moore, Union, and Wake. Company F, as with each of the others in the 26th, had drawn the bulk of its recruits from one or two counties, many of the men having known each other all their lives.

The men whom "Sam" and Keith now served with hailed, like the couple, from largely rural and agrarian backgrounds, only the recruits from Wake County, site of the state capital, Raleigh, from a region where a town numbered more than three hundred people. In every company, the occupations of the troops reflected their literal attachment to the land, as nearly 75 percent of the 26th's troops either worked the land they owned or that of their parents or in-laws. The farmers turned soldiers were by no means all from hardscrabble acreage: More than a third possessed land and accompanying holdings assessed at more than a thousand dollars, a decent amount for the era. Keith and Malinda's property on the Grandfather ran just over that figure.

Company F's officers, men such as Lenoir schoolmaster, scholar, and lawyer Nathan Rankin, came from the region's most affluent families, who still owned farms, but whose chief income derived from trade or "more genteel professions."[14] In several cases, the family assets of several of the 26th's officers ran over one hundred thousand dollars.

Back in the ranks, in addition to fellow "farm folk," the Blalocks' comrades included brick masons, coopers, a postmaster, mechanics, a minister, and students. The average age of the couple's mess-mates was twenty-three years and eleven months; however, a number of men in their thirties and forties had enlisted. At fifty-five, Joel Helton, a Caldwell County farmer whom Keith and Malinda had known for most of their lives, was the 26th's oldest recruit. On the other end of the age spectrum were dozens of teenagers, including three fifteen-year-old recruits who had either lied about their age or had known recruiters who had looked the other way. In "Little Sammy Blalock's case," she fooled "all the men except me," testified James Moore.[15]

At Camp Carolina, two miles north of Raleigh, Keith and "Sam" began their training, the base sprawling across the parade grounds of the Crabtree Plantation, close to the junction of the Raleigh and Gaston Railroad and Crabtree Creek.

For Keith, Malinda, and the other recruits, life at Camp Carolina posed a drastic change from the life they had known. They had never been away from home for so long—with no end in sight. More than eighteen hundred troops were spread in wooden huts and canvas tents across the plantation, more than half of the number of people who actually lived in Watauga County.

For recruits who had led pious or sheltered lives—not Keith and Malinda—the rough ways of some men opened eyes. "I have been in and at many places," wrote Private T. W. Setser, "but this is the goddamndest place that I ever Seen. . . . Some sing, Some get drunk, Some curse, Some play cards and all Sorts of devilment that men coulda think of."[16]

The business of the camp was to pound high-spirited or genteel men alike into soldiers. Keith and Malinda learned the complex system of marching and skirmishing maneuvers through endless hours on the drill field from November 1861 to January 1862. Shivering in the rain and wind, they drilled, marched, shot, learned the savage skills of the bayonet, and repeated the routines again and again.

Keith grasped it all with the aplomb of the born soldier, and "Sam," described by one of Company F's men as "a good-looking boy, aged 16 [sic], weight about 130 pounds, height five feet four inches," also proved a natural soldier.[17] "[Sam] stood guard, drilled and handled a musket like a man, and no one ever suspected," a Watauga man would later note.[18]

An officer of Company F would write that Malinda "drilled and did the duties of a soldier, as any other member of the company, and was very adept at learning the manual and the drill."[19]

Malinda proved adept in another aspect of camp life, though the reason was not what her fellow recruits would have imagined. "Sam was pretty handy with a cook-pot," a private would recall. "So he was assigned the position of Mess-Wife."[20]

The term jokingly referred to any soldier who cooked well enough that his mess-mates chose him to prepare rations for groups of five to twenty men. The "honor" in no way exempted Malinda or any other mess-wife from every other duty of a soldier. They did not learn until much later that they had the real wife of Keith Blalock cooking the meals.

The Blalock "brothers" attracted attention for their obvious devotion to each other, a bond that Company F's men had noticed immediately. The brothers tented together and spent every possible moment with each other. The men of Company F had shrugged off Keith's endless concern for "Sam" as an older brother's natural protectiveness. If any of their fellow soldiers thought it strange that Keith even tracked "Sam" when he walked to start some coffee over a mess-fire and that "Sam" never joined the other men in a swimming hole, no one mentioned the thought to the tall, broad-shouldered Keith. The fact that he had been the bare-knuckled terror of the Blue Ridge counties was common knowledge in the mountain companies.

Many of Keith Blalock's comrades would have been stunned if they had known that the man whose leadership abilities were so evident was consumed with the hope of deserting at the first chance—now with "Sam." If not for Malinda's own scheme, Keith would have already been wearing federal blue in Kentucky or Michigan, not rebel gray in North Carolina. If not for Malinda's devotion to him, the couple would not be in danger of dying together in a cause that Keith Blalock despised.

As Keith and Malinda's "miserable time in the Rebel army" dragged through the winter at the training camp, they drilled at least six hours a day even though the drill field and parade ground flooded ankle-deep in the incessant rain.[21] The constant presence of federal ships off the North Carolina coast spurred officers to drill the recruits even harder; most of the 26th was already on the coast or on Bogue Island, preparing to meet the imminent federal amphibious assault.

Keith and Malinda, when free from drill or sentry duty, wrote letters home as rain slapped against their tent's canvas walls, and mainly kept to themselves. As the weather grew colder, they and the other troops stayed inside their tents as much as possible, huddled under overcoats and as many extra blankets as they could find.

Many men sought refuge in religion, attending nightly prayer meetings and long services on Sundays. Neither Keith nor Malinda was especially pious, though they did attend Sabbath sermons.

Equal numbers of soldiers in camp sought solace in "gettin' tight"— drunk. Keith and Malinda kept a bottle of corn whiskey or brandy in their tent—a common practice to ward off the chill at night—but did so in moderation. With "Sam's" secret to hide, too much liquor could loosen one's tongue, and Keith did not want to lose "the soft comfort of Malinda."[22]

Until they faced enemy fire, the biggest threat facing the Blalocks and the men of Company F was disease. First to strike the camps from Raleigh to the coast were "the children's illnesses," measles and mumps. Measles, in particular, spread through the ranks, and while few of the victims died from the maladies, the ensuing weakness of men's immune systems left them prey to deadlier diseases such as dysentery and typhoid fever.

Impure drinking water and poor sanitation in camp led to the most common ailment, acute diarrhea. Keith's and Malinda's hardy constitutions and luck carried them through in good health despite the conditions.

At Christmas, the officers gave their alternately ailing and bored troops a welcome gift: For five days drill was cancelled, and the men only had to report for roll call and sentry duty. Still, as a Caldwell County soldier wrote, the break could not ease some conditions: "Winter with its chilling winds and its cold rains has come. 'Tis a dark and gloomy day, and the shivering sentinels as they walk their wary rounds painfully remind us that the soldiers' life is not altogether romantic."[23]

The gloom increased in late January 1862, when all furloughs were suspended. That emotion soon gave way to anticipation and fear with the news that a federal fleet had moved into Pamlico Sound. Vance was ordered to move the 26th to New Bern, on the Neuse River. At Camp Carolina, the 26th's most recent arrivals, including Keith and Malinda, would soon join the entire regiment at the Neuse.

CHAPTER FOUR
A Secret Revealed

B REVET SERGEANT Keith Blalock whistled once—Company F's
signal to halt. Moonlight had broken through the cover of rain
clouds a minute after he and a dozen pickets of the 26th North Carolina had waded several yards into the waist-high waters of the
Neuse River. As they strained to keep their balance in the swift current and
to hold their muskets above their heads, they offered snipers easy targets.

Blalock had orders from Captain Nathan P. Rankin to track a band of
pro-Union partisans and to scout for federal pickets screening the advance of
General Ambrose Burnside's regiments up the North Carolina coastline. At
any point, Blalock had permission to cut off the search and to return to Confederate General Lawrence O. Branch's encampment, at Kinston.

Nothing stirred on the opposite bank, a hundred or so yards away. But
Blalock, his instincts for survival honed over twenty years of hunting along
Blue Ridge trails that teemed with black bears and mountain lions, whistled
twice—the cue to withdraw.

As the skirmishers turned around and slogged toward the near bank,
Blalock and Corporal James MacAllister backtracked, but kept their faces to
the opposite bank, cocking their British-made Enfield muskets while lowering
them to shoulder level.

Tiny flames suddenly flared from the distant trees—instantly followed by
the deep reports of Sharps long-distance rifles. A ball tore into MacAllister's
throat and knocked him backward into the water.

Blalock and the rest flung their muskets the twenty feet to the near bank
to keep the weapons from getting wet and ducked beneath the surface as balls
whistled by where heads and chests had just been. Blalock stayed submerged
until his fingers touched the muddy bank. Then he clambered from the water
and rolled behind a pine as balls smashed into trunks all around and kicked
up sprays of splinters. From his right hand, he yanked a long sliver.

As the men returned fire and he crawled over to his musket, Blalock
looked for his "younger brother." "Stick to my side—always," Keith had ordered Malinda.[1]

Keith found her propped against another pine less than twenty feet away, cocking her musket's hammer with her left hand. Her other hand pressed against her left shoulder, torn open by a ball.

Keith crawled over to Malinda, wan and bleeding. The sergeant pulled a handkerchief from one of his jacket's pockets, pulled Malinda's hand from her shoulder, and carefully inserted the cloth into the hole. The makeshift bandage stanched the bleeding for the moment.

Keith scooped up the five-foot, four-inch soldier and stumbled along the dark, slippery trail toward the 26th's camp, his arms shielding his wife from the branches that ripped at his own face and hands.

Men of the 26th who had been rousted from sleep by the gunfire had rolled out of their tents, grabbed their muskets, and rushed toward the river, passing Keith and his "brother," who, in the grim slang of the era's soldiers, had "met the messenger"—a federal ball.

Finally, Keith reached the camp and sprinted the last few hundred yards past watch fires and rows of tents to the surgery. Dr. Thomas J. Boykin, some nine years older than the twenty-four-year-old sergeant, waited for the wounded in front of the medical tent's open flap, already wearing his leather apron. Inside, his scalpels, small mallets, clamps, and saws were spread out on a camp table. The volleys echoing from the Neuse meant that he was in for a long evening. As Keith Blalock neared, one of the strangest nights of Boykin's wartime service began.

Blalock dashed into the hospital and laid Malinda on a surgical table. As always, Boykin walked first to a basin of water, quickly scrubbed his hands with lye soap, and moved to the wounded soldier. Two orderlies, whose chief task was to hold down thrashing patients as the surgeon cut, sawed, and stitched with no anesthesia except corn liquor, joined him.

Keith would write to his stepfather: "I told Boykin, 'There's something you have to know about Sam.'"[2]

Boykin aligned a wooden peg between Malinda's upper and lower teeth so she could clamp down against the oncoming agony and would not bite her tongue, removed the saturated handkerchief, and inserted an iron probe into the wound to feel around for the flattened musket ball and for any bone fragments. Then he ordered Keith to leave the tent and to return to his unit.

Keith refused to budge. Boykin ordered his assistants to escort him from the surgery, but nobody moved.

Blalock turned and left the tent. An orderly closed the flap, and Boykin, who had sawed off more limbs in a year of warfare than most of his William and Mary medical professors had in their entire careers, went to work on Malinda.

A Company F private recuperating from a leg wound was leaning against a tree outside the tent as Blalock emerged and sat on a pine stump nearby.

The private would recall that Blalock hugged his knees, closed his eyes, and rocked back and forth.

Boykin was about to discover Keith and "Sam" Blalock's secret, which Keith had already tried to tell the doctor. All that Keith could do was wait.

Later, to a friend, Keith said that he had thought about how much Malinda had already faced in the 26th. That Blalock's "younger brother" soldiered nearly as well as did Keith himself was no secret in the regiment. From the day Malinda had enlisted to the fight along the Neuse, she had done her duty without complaint—happy just to be with Keith. Just three weeks earlier in front of New Bern, North Carolina, Malinda had worked sixteen-hour shifts with her comrades to erect breastworks with worn and broken shovels and axes and without benefit of picks or grubbing hoes. By the evening of March 13, 1862, the 26th had helped build nine forts, two miles of entrenchments, and redans—defensive bastions—and works for forty-one cannons, which included six massive 32-pounders.

Company F was about to see its first action, against Burnside's regiments, who had seized nearby Roanoke Island in a daring and bloody amphibious assault and were advancing up the coast against New Bern, a key target in the Union's campaign to tighten the blockade of the South's ports.

The anguish Keith Blalock faced less than three weeks later outside the surgeons' tent had nearly arrived twice on March 14, 1862, when Union General Ambrose Burnside threw 11,000 troops against the 4,000 men of Brigadier General Lawrence O. Branch's 7th, 26th, 33rd, and 35th North Carolina Regiments. "Sam" had stood alongside his brother in a rifle-pit as the 51st Pennsylvania and 24th and 26th Massachusetts stormed the North Carolinians' entrenchments. Confederate batteries poured grapeshot into the massed Yankees, and the swampy ground was soon littered with men whose screams and moans mingled with the cannons' din. But the blue ranks kept regrouping and closing up, pushing closer to the rifle-pits and artillery redans.

The order to fall back pealed through the rebels' jumbled ranks. The 26th retreated toward the second line of defenses, seven-foot-high earthworks bristling with rebel cannons and muskets.

The regiment stood at the bastion anchoring Branch's right flank. To the earthworks' immediate left was a brickyard that was held by a three-day-old New Bern militia regiment with weapons ranging from old Mexican War percussion muskets to shotguns of every size and make. Of the muskets' notoriously short range and inaccuracy, a Company F soldier said, "You could fire them at your target all day without his knowing about it."[3]

As the 24th and 26th Massachusetts and 51st Pennsylvania formed two-deep battle lines and surged at the North Carolinians, the men held fire until the federal troops were one hundred yards away. The Confederates' Enfields were lethal from that distance. The men of Company F could squeeze off five shots per minute: the mark of a well-trained company was four.

A battery of seven ten-pounder cannons mounted on dirt platforms along the earthworks and loaded with grapeshot depressed their muzzles at the on-rushing blue lines.

At one hundred yards, the 26th opened up on Lieutenant-Colonel T. S. Bell's 51st Pennsylvania, and half of the unit virtually disintegrated in the shower of musket balls and grape. Beside and behind the 51st, the Massachusetts regiments wavered.

To Company F's extreme left, a far different scene erupted. The 21st Massachusetts, led by West Pointer and Mexican War veteran Lieutenant-Colonel William S. Clark, swarmed upon the brickyard's defenders, and the militia broke and fled past the 26th.

Panic spread down the Confederate entrenchments. Burnside reinforced the 21st with the 4th and 5th Rhode Island and the 8th and 11th Connecticut, and as three-quarters of Branch's men abandoned their defenses and fled northwest of the town, only Company F and the 26th barred a complete envelopment of the Confederates by Burnside.

The Blalocks and their comrades held their positions for three-and-a-half hours, pinning down the Union troops in the brickyard until the bulk of Branch's shattered units reached a deep creek five miles northwest of New Bern. Colonel Vance ordered the 26th to abandon the earthworks and designated several companies to screen the regiment's retreat up Blind Road to the creek. Company F fought in the rearguard, firing, falling back several yards and reloading, firing again, and repeating the process all the way to Bryce's Creek.

When the Watauga and Caldwell men finally reached the bank, with Rhode Island skirmishers just two hundred yards away and picking off the rearguard, the rest of the 26th were on the opposite bank, and so were the flat-bottomed ferries that had taken them there.

Keith and "Sam" Blalock, having learned to swim in fast-flowing Blue Ridge rivers, made it to the ferries. Scores of other men did not. As the Blalocks clambered aboard a boat, a Minie ball tore through Malinda's baggy tunic at the right hip, but missed her.

In Captain Rankins' post-battle report, he lauded the Blalocks' company for their steadiness under fire. Lieutenant Joseph Ballew wrote that Keith Blalock was officer material.

Keith Blalock's comrades would have been stunned if they had known that the man whose leadership qualities were so evident despised his uniform. To Blalock, it was one more reminder of yet another secret that he was hiding: if not for Malinda's own scheme, Keith might have been storming a rebel redoubt on some distant front.

An hour after Blalock had carried "Sam" into the tent, the doctor stepped outside to tell him that "Sam" had survived the surgery, the wound not anywhere as serious as it had looked. Although a lot of blood had been lost, Boykin had removed the ball, which had not struck a bone, curtailing the chances of fragments causing infection. Keith would recall: "The physician said to me, 'You have a lot of explaining to do.'"[4]

Keith implored him not to say anything about Malinda until he was better composed to deal with the trouble he likely faced. Whether out of sympathy or out of sheer surprise at the night's events, the surgeon agreed, but for not more than a few days apparently. The orderlies were ordered by the physician to say nothing for the moment. That offered all the time Keith needed.

Although Malinda's wound would not have earned the usual soldier a permanent medical discharge, and perhaps no more than a furlough, she would be going home for good as soon as her gender was made known to Colonel Vance. One way or another, Keith was determined to accompany his wife. He was also resolved to fight for the Union, but his current straits precluded it for the moment. Even if "Sam" was not soon to be "a secret revealed," Keith's previous scheme that he and Malinda would "go missing" together had fallen apart.[5] He later said that he and Malinda had served in the 26th "only with the view of making [our] escape through the lines into the U.S. Army, but finding the Armies so situated as to make escape impossible at that time, and therefore [we] did not attempt escape."[6]

Out of desperation, Keith came up with a drastic solution. Late at night, he slipped past the pickets and crept through the woods and swamp until he found what he was looking for—a huge patch of poison oak. He stripped off all of his clothes and rolled around in it for half an hour or more.

By the morning muster, Keith would laconically state, "I was seriously poisoned and swollen from the effects of what is known as 'poison vine.'"[7] He reeled toward a hospital tent, already running a high fever. "The Physicians in charge of the Hospital supposed it to be Small Pox or a swamp fever," Keith wrote, "and refused to admit [me]."[8]

The surgeons feared that Keith's rash, temperature, and "many loathsome skin eruptions" might infect other patients in the hospital and spread throughout the regiment.[9] Ordering two undoubtedly terrified soldiers to escort Keith back to his tent and to stand guard over him, the doctors "allowed [Keith] to speak to no person on the way back."[10] Keith spent the night in quarantine, alternately sweating and shivering, "nearly out of my senses with it."[11]

Thomas Boykin visited Keith the next morning and, after examining the patient's fiery and worsening rash affecting him from face to feet, was even more baffled. "I also complained of being ruptured," Keith would relate. "He said it was hernia."[12] In all likelihood, Boykin's diagnosis of hernia was not hands-on.

Not long after rushing from the afflicted soldier's tent, Boykin recommended to Vance that he sign an immediate medical discharge for Keith to eliminate any possibility of contagion. On April 20, 1862, Keith received a paper bearing Boykin's and Vance's signatures and words that assuaged Keith's emotional, though not physical, torment: "Discharged for disability."[13]

Within hours of having approved Keith Blalock's discharge, Vance was visiting the 26th's wounded when Malinda, already apprised of Keith's successful "stratagem," informed the Colonel that she was woman. Vance did not recognize the short-haired "boy," and, putting the soldier's claim to the test, called Dr. Boykin.

Vance reportedly exclaimed, "Oh, Surgeon, have I a case for you!"[14]

Dr. Boykin's examination of "Sam" soon confirmed Malinda's gender "as strong as proof of holy writ."[15] Malinda's wound had not been sufficient to force her from the 26th ranks, but her "womanhood" was: "This lady dressed in man's clothes, volunteered, received bounty [$50] and did all the duties of a soldier before she was found out; but her husband being discharged, she disclosed the fact, returned the bounty, and was discharged April 20, 1862."[16]

Because Keith's discharge was one issued through regular channels, as opposed to his wife's, he was allowed to pocket his bonus. As for the doctor who had operated on her, no questions were asked, and Boykin wrote that "her disguise was never penetrated" until she mentioned it to Vance.[17]

In the *Confederate Veteran* in 1898, a humorous but garbled version of Malinda's revelation to Vance would appear, Malinda referred to as "Joe":

> "Colonel, I want to go home," said Joe, after the customary salutation.
> "Well, Joe," said the Colonel, "I suppose a good many of us would like to go home, but just now we are needed somewhere else."
> "But, Colonel, I ain't a man."
> "No, but you soon will be, and doubtless a brave one."
> "No, sir, I won't," Joe rejoined. "I'm a woman."
> "The devil you say!" said Colonel Vance, surprised and amused at the complete defeat of his proposition. "Here, Doctor!" he called to the surgeon of the regiment, "here is a case for you."[18]

Malinda would write that she met "Colonel Zeb Vance at the hospital and told him that I was the wife of William Blalock and wanted to go home."[19]

"Yes," she continued, "I had on a Soldier's uniform at that time and had boy hair cut short and passed as a man. Colonel Vance first said he would keep me as an orderly, but went and got me a medical pass home, and I did go home."[20]

The Blalocks' neighbor and fiery Confederate Carroll Moore would contemptuously write that "Blalock and his wife enlisted only for the sake of the bounty and only as long as it suited them."[21]

Malinda, referred to as "Mrs. L.M. Blaylock [*sic*]" in the 1863-64 North Carolina Confederate Roll of Honor (a mistake, along with an erroneous reference to a camp muster date causing some later confusion—see endnotes for Chapter 4), would write: "We were sent home rejoicing after about six months in service and three fights."[22]

The Blalocks would have to walk most of the long route back to the Grandfather, as Keith's horrifying appearance prevented their boarding a train or even hitching a ride on the back of a farmer's cart.

Neither one minded, but their joy was tempered by ominous words that Vance had said to Malinda just before she left Kinston. "When they [the 26th] wanted him [Keith]," Malinda noted, "they would call for him."[23]

PART TWO

Tories, Yankees, and Outliers

CHAPTER FIVE
We'll Be Back

IN early June 1862, mountain folk slogging along the rutted Morganton Road gaped at a man and woman headed west toward Coffey's Gap. The man, his face and hands laced with "scarlet welts and fiery eruptions," looked familiar but hard to place.[1] So too, did the slight woman, her dark hair short and her left arm in a sling. She was "stick thin" and drawn, but with a second look, locals recognized Malinda Blalock more quickly than they did her husband.[2] And when they did realize that the man was indeed Keith Blalock, most recoiled and got out of the way—not, for once, because they were intimidated by him, but because they feared he had contacted some virulent and likely contagious case of swamp fever.

With each step the couple put between the 26th's hospital tents and the looming mountains, Keith and Malinda felt as if they "wanted to burst with relief."[3] The air grew cooler as they approached Watauga, "colder in both summer and winter than in any other county in the State."[4]

When they encountered farmers in their fields or on the path, Keith hung back, so as not to chase away anyone staring at his rash, as Malinda, still posing as a boy, persuaded people to spare a few pieces of cornbread or fruit, a cup of water or buttermilk, and sometimes even a bowl of meat or stew. Locals whose own sons had marched off with the 26th or the 58th proved especially amenable when Malinda showed them her discharge paper, earning homespun plaudits for her "devotion to the Cause."[5]

As Keith and Malinda climbed into the foothills of the Blue Ridge, the sights, sounds, and smells by which they had measured their entire lives surrounded them.

As they neared Boone, a hamlet of several log cabins, a few substantial homes, an inn, and a general store, "a land close-hedged on either side with gnarled and twisted old laurel trees . . . spread before them."[6] The air was redolent with the laurels' "bitter, tonic fragrance."[7]

Then the path turned into the open, a panorama of "wide, rolling slopes, green hills and valleys dotted with roofs, and beyond these the great blue mountains soaring up to the sky."[8]

At Coffey's Gap, the pair stopped briefly at the home of McCaleb Coffey, who took a look at Keith's condition and offered a curt greeting. Although his dislike for his unionist brother's stepson had not ebbed, Coffey could say little, as Keith had served in the 26th despite people's suspicions about his loyalty.

For Malinda, Coffey had nothing but admiration for the sheer "pluck" of the wounded young woman, who had "literally traded her hoopskirt for a Confederate's shell jacket."[9] His hopes that all four of his boys—Jones, Thomas, Ninevah, and John—would walk again up the same path where Keith and Malinda stood would prove futile.

Minutes later, the couple headed up that path to Keith's boyhood home.

When they stepped onto Austin Coffey's porch, Keith and Malinda received a warm greeting from his mother and from his stepfather, who was even more delighted when Keith proffered the couple's discharge papers. Never again, Keith vowed, would he wear Confederate gray. "[I'd] rather have died than serve the Secesh [sic]," Keith would remember.[10]

One of the first things Keith had done when back on his family's porch was to let them know the real cause of his "swamp fever." For weeks, however, other people he had known his entire life avoided him, fearing contagion and half-expecting news of Keith's death from his ailment any day.

Keith and Malinda departed his stepfather's home almost immediately and climbed the narrow, familiar path leading to the Grandfather. They "knew the route as well as they knew their own faces."[11] For the first time in months, the mountain's splendor rose in front of them, the Grandfather's "calm and noble form . . . its rocky top drawn in a series of curves against the western sky."[12] The husband and wife knew and had missed every inch of "the long spurs like buttresses" and the forests that "clothed it as with a garment to where the black rock surmounts them."[13]

Keith and Malinda ascended a steep, mossy path shrouded by balsam firs and cliffs. Somewhere above them gushed the famous Grandfather Spring, only ten degrees above freezing even in the summer. Several more turns and they reached their cabin. They were home for the moment, and safe. Or so it seemed.

For a few days, the couple recuperated from their grueling trek. Keith, once his fever broke, began tending to the self-induced rash that had caused it. Employing a traditional mountain treatment for the poison oak, or "vine," Malinda applied and reapplied brine-soaked poultices to "all of Keith's affected parts."[14] He also soaked several times a day in warm water into which Malinda heaped salt. The crimson blotches first turned pink and then faded, any traces of the rash on his hands and face eventually disappearing in his sun- and wind-burned skin.

Malinda, too, recovered, and within a few weeks, she and her husband resumed the lives on the mountain they had left behind for the 26th. She dried apples, peaches, pumpkins, and blackberries for pies, and they both cleared their overgrown plots and laid in new beds of beans, turnips, and sweet and Irish potatoes. Keith and Malinda also returned to the hunting trails of the Grandfather, tracking deer and wild hogs.

Clad in the broad-brimmed cap, the long homespun hunting shirt, and moccasins of "the backwoods hunter of this period," Keith and Malinda both reveled in "the wild, free life" that stood in such stark contrast to the regimentation of the soldier's routines.[15] The husband and wife, as with all who prowled the Grandfather's forests for game, "sang and danced and frolicked when they came in from their traps and camps in the peaks and crags."[16] While hunting, Keith and Malinda spent nights in their "ranges," huts of unhewn logs spread throughout the mountain and buttressed against the omnipresent winds by boulders. The couple hung the skins of deer on the huts' outer walls to dry, and, later, Malinda's sewing needles and scissors would turn the hide into clothing.

Over the door of each hut, the Blalocks hung their hunting rifles on wooden pegs, the weapons always loaded and easy to reach.

Keith and Malinda kept to themselves in the weeks after their return, occasionally visiting Austin Coffey and Keith's mother, but avoiding other locals, most notably rabid Confederates.

Even though Keith's discharge was valid and, as he said, "I should have been left alone," he was not shielded by "that bit of paper" from the escalating conflicts.[17] Once again, his unionist beliefs would thrust him against many of his Confederate neighbors. "In time," wrote a historian, "the Confederate authorities would come to wish that they *had* left Keith alone."[18]

Keith's dilemma simmered again as he encountered other hunters in the mountains and Austin Coffey's brothers on the Morganton Road. They noticed that beneath the hunter's cap, Keith's rash had vanished and that he appeared as robust as ever. They muttered that he was healthy enough to reenlist.

As further proof of Keith's health, Carroll Moore charged that "soon after his [Keith's] discharge from the Confederate service, Blalock and his brother-in-law William Pritchard beat and robbed a man by the name of Lassen Farr, taking an ass from him among other things."[19] Moore further alleged: "This was about the first of his [Keith's] acts of depredation that [I] remember."[20] Keith would vehemently deny the allegation and was never actually charged with it.

"I saw them [Keith and Malinda] when they went off with the 26th," said Jesse Moore, "and I saw them when they came back. Keith soon was healed."[21]

To Keith's mounting anger, his stepuncles contended that he should join either the 58th Regiment's Company I, mustering in summer of 1862 in Boone, or the same regiment's Company D, organizing in nearby Valle

Crucis, the Valley of the Cross. If Keith did not want to endure the life of a foot soldier again, they reasoned, why not join the twenty-five or so Watauga men who joined Company A of the 6th Cavalry regiment? Keith's uncles and other local Confederates surmised that there was but one reason for Keith Blalock's obstinance in not reenlisting: "His Unionism was particularly obnoxious to us all," said Carroll Moore. "He knew that."[22]

As the summer wore on, McCaleb Coffey, Carroll Moore, John Boyd Sr., and others whose sons were off with the 26th and the 58th once again challenged Keith's loyalties in front of Austin Coffey and, on the rare occasions they encountered Keith off the Grandfather, with "the healthy specimen" himself.

Strengthening local Confederates' case against Keith's "sitting it out" was not only his recovery from his "swamp fever," but also the Conscription Act of 1862. The edict guaranteed trouble for the recalcitrant Keith.

Enacted in April 1862, the Conscription Act of North Carolina was designed to combat the disaffection and unionism roiling the central and western counties of the state. In November 1861, the explosive situation in Watauga and the other mountain counties had compelled Governor Henry T. Clark to send an urgent dispatch to Confederate President Jefferson Davis, in Richmond. The governor informed Davis that the Raleigh legislature was inundated with "numerous communications from the North Carolina counties bordering on East Tennessee requesting help against traitors, Unionists, and deserters."[23]

With the exception of diehard Confederates, the fury of the mountain folk against the Conscription Act was pronounced. Historian John G. Barrett notes that conscription "was particularly obnoxious."[24]

"For mountain folk," he writes, "accustomed to individual freedom, the act was especially galling. . . . Having responded most generously to the early calls for troops, the mountain counties in many cases were already stripped of young men by the time conscription went into effect. The additional demand for troops, therefore, met with considerable opposition, as did future legislation expanding the draft."[25]

With his discharge paper, as well as that of "Sam," Keith Blalock could claim that he had "responded most generously" to the Cause, his avowed unionism notwithstanding.[26]

Other mountain unionists who had placed region above ideology and had enlisted in Confederate regiments deserted in ever increasing numbers in the summer of 1862. Most headed west, where unionists and, now, many neutral people simply opposed to conscription helped hide and feed them on their way to the mountains. "Many western Carolinians place little or no stigma on desertion," wrote a local man, "and the warm welcome they accord army deserters causes the mountains to fill up with the disloyal from all of the Confederate states."[27] Rebel soldiers gone "over the hill" could find a heartfelt welcome at the cabin of Keith and Malinda Blalock. The couple began guiding deserters as far as the Grandfather's wind-whipped summit and pointing out the route to safety to Union-controlled territory in eastern Tennessee.

Keith would attest: "I was reported to the Home Guards as being a Lincolnite and a pilate [*sic*—pilot] for Union men through the lines to the U.S. Army, which was correct."[28]

Mountain pilots drew special attention from the local Confederates, as well as the government in Richmond, by the summer of 1862.

Confederate Secretary of War J. A. Seddon wrote to Zeb Vance that "our armies are so much weakened by desertion . . . that we are unable to reap the fruits of our victories."[29] In a letter to the Secretary of War, Robert E. Lee, who counted the 26th North Carolina among his regiments in the Army of Northern Virginia, mentioned that "desertion of the North Carolina troops from this army is becoming so serious an evil that, unless it can be promptly arrested, I fear the troops from that State will be greatly reduced."[30]

Despite Confederate locals' reawakened suspicions about Keith Blalock's disloyalty, he could not be branded a deserter—yet. To Austin Coffey, Malinda, and others, Keith swore he "would die at home before being forced off" to a rebel regiment again.[31]

Keith and other unionists in the mountain counties were also swept up in the divisive North Carolina gubernatorial election of 1862. Running against staunch Confederate and "Jefferson Davis man" William J. Johnson was Keith and Malinda's former commander, Zeb Vance.[32] Vance, his campaign championed in newspaper editor W. W. Holden's diatribes against secession, conscription, and the war in general, attracted unionists such as Keith Blalock to his side. Although that support led his many critics to label Vance the "Northern or Federal candidate," he publicly eschewed the Union men of the disaffected mountain region.[33] To the *Fayetteville Observer,* Vance stated: "Believing the only hope of the South depended upon the prosecution of the war at all hazards and to the utmost extremity so long as the foot of the invader pressed Southern soil, I took the field at an early day, with the determination to remain there until independence was achieved. My convictions in this regard would remain unchanged."[34]

Despite his belief in fighting on, Vance attracted the votes of the Austin Coffeys and the Keith Blalocks with bitter harangues against the "Conscriptive Act."[35] Vance decried it as "unjust and impolite."[36] For Keith, to say the least, the legislation posed a threat that he would have to face. At some point, the recruiting officers who had "persuaded" him to enlist in the 26th would return—this time as conscription officers sanctioned to truss him up and haul him back to the ranks. "The die is cast and the dog is dead and the baby is born," wrote a local "recruit," "and his name is conscription."[37]

In Watauga County, conscription parties composed of militia—the soon-to-be infamous Home Guard—declared that former Confederate soldiers wounded seriously enough to preclude their return to the army but healthy enough to ride and shoot must join the conscription men, and dozens of discharged Confederate regulars did. Two Watauga men who joined the guards professed their particular contempt for "outliers [deserters]." The pair's names were William and Reuben Coffey, and in their view one of the county's biggest "shirkers"—"a prime healthy specimen"—lived up on the Grandfather.

Knowing where Keith Blalock's mountain cabin lay and finding him there were two entirely different propositions. "I knew those mountains better than anyone," Keith would say, "and could disappear before you knew I'd ever been there."[38]

As always, Keith and Malinda had devised plans revolving around his "dogged determination not to serve in the Confederate ranks."[39] Keith, with his knowledge of virtually every cave, every hidden path, and every crag of the Grandfather, eluded the conscription officers in the beginning. "[Keith] had little to fear so long as he avoided public places, or even gave the conscription officers an excuse for not seeing him."[40]

In Keith's case, that excuse was that the conscription parties literally could not see him high on the mountains, while he enjoyed "an eagle-eye view" of anyone riding up from the valleys. Keith and Malinda usually glimpsed the Home Guard long before "the motley array thundered" up to the cabin.[41] When they did, they found a smiling Malinda and no sign of Keith. Malinda could point toward the Grandfather's jagged profile and truthfully and enigmatically say that Keith was "somewhere yonder."[42]

"Yonder" could mean a few hundred yards away and a perch where Keith's rifle-gun was trained on one of his step-uncles. Chances were, a descendant relates, that Keith "was watching from a nearby thicket and trying not to give himself away by a fit of laughter."[43]

The fact that Keith was "living much the same life as usual and always had abundant warning to stay out of sight" until the Home Guard rode off in frustration galled his step-uncles, Robert Green, Carroll Moore, and every other local Confederate man.[44] And Keith and Malinda knew better than to underestimate the tenacity of the conscription parties. When more than a handful of riders materialized along the mountain's lowest trails, Keith climbed high into the dense, tangled woods and gorges, spots where no horse could pass. "If he feared pursuit by dogs," a conscription agent wrote, "he rubbed the soles of his feet with onions or odorous herbs in order to confuse the scent."[45]

Sometimes when the Home Guard combed the slopes in earnest, Malinda would vanish with Keith under cover of the thick blue mists frequently shrouding the mountain. More often, however, she remained in the cabin to "greet" the riders as they "repeatedly searched" for her husband.[46] "The deserter or shirker's wife had not only to bear more anxiety for her husband's safety than the soldier's wife did, for the sight of armed men seeking his capture or death was almost an everyday occurrence," a Home Guardsman noted, "but she must, by her own almost unaided labor, cultivate the crops and raise the food."[47]

When Keith had to remain "hid out" for several days at a time, Malinda prepared food for him "in the deadest hours of the night and smuggled it out to him."[48]

Malinda's lot in the summer of 1862, in an observer's opinion, "was but another proof of the truism that, after all, it is women who have to bear the brunt of the ills that befall mankind."[49]

Malinda held a different view. "She would have marched into the very jaws of death itself in her devotion to that which she held dear—Keith."[50]

Malinda had to be always aware that her movements and those of other local women whose husbands, brothers, and sons were hiding out came under constant scrutiny by the Coffeys and other conscription men. While local Confederates deemed Keith Blalock highest-priority prey, they rounded up other outliers and shirkers throughout the county. The Home Guard did seize many, but many more "took to the woods and mountains, lying out day and night to avoid arrest, and although the militia officers have exerted themselves with great zeal, yet these skulkers have always had many more active friends than they need, and could always get timely information of enemy movements to arrest them and so avoided it."[51]

"Timely information" about the activities of his Confederate step-uncles and the Home Guard's sallies onto the Grandfather often came to Keith via Austin Coffey, who carefully monitored his brothers' activities. At first warning from his stepfather, Keith would melt into the forest, gorges, and caves, always one step ahead of his trackers.

Still, Keith relied mainly on his own eyes and on "the contrivance and cunning" that Malinda was "driven to exercise" against the Home Guards.[52] Malinda and Keith devised "her own code of signals to guide the movements of her husband."[53] The Blalocks' system featured cues steeped in domestic routines that seemed innocuous, but proved anything but that. "Sometimes a certain bed-quilt hung on the fence meant danger, and another of a different color or pattern meant safety, or a certain song sung on the way to the spring conveyed the necessary information."[54]

On Grandfather Mountain, which teemed with hogs set loose by locals to forage along the slopes, hog calling was the favorite signal of Malinda and of the other women whose husbands or sons concealed themselves amid the ragged slopes. "In those days of scarcity," a Home Guardsman wrote, "the hog became of even more than his usual importance. The neighborhood constantly rang with shrill voices imploring him to hasten home to be fed. A slight change in the habitual mode of calling apprised the deserter a mile distant when he could approach his home and when he must keep close underground."[55]

Keith was sometimes compelled to hide in a cave or a concealed mountain clearing for several days at a time and did not dare hunt or forage for fear of revealing his whereabouts to the Home Guards. Malinda, "clad only in limp homespun," would sneak from the cabin at nightfall with "concealed provisions about her person that would give lessons to the deftest importer of dress silk and kid gloves, aided by crinoline, bustles, and all of the paraphernalia of fashion."[56]

"[Malinda] knew the Grandfather so well that she could make her way around even in pitch-tar dark," a descendant wrote of Malinda and other Watauga women who spirited away food and provisions to unionists and outliers in hiding.[57] Even a Home Guardsman grudgingly conceded: "Many a wild goose chase did they lead those who followed a will-o'-the-wisp of a faded, checked homespun [dress] for miles through bush and briar. . . . Indeed, these women, in their way, proved quite as true and sacrificing as their more refined sisters who sent their husbands, sons, and brothers to the field instead of the woods."[58]

As Malinda had proven in the guise of "Sam" Blalock, she would sacrifice and endure anything for her husband.

In the summer of 1862, a man who would endure anything to put Keith back in a Confederate uniform or in a Confederate prison took command of the Watauga County Home Guard Company. Setting up his headquarters at Camp Mast, near Boone, twenty-three-year-old Major Harvey Bingham knew how "to soldier."[59] Bingham, a Caldwell County native who sported a thick goatee and possessed an intimidating stare, had seen hard duty as "a boy officer" with the 37th North Carolina Regiment.[60] Wounded twice and suffering the effects of a camp fever, he had been honorably discharged and sent home.

Bingham chafed at the idea of sitting out the rest of the war, and when Robert Green, Carroll Moore, and William, Reuben, and McCaleb Coffey approached him with the offer to take command of Watauga's militia, Bingham jumped at it.

Within weeks of Bingham's arrival at Camp Mast, Keith and Malinda encountered a different caliber of Home Guardsman. Bingham selected fellow veterans who also had been honorably discharged for wounds or illness and men too old for regular service but eager to track down traitors and deserters.

Training his recruits to operate as a cohesive unit employing mounted infantry tactics, Bingham turned the Watauga Home Guard into a hard-riding, disciplined outfit that bore no resemblance to the "comic-opera jokes" that many other militia units were.[61] Keith and Malinda now faced foes as tough and wily as they were and nearly as familiar with the terrain of the Grandfather and nearby Blowing Rock. Bingham's determination, obsession in many people's view, to scour the region of all outliers, deserters, and unionists echoed in a shoot-to-kill policy. Whenever his men spotted a healthy man in civilian garb, Bingham ordered the guardsmen to call out "halt"—once. If their quarry kept moving, Bingham and his men opened fire. They offered no second chance.

Keith came face-to-face with Bingham's company in late August 1862, when early in the morning, the Home Guard finally caught up with Keith. A dozen or more riders burst up to the Blalocks' cabin, the thuds of hooves, the jangle of spurs, and shouts pealing across the clearing. Keith and Malinda stepped onto the porch and straight into the leveled barrels of Enfield muskets, cavalry carbines, and rifle-guns.

"I let my guard down just for a moment," Keith later told a relative, "and it cost."[62]

As Keith scanned the conscription party, some wore the gray shell-tunics of regular cavalry; others were clad in homespun shirts and knee-length woolen jackets. He peered at the craggy, grinning faces of William and Reuben Coffey and of Robert Green. Bingham, still wearing the officer's kepi and the bluish-gray, knee-length jacket of the 37th, glowered down at Keith.

Keith produced his discharge paper, claiming he had "done my bit."[63] The conscription men retorted that the "swamp fever" listed on the dog-eared document had cleared up just weeks after the ink was dry and that he was fully recovered.

"They told him that he had to reenlist or suffer the penalties for desertion," Malinda recalled.[64]

Under the provisos of the Conscription Act, if Keith refused to serve, the draft agents could bind him and deliver him to the army, or clap a noose around his neck, or put a bullet in him.

Beseeching his "kin"—the Coffey brothers—to grant him one night to "get ready," giving them his "blood-word" that he would report for duty the next morning, Keith, "a splendiferous talker when he wanted," somehow persuaded them that he would honor his promise.[65] After all, he reminded them, he had fought with the 26th even though branded a unionist. And if they needed additional proof of his loyalty to the country, he had even allowed his wife to serve the Confederacy as "Sam" Blalock.

With Bingham's warning that militiamen were perched along every trail leading from the Blalocks' home and up the Grandfather, the Home Guard camped near the cabin in the belief that, for Keith, flight was impossible. The conscription party thought they had barred any possible escape route.

That night, Keith and Malinda gathered a sack of food, provisions, and ammunition and waited until the predawn mist rolled upward from the Grandfather's gorges. Then the couple shouldered their rifle-guns, stole from the cabin, and sneaked past the slumbering militia "watching" the cabin.

As dawn broke across the Blue Ridge, the Home Guard discovered the cabin lay empty. According to Malinda, "We weren't going to let Keith be arrested in his front yard."[66]

There was little doubt whom Keith chiefly blamed for the Home Guards turning up on his property. "Blalock had a grudge against William Coffey," Keith's friend George Perkins wrote, "because he had been so hard on Union men of who Keith was one."[67]

McCaleb Coffey tried to downplay his brother's role in Keith and Malinda's plight, even attempting to soften William Coffey's avowed secessionist stance. "A squad of home guards came over in search of him [Keith]," testified McCaleb, "and my brother, a quiet, peaceable old man of the neighborhood, was taken along with them to show them the way to Blalock's house and hiding spots. Blalock was in revenge for his [William Coffey's] having shown the home guards the most secret way to his [Keith's] house when they were in search of him."[68]

McCaleb added that when the Home Guard "sent for William Coffey to pilot them through the mountains to Blalock's, his brother was reputed one of the most experienced woodsmen in the country."[69]

Major Bingham, enraged that Keith had duped him, despite William Coffey's piloting expertise on behalf of the Home Guard, within days posted notices of a $500 cash bounty for the capture of Keith Blalock as "a shirker and deserter"—dead or alive.[70]

CHAPTER SIX
A Ragged Band

I N the impenetrable forests and crags of the Grandfather, Keith and Malinda climbed to a spot they had selected weeks ago. They had laid in provisions and ammunition in a rude hut near an abandoned rail pen tucked amid "primeval wilderness unbroken save for one mere clearing."[1]

"Our enemies could hardly see their own hands in front of them that high on the mountain," Keith chided.[2]

A local's words testified to the Home Guards' obstacles in pursuing the Blalocks. "There are many tangles and thicketty [sic] places in the coves of the mountains, and others where there is laurel and ivy in small spruce pines that so cover the banks of the streams as to render locomotion along them impossible. Axes are necessary to hew a way into many places, and woe to the men who ventures too far into their depths by crawling or creeping between their rigid branches."[3] Locals called the thickets "hells."

With their knowledge of the mountains, Keith and Malinda never needed those axes, navigating ancient Cherokee footpaths no more than a foot wide at points. The thuds of Home Guards' axes echoing up the Grandfather brought little more than laughter to the Blalocks, who figured that their trackers would never reach them and that, on the remote chance that the Confederates lurched upon the tiny log cabin, the couple would have disappeared hours earlier in the bluish haze rolling across the mountain's five peaks.

To Keith and Malinda, their lives as fugitives on the Grandfather offered much despite the dangers. "It suited them," wrote a local. "Both loved the mountains, and they both welcomed a good scrap almost as much as they loved each other."[4]

The Home Guards did not relish the real possibility of a scrap in which Keith and Malinda held their favorite spot—"high ground covered by their rifle-guns."[5] Both were crack shots with the mountaineer's traditional weapon. With a far greater range than the standard-issue Enfields carried by Confederate regulars and many Home Guards, the rifle-guns' caliber ranged from 80 to 140, the ball big enough to blow a fist-sized hole in a man. Keith and Malinda could fend off their foes indefinitely from the right vantage point, and the couple knew every "sniper's-perch" on the Grandfather.[6]

Drifting down from the mountain, the distant din of hunting rifles galled William, Reuben, and McCaleb Coffey and especially Major Harvey Bingham. "Keith and Malinda were up there, taking down game and doing what they pleased with a war on and all those Watauga boys off fightin' the Yankees," a neighbor said.[7]

Every time Keith's pursuers stared up at the Grandfather, they knew he was up there. But they had no idea where his hiding place lay.

Keith and Malinda did find the life of the fugitive thrilling: "There was novelty, excitement, and a spice of danger which added zest to it. Perhaps, as men who had been both [deserter and soldier] declared, it called for more courage to be a deserter than a soldier, but the former enjoyed a freedom impossible to the latter, and the deserter availed himself to his long holiday of two years or more to loaf, hunt, and fish to his heart's content. Owing to the scarcity of ammunition and the absence of such a large proportion of the male population, game became so tame and abundant as to be taken without trouble."[8]

The need to replenish ammunition, and Keith's confidence in his knack to elude the rebels led him and Malinda to sneak at night to Austin Coffey's house numerous times for shot, extra clothing, and news of the war and neighbors. By dawn, the couple would scamper back up the Grandfather, hidden in the billowing morning haze.

After a few locals reported ghostly sightings of the Blalocks coming and going from Coffey's Gap, the Home Guard placed a watch on Coffey's home, and Austin's brothers began paying visits at odd hours of the morning and evening. No Confederate, not even Bingham, however, proposed arresting Austin Coffey, who was, in the region's venerable custom, "looking after his kinfolk."[9] Ameliorating some neighbors' anger at him was the genuine fondness and respect people accorded him. "Though a Union sympathizer, he was respected by the rebels, having never refused food and shelter to anyone regardless of their convictions."[10]

Still, as the war dragged on and Watauga men died on the battlefields from Virginia to Tennessee, many neighbors' good will toward Austin Coffey eroded with each rumor that his wanted stepson Keith and Malinda had "come off the Grandfather yet again."[11] Confederates' hatred of Keith and the Home Guards' determination to haul him in or kill him in the attempt placed his stepfather in burgeoning danger. A local mountain man wrote: "The old man frequently hid Keith and Malinda, and in so doing risked his own life."[12]

The lives of those futilely tracking the Blalocks proved also at increasing risk by fall of 1862. Ever-growing numbers of Confederate army deserters from western North Carolina and local men dodging conscription sought refuge in the mountains. Governor Vance estimated that more than 1,200 men were holed up in the Blue Ridge by the end of 1862. The Home Guard faced not only tough and wily individuals such as Keith and Malinda, but also bands of deserters who were "heavily armed."[13]

Among Watauga unionists who had supported the Confederacy out of regional loyalty in the conflict's early days, rising anger at the Conscription Act erupted. In the Confederate Congress's lower house, the only two North Carolina votes opposing the Conscription Act had been cast by delegates from western North Carolina. Roiling the people of the mountain counties further, the Conscription Act's "slave" clause, added on a few months after the original bill's enactment, fueled charges that the conflict was "a rich man's war and a poor man's fight."[14] The clause, known as the "20-Nigger Law," allowed men of property, plantation gentry who owned at least twenty slaves, to sit out the war.[15]

Another legality—"exemption"—allowed men of means to hire a destitute neighbor to fight in the wealthier man's place. Of the mountain men, a regional historian writes: "None of them held exemptible jobs, owned twenty or more slaves, or could dream of hiring a substitute. Conscription stuck this class of people with staggering force."[16]

Just as Keith Blalock had rolled in poison oak to gain his medical discharge months earlier, local men he knew hatched similar or even more drastic schemes to avoid the conscription agents. Some "shirkers" cut off a finger or two or scaled their skin on blades or washboards until fetid sores appeared, risking infection and death to avoid service. One man pleaded to army surgeons that he suffered from "a condition of disease as great as any man had."[17] The doctors did not agree, saying he had a cold only and packing him off to the front.

Keith and Malinda knew men who even dressed in women's clothing as they worked their land, but the ruse rarely worked as riding with the conscription parties were at least a few locals bound to recognize the "female" farmers. Unlike with Malinda at Kinston, a quick "body inspection," as the Home Guard called it, revealed no feminine features on these "volunteers."[18] They soon exchanged their calico dresses for a gray- or butternut-hued uniform.

As increasing numbers of men sought refuge in the mountains from the Confederate army, Bingham and his men stepped up their efforts to capture them. Keith did not have to worry much when on the Grandfather's upper reaches, but on the lower slopes, where the Home Guard prowled daily, he had to take greater caution. Several times alone or with Malinda, he hid in caves as Bingham's mounted men pounded up nearby paths.

Keith's luck in evading the militia seemingly ran out in mid-September

1862. Returning alone from Austin Coffey's house, Keith crawled into a small cave and huddled there while the rebels scoured the outside woods. The search continued without letup, for the militia had spotted Keith somewhere between Coffey's and the approaches to the mountain.

Eventually, they found Keith. The jubilant rebels hauled him from the cave, debating whether to hang him from a nearby limb or to drag him off to a Confederate prison. They chose the latter course of action.

Keith would recall: "[I] was arrested by Major Bingham's command, my hands were tied behind me, and I was sent to headquarters in Watauga Co., N.C."[19]

Bingham's headquarters lay alongside Cove Creek, four miles above Valle Crucis and several miles from the Grandfather. The Home Guard's encampment, a collection of wooden shacks and leaky tents used during the Mexican War sprawled around an old mill, featured a ramshackle "Guard House," into which they pitched the trussed-up Keith.[20] He languished in the damp, fetid jail "for a term of eight days."[21] On the ninth day, several guardsmen shoved open the door and hauled him outside, once again tying his hands behind him.

Tethering him behind a guardsman's horse, they "started to Castle Thunder [a Confederate base to the east]."[22] Bingham curtly informed Keith that his war was over. "I was to wear the Ball and Chain," Keith would say.[23]

Keith trudged behind the horse for two days and nights, the specter of a Confederate prison's disease, beatings, and a high likelihood of death for "such a notorious character" awaiting him.[23] As always, Keith had other ideas.

His words uttered with brusque bravado, Keith would relate: "On the third day after starting for Castle Thunder, I made my escape out of their hands and returned to my home again."[25] He did so at night, as his captors slept.

Bingham, seething at the news that Keith Blalock had once more escaped, deployed the Home Guard along the paths of the lower Grandfather, but Keith slipped past them and climbed to his hidden hut, where Malinda, "much troubled by his absence," had "taken to the woods while Keith was gone."[26] With the mountain crawling with outliers and Confederates alike, Malinda, though resourceful and a fine shot, was too smart to risk being caught alone by any band of men—especially strangers who had not seen a woman for many months.

Keith and Malinda's latest reunion lasted less than a week without interruption. Another Home Guard contingent, from Burke County, joined with Bingham's men in a sweep of the Grandfather and Blowing Rock, and Keith was once again nabbed on the Grandfather's bottom trails, headed to his stepfather's house. Fortunately for Keith, the Burke County riders caught him: Bingham had issued orders for his men to shoot him on sight.

"In a few days after returning home [following his escape on the road to Castle Thunder]," Keith recorded, "I was again captured, by Maj. Walton's command of Burke Co., N.C., and on the first night after being arrested, again made my escape."[27] Again, Keith made his break under cover of darkness, as the guards dozed.

Keith's uncanny or incredibly lucky ability to slip away from his captors twice in less than two weeks did not lull him into any sense of invulnerability. With the increased vigilance of the Home Guard and the certain knowledge that the next time he was seized, execution loomed, Keith devised a scheme that would allow him and Malinda to remain on the Grandfather for the moment. Strength in numbers, in Keith's view, was the key to holding off Bingham and Walton. Those numbers lay with the other fugitives in the mountains.

A dozen or so deserters and shirkers who slipped individually at various junctures onto the Grandfather and worked their way to its higher reaches still found themselves gaping at gun barrels. Those belonged not to the Home Guards, but to Keith and Malinda. Some of these deserters convinced the glowering Keith—his visage even more formidable courtesy of the barbed goatee and mustache he now favored—and the diminutive but dangerous woman alongside him, that they loathed the Confederacy. The couple uncocked their weapons and led them to the concealed hut, or "range."

With the Home Guard's incessant forays into the mountains, "I saw the need for men we could trust and who could shoot," Keith recalled.[28] Some of the outliers were men Keith had known his entire life, mountain men such as gaunt but tough Harrison Church, crack shot Jim Hartley, and clever Joseph Franklin. All three despised the Confederacy as much as Keith and would have no problem pulling a trigger on longtime friends and neighbors wearing gray.

Although several of the fierce outliers arrayed near the Blalocks' range knew the mountains as well as Keith, they deferred to "the young giant." He set up a wide perimeter around the cabin, day and night posting shifts of lookouts and pickets including Malinda and himself.

Eating wild berries and roots, cooking game and fish only when dense haze could conceal their campfires from Confederate eyes in the valley, the Blalocks and their gang, some of them toting Enfields they had deserted with, lived off the land. Keith and Malinda continued their nocturnal forays to

Austin Coffey's home, relying on the same type of signals—clothes hung a certain way on the line or a candle lit in a certain window—to let the couple know if they could safely sneak into the house. Through their cunning and a healthy dose of luck, Keith and Malinda would slip in and out despite the watch maintained on the house by Coffey's stepbrothers. "No one, not even the Home Guards," said a Coffey relative, "expected Austin to turn them in or to turn them away."[29]

The Home Guard continued to hope that they would surprise Keith at his stepfather's rather than on the Grandfather, as he would undoubtedly make a bloody stand on the mountain. With his stepfather and his mother present, however, he would never risk a shootout. "That's the only way I'd have laid down my rifle-gun," Keith would say.[30]

Keith and Malinda always returned to their new comrades with a satchel of bread and ammunition and any pieces of news: the Confederates were still rounding up conscripts—"cannon fodder"—in earnest, and the local rebels wanted to bag Keith as a trophy to their patriotism and an example to other shirkers.[31]

Since Keith and Malinda's cabin could not house many and since the gang's leader had no intention of letting anyone disturb his and Malinda's privacy once they shut the rough pine door, his men fashioned crude huts of their own in the woods and slopes nearby. Each site "being carefully selected and reconnoitered from every possible way of approach," two or three deserters and "runners" crawled into their "dismal abode."[32]

The deserters, wrapped in woolen blankets, slept on pine needles, "which made a very good carpet."[33] On moonless or cloud-wrapped nights, they lit tiny fires inside the caves, the wan light "an indispensable companion," especially in rainy weather, when water seeped from the caves' walls.[34]

For the small fires Keith and Malinda tended in their range's hearth and those in their comrades' caves, the gang chose the driest and least smoky wood. As one deserter noted, however, every time they lit a fire, they risked detection by the militia, and "various plans were hit upon to minimize the danger of betrayal from the source [fire]."[35]

Some of Keith's men masked camp fires by choosing caves near a dead tree, which outliers charred near the hidden entrance to their dank homes. If the Home Guard happened to track whiffs of smoke to the sites, "the smoke would be attributed to the blackened tree."[36]

Keith's men took equal care in hiding their caves' openings. A Confederate militiaman remembered: "In addition to the leaves always kept on it [the cave's mouth], a tree would often be felled over the spot, the boughs serving not only to screen the entrance from view, but likewise to lessen the danger of any one walking directly into the cave. As it was all important that no trace of path should be seen thereabout, the trunk of the tree afforded a safe walk-way, care being taken always to approach from different directions. The presence of a newly felled tree, like a burning one, attracted little suspicion."[37]

Keith and Malinda, by their own account, were glad that they spent most of their nights in the late summer and fall of 1862 in their hut or in other hidden hunting ranges along the mountains rather than shivering in the caves' "Egyptian blackness."[38] A Confederate deserter turned "cave-dweller" wrote: "Even under the best of circumstances, in the fairest, warmest weather, and in the driest soil, a cave was dismal. There was a darkness, a chilliness, a strange and grave-like silence down there."[39]

Keith's men avoided hours in their caves whenever practicable, as a rule, one deserter noted, "putting dependence on good eyesight and legs . . . when no especial danger was apprehended, to betake themselves to the woods during the day and use the caves only as sleeping-places."[40] Most nights, Keith, Malinda, and their comrades gathered outside the hut to eat game or fish taken that day and to swap stories about family, friends, foes, and war. The camaraderie assuaged the fear and tedium that proved constant companions for the fugitives, even for Keith and Malinda, who had "the matrimonial comforts of each other's company."[41] If any of the "ragged band" looked at or thought of Keith Blalock's pretty wife with any sort of longing, they never acted on it.[42] As Malinda would say, even if they had tried, "Keith and I could stop any of that."[43] That Keith or Malinda alike would have put a bullet in anyone taking liberties toward her was a given among the Grandfather's deserters and shirkers.

Keith and Malinda still roamed the mountain alone when they sneaked down to Austin Coffey's home, but otherwise they now prowled the trails and passes with four or five compatriots armed with revolvers and Enfields. Along with the added strength in manpower, a new worry for the couple emerged: alone, they had eluded their trackers since fleeing the conscription party, covering up their whereabouts at every following juncture; however, the Blalocks could not monitor every movement their new companions made.

Keith said that no one had ever trailed him and Malinda to their mountaintop lair—"we'd have heard him and killed him."[44] But in late October a column of militia and conscription agents, their Enfields and Colt revolvers loaded, mounted up in a thick fog covering Blowing Rock and plodded up a narrow trail on the back slope of the Grandfather.

A third of the way up, they dismounted, tied their horses, posted a guard over their mounts, and on foot, pushed up an even narrower trail, Keith's foe Robert Green among them. They had discovered the site of the Blalocks' main encampment.

Shrouded in the fog, their movements muffled, they climbed closer to their prey.

Chapter Seven
High in the Hills

"COME out, Blalock!" was what they said, according to Malinda.[1] The voice boomed across the clearing near dawn and rousted Keith and Malinda from their bed. They pulled on their clothing, grabbed their rifle-guns from the wall pegs, and ran to firing slots just big enough to poke a gun barrel through and still be able to see out.

Across the clearing, they could make out men and their Enfield barrels moving about the tree line. Keith recognized Robert Green and two of the Moore boys.

Outside the cabin, several of Keith's men, startled from sleep in perches behind tree trunks, had already rolled from their blankets and found firing positions behind stumps and fallen trees near the hut. They could only hope the militia had not surrounded them.

Long moments passed with no reply from Keith. Locals had spotted the gang on several occasions, so the conscription officers expected to meet with "stubborn and organized resistance" from Keith, Malinda, and their band. Several Confederates, the Moores and Robert Green chief among them, likely preferred that Keith and his "desperadoes" would open up on them.[2]

Suddenly two flashes spit from the hut's firing ports, followed by the rifle-guns' roar. Keith Blalock had given his reply.

The other outliers joined in, and within seconds blasts erupted from the tree line around the hut. Enfield balls slammed against the pine walls, kicking up sprays of wood and tar paper.

"I counted fifty or more men firing at us from three sides," Keith would say.[3]

For several minutes, he, Malinda, and their friends blazed back, no more than a dozen in strength. Then the conscription party's fire slackened. The Blalocks spied movement away from the trees as their foes' fire stopped.

The waning action did not fool Keith. His outgunned band had repelled the Confederates for the moment, but the flitting shapes that rustled in the woods and thickets signaled that Green, Moore, and the others were moving to encircle the deserters and shirkers.

"Only one thing to do," said Malinda. "We had to deertail it out of there."[4]

Everyone in the Blalocks' band came to the same decision—every man for himself. As soon as their attackers made a rush for the cabin, they could overwhelm the defenders.

Once Keith and Malinda gauged which direction—northwest of the cabin—was not yet covered by the militia, they burst from the hut and toward the woods. Malinda took the lead so that Keith could cover her back: Keith figured that in the few seconds before the startled conscription men could react and pull their triggers, the fleet Malinda would cover the sprint to the woods and any bullet would find him rather than his wife.

Keith was right on both counts. As Malinda dashed into the cover of the woods with Keith a few steps behind, the Enfields and squirrel rifles opened up again. A ball tore into Keith's left arm. He staggered, rolled into the forest, and lurched after Malinda as balls whistled around him and smashed into branches and trunks.

The couple worked their way to the Grandfather's summit along a tiny trail they had scouted as an escape route in the event that they were surprised by Confederates just as they had been that very morning. As the din of the Enfields ebbed, the Blalocks stopped for a few moments and bound Keith's arm. Fortunately, the ball had passed cleanly through the flesh.

Keith and Malinda then trudged higher up the slopes, crawling in spots along steep boulders slippery with lichens, one misstep likely to send them sliding down the rock face. If they thought, however, that their enemies had given up the chase, shouts still distant but drifting ever closer proved the couple wrong.

With Keith weakening from blood loss, the couple neared the Grandfather's "black, rocky top," eight miles long.[5] They clung to "Indian ladders," tall tree trunks with lopped branches that served as rungs to help them up "otherwise insurmountable cliffs."[6] Eventually, near twilight, Keith and Malinda reached an old hog pen screened by rocks and a stand of balsams. Exhausted, the couple tumbled into the pen, in reality a pit, and huddled there as nightfall came.

Though sheltered somewhat from the fall gusts, the hog pen offered scant protection against the sodden evening mist of the Grandfather's summit. Keith and Malinda could only shiver and listen to their hunters' voices pealing closer and closer.

As the night dragged on, Keith and Malinda had company, "hogs which had bedded up against the rocks" of the pen.[7] The creatures were actually welcome, as they were domestic hogs turned loose on the mountain every fall and winter "to root," and provided additional warmth for the weary couple.[8]

Keith and Malinda had chosen their hiding place well. The Grandfather's upper reaches were strewn with such pens, and to search for every one would have taken the militia days or even weeks. Still, the Confederates did come close enough to the Blalocks' refuge that the couple could hear what the men were saying.

Sometime during that seemingly endless evening, the search party's clamor waned, then stopped. By morning, Keith and Malinda could breathe more easily as it became obvious that the militia had headed down to the valley, abandoning the chase—for the moment.

With Keith wounded and their band scattered or seized, Keith and Malinda could only wonder how their enemies had found them. Keith attributed their dilemma to "plain bad luck," carelessness by one of their companions, or perhaps a campfire spotted by a Confederate neighbor.[9] No matter the reason, Keith and Malinda had to flee the Grandfather, and soon, for the Home Guard would come back to the mountain's crest.

The couple, with only their rifle-guns and each other, crawled from the hog pen and climbed down the Grandfather. Their destination was Tennessee, where fellow unionists in the Great Smoky Mountains could guide them to the federal lines. Unaware as of yet that his enemy Robert Green had also been wounded in the arm during the clash at the hut, Keith vowed to take revenge against the entire Green and Moore clans, as well as his rebel step-uncles. In particular, he believed that once again, William Coffey, whose knowledge of every hidden thicket and gorge on the Grandfather rivaled Keith's own, had piloted the rebels to his hideout. Keith had not seen the "peaceable"[10] old man in the fight, but, as William Coffey's wife would say, "He [Keith] always blamed William Coffey for bringing the home guards to their [the Blalocks'] place."[11] Mrs. Coffey did not deny Keith's contention, nor did the stepbrothers.

Besides his decision to retaliate against William Coffey at the first opportunity, which could not arrive soon enough for Keith, he had also chosen to join the Union forces in Tennessee. So, too, had Malinda.

CHAPTER EIGHT
An Awful Time for Us

A VOIDING anything that resembled a main trail, Keith and Malinda worked their way down to Shull's Mill, near the Watauga River. The couple crawled over Buzzard's Rocks and the jagged Dog's Ears, the Grandfather and the Hanging Rock towering in the distance, each step tortuous for the wounded Keith.

Below Shull's Mill, an old stone bridge spanned the Watauga River, but Keith and Malinda could not take the chance of crossing the structure, which was used by the Home Guard. They forded the frigid mountain current at an isolated, tree-shrouded spot and, screened by the woods, loosely followed the Caldwell and Watauga Turnpike.

Keith and Malinda subsisted on gooseberries and spring water, afraid to take a shot at any game for fear of alerting Confederate sympathizers. Even in winter on the Grandfather, the couple could have easily waited it out until spring, knowing just where to find game even in the snow and having "laid in some corn, vegetables, and such larder at the cabin."[1] But on the run from the militia, Keith and Malinda had no such reserves. "We ate whatever we could find, and it wasn't much," Keith said.[2] A friend and fellow unionist described the plight that confronted Keith, Malinda, and every other refugee from the rebels in the late fall and winter in the mountains: "No person knows what they could be induced to eat until they suffer for several days and nights with the most excessive hunger. In that sort of an extremity, the most fastidious and delicate taste very willingly accommodates itself to articles of food which otherwise would be most wretchedly abhorrent."[3]

Their growling stomachs constant and unwelcome companions, Keith and Malinda trudged west. They waded across Dutch Creek near a waterfall that gushed over an eighty-foot boulder. Always, their rifle-guns were loaded, their ears alert to any distant hoofbeats.

Between gaps in the mountains' "abrupt, tree-clad walls," they trudged through Valle Crucis and followed Crab Orchard Creek toward Banner's Elk.[4]

At Banner's Elk, Keith and Malinda found aid from two unabashed unionists, Lewis and Martin Banner, whose homes and land would soon become key stops along the region's so-called "underground railway."[5] The Banners "would pilot many an escaped federal prisoner and Union man trying to get through the lines to Tennessee."[6] Keith and Malinda were among the earliest arrivals at the Banners' doorsteps.

"Lewis Banner was a strong Union man," Keith would tell a friend in Watauga County. "None stronger."[7]

One of the many other unionists whom Banner helped to safety lauded: "His [Lewis Banner's] home was the home of the oppressed and struggling Union sympathizer trying to get through to the federal lines . . . and many a time through great personal sacrifice did he pilot men through the mountains so as to avoid the vigilance of the Home Guard. . . . Mr. Banner, or 'Uncle Lewis,' as we all are ever wont to affectionately call him, was our deliverer."[8]

Sizing up Keith as a man who might prove helpful in future missions to help fellow unionists, the Banners, Keith said, "admitted me into the inner temple" of their secret escape routes.[9] Although Keith's focus at the moment was to escape the Watauga County conscription parties, soon he would more than justify the Banners' gamble on his ability to guide other men to safety and to do so "without letting on to any Rebels."[10]

"Uncle Lewis took us on a horse in the dark up and down hidden trails in the mountains," Malinda told a friend.[11]

With Banner's aid, Keith and Malinda slipped into Tennessee in November 1863. It was time, in Keith's words, "to get back in it."[12]

Once into eastern Tennessee, Keith and Malinda's danger did not ebb. In several ways it increased, for the unionists and rebels of the region were locked in guerrilla warfare that had not yet hit the couple's home county full-bore, but soon would.

"Rebel gangs of soldiers were now prowling through the county in every direction, ransacking and plundering, and murdering many of the citizens," wrote a friend of Keith. "They took every weapon that they could find, and hauled off the small stock of provisions which the people had to live upon; and where the county was too mountainous for them to go with wagons, they would go on horseback and pack off the scanty provisions from the most humble cabin in the mountains."[13]

For the exhausted North Carolina couple, few unionists in the cabins that Keith and Malinda risked to approach had much food to spare. But, perhaps because one of the ragged strangers was a woman, they found a bit of bread or a cup of milk along their trek westward. They still foraged for berries and downed game on occasion.

"It was an awful time for us," Malinda would say.[14]

With the mountain winds whistling colder each night and the first flecks of snow drifting across the peaks, Keith and Malinda still languished several hundred miles from real safety—federal lines in Kentucky. "Cold, bleak winter was at hand," a friend holed up in the Tennessee slopes wrote, "and it was almost impossible for men to lay out alone in the mountains; for if, by doing so, they could succeed in hiding from the Rebels, there was nothing which could be procured to eat. Their only alternative was either to go through the lines or remain."[15]

Keith and Malinda chose to stay in the mountains of Carter County, which bordered western North Carolina. But they would not endure the winter alone.

✍

Believing federal troops would push into east Tennessee in the spring of 1863, unionist scouts, or pilots, rebel deserters, and various other "Lincolnites" had formed guerrilla bands by mid-1862. The bands raided Confederate camps and depots, burned bridges across the Watauga River, and tore up rebel railway tracks. Keith and Malinda, with the help of such Carter County residents as William Lewis, "a good Union man residing on the waters of the Watauga River," were guided to the mountain encampment of Yankee partisans, or "bushwhackers" in Confederate eyes.[16]

In a remote gorge, the couple hunkered down for the winter in a wooden "camp-house" concealed in a huge thicket of ivy and laurel bushes that covered the dwelling and served as natural insulation.[17] The unionists covered the earthen floor with leaves to provide "a tolerable good bed to sleep on."[18] For warmth, the company tended a fire near the building's door; they posted lookouts round the clock to make sure that Home Guards or Confederate regulars were not tracking the smoke to the guerrillas' lair. The abundance of wood allowed the fugitives to bank the fire day and night.

Keith, Malinda, and the rest of the band took turns climbing down to unionists' homes for what provisions their allies could provide and hauling a bushel of cornmeal or a pound or two of bacon and flour back to the camp to augment the dried game the men had "lain in" during the warmer months.[19]

Malinda baked bread for the company by spreading the rough, bran-flecked dough on a flat stone and laying it alongside but never in the fire. To prepare the dough, she had measured meal into a kneading trough, poured water from a nearby creek into it, and worked the mixture by hand until it thickened.

They cooked their meat on the fire coals and drank water from tin cups. The Blalocks and the others craved a cup of coffee against the chill, but, as one of the band remembered, "the luxury of coffee, we did not think of endeavoring to procure it, as the infamous rebellion had deprived the county of a supply of the genuine article, and we did not want to substitute in its place the coffee which was used by the Rebels, which was wheat and rye."[20]

As the winter wore on, Keith, chafing to head back to western North Carolina to settle scores with his step-uncles, the Greens, the Moores, and Bingham's Home Guard, persuaded the other unionists that his knowledge of the mountains, his cunning, and his toughness comprised the ideal traits of a partisan captain. Strengthening his case was the fact that he and Malinda had piloted several of his current companions from the Grandfather to the Tennessee border, where Daniel Ellis and other guides had taken the fugitives in hand.

Any doubts that Keith would lead the others disappeared with the visits of two Union men to the encampment during the winter of 1862–1863. The first, a young Yankee officer from Michigan, told the band that he needed pilots to guide potential recruits out of North Carolina for a proposed regiment of cavalry, the 10th Michigan. Keith offered his services and those of "his men."[21]

By the time the first thaw began, Keith had been appointed "recruiting officer and scout Captain" for the Michigan regiment.[22] As his aide-de-camp, he selected Malinda. No one objected, for the other partisans had seen how Malinda bore every physical hardship and handled a rifle-gun as well as any of them. Besides, she had "soldiered" before. Of equal importance, in all likelihood, to their acceptance of the diminutive woman as one of them was the fact that husband inspired both respect and fear in the rest of the band.

Keith now donned a dark-blue recruiting officer's tunic, replete with braid and gilded buttons, as well as a wide-brimmed cavalry hat, all provided by the Michigander. Malinda likewise wore a federal uniform. If captured in their home county in the blue garments, both knew that they would be shot or hanged as traitors. "We weren't afraid," Keith told a relative. "They wanted us dead no matter what."[23]

Even more portentous for Keith and Malinda than the Michigander's visit was that of the second man, George W. Kirk. In this fierce and daring Union officer, Keith met not only a kindred soul, but also a martial mentor.

Kirk, described by Confederate General Robert Vance as "chief of military marauders in North Carolina," was born in Greene County, Tennessee, on June 27, 1837.[24] Confederate histories of the war in the mountains would portray Kirk as a traitor, a bushwhacker, and a ruthless killer. A case can be made that he was all of these, but Kirk also proved a bold, brilliant, and zealous Union officer whose very name would spark fear among rebels in east Tennessee and North Carolina.

In the winter of 1862–1863, Kirk had been commissioned by the federal army to set up escape routes—safe houses, caches of food, and mountain hideouts—for unionists and deserters fleeing from the rebels. His main charge was to recruit as many of these men as possible for the Union ranks, and he did so with a high degree of success. Kirk's other mission was to organize local unionists into partisan bands for raids into North Carolina, tying down as many Confederate soldiers as possible.

When the stocky, broad-shouldered Kirk and rangy Keith Blalock first met, they soon learned that they possessed more in common than fierce hatred for the Confederacy. Kirk, like Keith, had bowed to local Confederates' pressure to join a rebel regiment, but had intended to desert to federal lines at the first opportunity. Before his unit had seen action, Kirk had "gone over the hill" in central North Carolina and had "scouted his way back to Kentucky," where he joined the Union army.[25] General John M. Schofield, impressed by Kirk's nerve and his knowledge of east Tennessee, viewed him as the perfect man to build a guerrilla network in the region. Kirk was also attracting the attention of another officer, General William Tecumseh Sherman, as "an officer to watch."[26]

Keith Blalock, having already signed on as a recruiting officer, eagerly accepted Kirk's offer that the Watauga man help organize a new "mountain railway" for unionists, deserters, and federal captives who escaped from the hellish Confederate prison camp in Salisbury, North Carolina. For Keith, the scenario seemed perfect: not only could he seek officially sanctioned revenge against neighbors and the Home Guard, but he could also lash out at the Confederates whenever he chose. "We could fight the Secessionist on our terms," Keith said. The ground that he and Kirk chose was Watauga, Caldwell, and Burke Counties.[27]

Keith and Malinda would return home in the spring of 1863—at the head of a unionist guerrilla column.

George Kirk, having selected Keith as "a trusted lieutenant" along with Jim Hartley, Harrison Church, and James Voncannon, all of them men from the western mountains of North Carolina, supplied Keith with the finest weapon he had ever owned—a Spencer repeating rifle—and a Colt revolver.[28] Because Keith and his company would be outnumbered in most actions against the Home Guard and Confederate regulars, the partisans needed superior firepower. Kirk had found it in the Spencer. A mere forty-two inches long from stock to barrel, which made it shorter even than a cavalry carbine, the lever-action rifle carried eight rounds, one in the chamber and seven inside a tubular magazine in the stock. To Keith and Malinda's amazement, they and their men could fire their .52 caliber rounds at a rate of twenty per minute. The percussion cap muskets the couple had carried in the Confederate ranks could fire five rounds per minute if the soldier was extremely skilled.

Proving the further wisdom of Kirk's choice of weapon, the Spencer "always came up firing" no matter how dirty and wet the conditions.[29] In the rugged terrain and weather in which the Blalocks and their band would soon operate, the state-of-the-art Spencer was, indeed, the ideal weapon—one that, because it was not standard U.S. Army issue, had to be ordered and paid for by officers and their men. Kirk did so for the Blalocks and would similarly pay to equip his men with the rifle by using the proceeds from his raids' plunder. In the hands of both husband and wife, the "repeater" would terrify Confederates throughout the Blue Ridge.

Under Kirk's orders but given the greatest latitude, as Keith said, to "freewheel," the Blalocks planned their first incursion into their home state. Kirk's guerrillas did so under the nominal protection of the federal army's Article LXXXII, General Orders 100, which, because of their authorization to act "under Kirk's commission," gave them legal military status: "Men or squads of men, who commit hostilities, whether by fighting or inroads for destruction or plunder or by raids of any kind without commission, without being part and portion of the organized army, and without sharing continuously in the war, but who do so with intermitting returns to their homes and their avocations, or with the occasional assumption of the semblance of peaceful pursuits, divesting themselves of the character of appearance of soldiers—such men, or squads of men, are public enemies, and therefore, if captured, are not entitled to the privileges of prisoners of war, but shall be treated summarily as highway robbers or pirates."[30]

Keith and Malinda were not coming back to their homes and avocations for peaceful pursuits and were acting with Kirk's fully commissioned military sanction; Keith's duties also included those of an official recruiting officer for both Kirk and the 10th Michigan Cavalry. But none of that would matter if the Home Guards or Confederate regulars captured the Blalocks. A rope or a bullet to the brain would supercede any military "privileges of prisoners of war," as the couple had fled the Grandfather as Confederate traitors. Now, they planned their return—as Union partisans.

Their rebel neighbors would view them as something else: "a lawless gang of deserters, traitors, and bushwhackers, uniforms or not."[31] In "blue federal uniforms, armed with Spencers and Navy [Colt] revolvers," the Blalocks slipped back toward the Grandfather.[32]

PART THREE

Like Corsican Brigands

CHAPTER NINE
A Trusted Lieutenant

IN the early spring of 1863, Keith and Malinda led twenty-five men on horseback out of the encampment, through the passes, and across the Watauga River. Word that Keith had been spotted in "a federal officer's uniform" and that Malinda similarly wore the blue spread throughout their home counties.[1] Kirk's other guerrilla bands infiltrated western North Carolina at the same time. His riders were on the move.

As Keith and Malinda would soon discover, the military and economic situation in the Blue Ridge was even more volatile than when the Home Guard had chased them into Tennessee. By December 1862, when they joined the encampment in Tennessee's Blue Ridge region, most mountain families' romantic sentiments for the Confederate cause was eroding daily. Keith and Malinda encountered small bands of deserters from the moment the guerrilla company entered North Carolina. He offered such outliers the chance to join his unit or, if they preferred, to wait a few weeks until he could pilot them into Tennessee and entrust them to Daniel Ellis and other men who could take them to the federal lines. To the later delight of Kirk and of the Michigan cavalry, Keith, carrying enlistment papers, convinced dozens of men to sign them and risk the flight through the mountains. Several, who were spoiling to fight the Confederacy and eyed the Spencers that Keith and his men held, opted to take their chances with his raiders.

The mountains, seething with unrest, proved increasingly fertile for the Blalocks' purposes. Confederate General Kirby Smith wrote that the Blue Ridge and the Smokies were "an enemy's country."[2] He added, "The people are against us, and ready to rise whenever an enemy's column makes its appearance. The very troops raised here cannot always be depended upon. They have gone into service, many of them to escape suspicion, prepared to give information to the enemy, and ready to pass over to him when an opportunity arises."[3]

Keith and other unionist recruiters found another brand of ally in the mountain counties. Describing these "part-time" recruits that Keith, Kirk, Hartley, and other "Yankee men" employed, a historian wrote:

Many of the mountaineers stayed in the valleys in which they had been born and raised. Many were trapped inside the Confederacy and had little choice. Most would try to avoid service to one side or the other; they would try to live on and hope that their steep ridges would hold back the tides of war. Out of this population, however, it was easy to raise armed men to prey upon the Confederates. The advantages of such service to these men were clear. They could fight when it suited them and yet comfort themselves with the thought that they were protecting the "Grand Ole Flag" and the "Union of their Fathers." They could foray quickly against Rebel railroads, bridges, and supplies and then vanish swiftly into the security of the mountains and return to the comforts of home. There was none of the endless boredom of regular service in faraway camps. No strangers to order a man about. No fighting in terrain chosen by some fancy pants officers. No death in some unknown field or a nameless grave far away from home, friends, and family. No constant worry about the survival and comfort of those at home while one served helplessly hundreds of miles away. This sort of fighting had its advantages. A man could stay in the mountains he loved. It seemed that he could almost choose when and where the war would happen to him.[4]

That sort of fighting, which Keith and Malinda could offer a man, did not always allow him to pick and choose his own war; as the Blalocks had learned, not even steep ridges and remote valleys could hold off the war from mountaineers. And the couple also knew that riding with the Home Guard offered some men a similar way to choose their own war in exchange for either solid rebel beliefs or even lukewarm ones. But what enticed many of the less than rabid rebels or neutralists to bands such as that of the Blalocks was the fervent desire to avoid Confederate conscription. That was something against which many apolitical mountain men would fight—even if only as "part-timers" in guerrilla companies.

Adding to the hatred of conscription and the general disaffection that Keith and Malinda found in Watauga, Caldwell, and Burke Counties were two laws enraging local unionists and all but the most rabid secessionists alike. The Tax-in-Kind Act forced local farmers to pay the Richmond government a war tithe of one-tenth of all produce to the Confederate army. Even more heavy-handed, the second law granted local committees the right to seize livestock, provisions, wagons, and horses for the rebel forces at any price they deemed fit. The increasing worthlessness of Confederate specie and the unfair prices hardened many mountain families' collective sentiment against Jefferson Davis and the war. Though most never embraced unionism, they adopted a neutral stance fueled by contempt for both sides and a desire to be left alone. The latter hope proved futile as both the Confederates and the guerilla units of the Blalocks and other unionists, and vicious gangs of bushwhackers that preyed upon everyone roamed the mountains in 1863.

The Conscription Act remained the most galling law in the mountain counties. "Pronounced Southern men William and Rueben Coffey" rampaged across Watauga and seized every potential soldier.[5] As a result Keith's recruitment papers or just his offer to scout men to safety attracted many outliers whose feelings about the Yankees were, at most, lukewarm, but whose affinity for the rebels was nonexistent.

The feeling among mountain families that they had furnished more than their share of manpower to the Confederacy was justifiable. "Having responded so generously to the early call for troops," wrote John Barrett, "the mountain region was pretty well depleted of young blood. . . . This additional demand for troops, therefore, met with considerable opposition."[6]

From January through June 1863, Governor Vance, sensitive to the concerns of the mountain counties and worried about the depredations of conscription parties, offered deserters something of a blanket pardon if they returned to their units. Still, he threatened punishment to those who resisted:

By the Governor of North Carolina
A Proclamation
 Whereas, I have learned with great pain that there have been latterly numerous desertions from the ranks of our gallant army, and that there are many persons in the country who incite and encourage these desertions and harbor and conceal these misguided men at home, instead of encouraging them to return to duty.
 Now, therefore, I, Zebulon B. Vance . . . do issue this my proclamation, commanding all such evil disposed persons to desist from such base, cowardly, and treasonable conduct, and warning them that they will subject themselves to indictment and punishment . . . as well as the everlasting contempt and detestation of good and honorable men. Certainly no crime could be greater, no cowardice more abject, no treason more base, than for a citizen of the State, enjoying its privileges and protection without sharing its dangers, to persuade those who had the courage to go forth in defense of their country vilely to desert the colors which they have sworn to uphold, and when a miserable death or a vile and ignominious existence must be the inevitable consequence: no plea can excuse it. The father or the brother who does it should be shot instead of his deluded victim, for he deliberately destroys the soul and manhood of his own flesh and blood. And the same is done by him who harbors and conceals the deserter, for who can respect either the one or the other? What

honest man will ever wish or permit his brave sons or patriotic daughters . . . to associate . . . with the vile wretch who skulked in the woods, or the still viler coward who aided him when his bleeding country was calling in vain for his help? Both are enemies—dangerous enemies—to their country. . . . Rest assured, observing and neverfailing eyes have marked you, Every one. And when the overjoyed wife welcomes once more her brave and honored husband to his home, and tells him how . . . in the lonely hours of the night, you who had been his comrades rudely entered her house, robbed her and her children of their bread, and heaped insults and indignities upon her defenseless head, the wrath of that heroic husband will make you regret . . . that you were ever born. Instead of a few scattered militia, the land will be full of veteran soldiers, before whose honest faces you will not have the courage to raise your eyes. . . . You will be hustled from the polls, kicked in the streets . . . and honest men everywhere will shun you as a pestilence. . . . Though many of you rejected the pardon heretofore offered you, and I am not now authorized to promise it, I am assured that no man will be shot who shall voluntarily return to duty. . . . Unless desertion is prevented, our strength must depart from our armies; and desertion can never be stopped while . . . they receive any countenance or protection at home. I therefore appeal to all good citizens and true patriots . . . to assist my officers in arresting deserters, and to frown down on all those who aid and assist them. . . . Unless the good and patriotic . . . arise as one man to arrest this dangerous evil, it will grow until our Army is well nigh ruined. . . . You can arrest it, my countrymen, if you will but bring to bear the weight of a great, a patriotic, and united community in aid of your authorities. . . .

> *Done at the City of Raleigh, this 11th day*
> *of May, A.D. 1863*
> *(Proclamation of Governor Vance, 11 May 1863,*
> *Governors' Papers.)*[7]

The drain of manpower imposed concerns both of subsistence and safety on families Keith and Malinda had known all their lives. "If all the conscripts from my county are taken off [by the conscription parties]," a neighbor wrote, "it will be impossible for those left behind to make support for another year."[8]

The incursions of Keith and Malinda's company and Kirk's other operatives terrified their home counties. A Blue Ridge man lamented: "In Western

North Carolina, the safety and security of homes and property are seriously menaced and openly assaulted by herds of disloyal citizens and gangs of deserters from the Confederate army. In the event, the conscripts are taken into Confederate service, we shall doubtless fall an easy prey to the malicious hands of marauders, which now openly parade themselves in the different counties, west of the Blue Ridge."[9]

Among those marauders, Keith and Malinda, while always on the lookout for the Greens, the Moores, and the Coffey step-uncles, moved cautiously at first in Watauga County. They followed Kirk's directives to the letter, establishing a network of informants and unionist friends from one corner of the region to the other. Their chief hiding spots lay near Blowing Rock. Burying caches of ammunition, food, and fodder for their horses—"splendid animals from Kirk himself," according to Keith[10]—they slipped in and out of "a thousand tree-clad hills and ridges that become higher and wilder towards the encircling wall of the Blue Ridge."[11] Four thousand feet above the cultivated valleys, "we scouted men out to Tennessee and to federal regiments," related Malinda.[12]

As news of more sightings of the Blalocks reached Camp Mast, Major Bingham stepped up his campaign "to capture all slackers and send them to the service; arrest deserters from the army and return them to their commands; and to keep down those lawless bands."[13]

Eager for the chance to train their Spencers on the Home Guard, Keith and Malinda nonetheless restrained themselves and the other men, unwilling to blunder into an action in which not even their repeaters could compensate against the militia's numbers. "We passed on some chances to fire at the guards," Keith recounted, "until we were ready."[14]

In June 1863, news reached the Blalocks and fellow scouts Harrison Church and Jim Hartley that "men stationed at Camp Mast . . . and commanded by Major Harvey Bingham had halted a man, and he did not stop."[15] The guards opened fire—"many shots"—and killed him.[16]

"On this account," wrote Shepherd M. Dugger, a teenaged friend of Keith, "retaliating squads were formed, headed by federal recruiting scouts."[17]

The opportunity for Keith and Malinda to employ their Spencers had come.

As the early morning mists began to lift from a trail leading up to Blowing Rock in mid-June 1862, twenty-five of Camp Mast's militia rode in single file, combing the route for outliers. A dozen men and a woman peered down from tree-lined spurs on both sides of the path and picked their targets.

Suddenly the Spencers roared. Three riders toppled from their saddles;

screams and shots rose toward the ridge. Most of the guards wheeled around and careered down the trail; several others abandoned their horses and escaped into the woods.

After waiting several minutes, the snipers climbed down the path, gathered up the riderless mounts, and headed to one of the band's mountaintop hideouts. The three downed guards lay crumpled in the dirt behind them.

A few weeks later, Keith's first chance to settle a personal score unfolded. One of his informants in Caldwell County told him that Robert Green, who owned several homes in the region, was heading to his "finely appointed lodge" near Blowing Rock. Keith, Malinda, and a handful of his company immediately saddled up and galloped off to meet him.

"We found him on the way to Blowing Rock," Keith said.[18]

Having selected a secluded bend in the trail, the Blalocks and the others waited several hours. They did not expect Green to ride alone.

Early in the afternoon, a wagon lurched into view. Even before Keith could see the man's face, the stocky build and the fine workmanship of the vehicle confirmed the arrival of the prosperous Robert Green. Surprisingly, he was unaccompanied.

Keith burst alone from the brush and onto the road just a few yards in front of the oncoming two-horse wagon and leveled his weapon at Green. For this job, Keith had left his Spencer at camp and had chosen a Sharp's rifle, whose gaping bore and huge ball were the favorites of buffalo hunters because of their stopping power.

Green leaped from the wagon and dashed for the woods. Keith did not move a step. Taking aim, he fired. Green shrieked as the ball slammed him down into a bed of bracken. He rolled onto his back and clutched his left thigh, the bone cracked cleanly in half and protruding through the flesh.

Keith strode over to the prone man and stared down at him, pointing the Sharp's bore inches from his face. An instant later Green passed out.

Two versions of what followed would spread across Watauga County. J. P. Arthur, who would interview the Blalocks extensively, wrote: "Green's friends say that Blalock's crowd left him [Green] lying as he had fallen, and that he managed to regain his wagon, turn it around, and drive back home.

"Blalock's friends say that after he had wounded Green, shooting him through his wagon body and afterwards bragging on his marksmanship, he went to him, and finding him unconscious, took him to his wagon, put him in it, turned it around, and started the team in the direction of Green's home.

"This is doubted by Green's friends, however."[19]

Keith always asserted that he "had aimed to wound, not to kill,"[20] and that the ball Green had earlier put in Keith's shoulder was paid off by the one Keith put through his foe's thigh. Although Green, in turn, claimed that he had never shot Keith and had never even taken part in the action that had dislodged the couple from their hut on the Grandfather, Malinda simply countered that she and her husband had seen him that day and knew that the man's shot had struck Keith. "No one could tell them different," says Murray Coffey.[21]

While Keith and Malinda began to combine their vendettas and Kirk's partisan warfare, Harvey Bingham was more determined than ever to hunt down and execute Keith as an example to other unionists. The Blalocks and their band responded with a series of hit-and-run ambushes that demoralized the Home Guard. "Bushwhacked from behind every shrub, tree, or projection on all sides of the road," Bingham and other beleaguered Home Guard commanders implored Richmond for help in the form of regular army units.[22]

Since the summer of 1862, the 69th North Carolina Regiment had pulled duty in eastern Tennessee, Keith and Malinda always wary of its companies as they piloted men to the border. But the regiment, scattered in camps and outposts from the North Carolina border to Chattanooga, Tennessee, was stretched too thin to chase every bushwhacker and Tory, or to ferret out every "den of marauding thieves."[23] For the first time, the government in Richmond seriously mulled the prospect of sending several regiments to the mountains to fight guerrilla units such as the Blalocks'. They were carrying out George Kirk's brand of warfare and adding their own brutal touches to it throughout the Blue Ridge spring and summer of 1863.

As James Moore, the Blalocks' erstwhile messmate in the 26th North Carolina, pointed out, the couple had become "the terror of the county."[24]

His brother, Jesse Moore, added: "Keith Blalock's name was a fright to the neighborhood on account of his numerous depredations."[25]

The patriarch of the Moore clan, Carroll, never tempered his hatred for and disdain of the Blalocks: "They continued their raids off and on, but steady like, the greater part of the time having a gang of something like a dozen or fifteen lawless fellows under them."[26]

Even some local Union men such as young Langston L. Estes, who "resided near the Globe, on the John's River," felt that the Blalocks sometimes carried out their raids "on account of the federals" with a harshness that invariably sparked retaliation upon other unionist, as well as neutral, families.[27] "In [my] judgment," Estes would state, "Blalock did much for the Union cause, but did a great deal that he ought not to have done, such as robbing and plundering Rebels throughout the country. He and his men were some protection to the Union people at the time, but would occasionally bring on them the vengeance of their enemies by way of revenging for what the Blalocks had done to Rebel citizens."[28]

That sentiment came from a man who had served in a Confederate regiment for a year before deserting and had ridden with Jim Hartley's unionist band, which had a well-earned reputation for striking rebel farms and the Home Guard with ferocity equal to that of the "Blalocks' gang."[29]

Confederate neighbors and relatives alike denounced the Blalocks' incursions throughout the mountain counties, but naturally viewed the outrages of the Home Guard as patriotic. From McCaleb Coffey's wife came the following sentiments toward Keith and Malinda: "They were angry at William Coffey and desired to get rid of him, as well as my husband, because of the aid they might render the Home Guards in heading off him [Keith] and his raiders in getting through the mountains with their stolen property and plunder. . . . He returned again and again to the neighborhood, and getting a gang of the worst kind of men [unionists] under him . . . and continued to raid and plunder up and down the John's River and the surrounding country."[30]

Whether one described the actions of Confederate cavalry or unionist guerrillas like the Blalocks in the mountain war, cattle- and horse-stealing proved constant torments for locals. "Among others that Blalock and his party robbed and stole stock from on the John's River," Mrs. McCaleb Coffey recalled, "within a few miles of me, were Daniel, Job, and Carroll Moore, Lott Estes, and Robert Green, and on the Mulberry Fork were Colonel Discon and William Coffey."[31]

In the summer of 1863, Mrs. Coffey and other local Confederates who loathed the Blalocks would soon have even more reason to want them caught and killed. Dreadful news for the mountain clans was on the way from a battlefield in Pennsylvania.

CHAPTER TEN
A Tense, Violent Season

IN mid-July 1863, Keith and Malinda heard the stunning news of the Confederate defeats at Vicksburg and Gettysburg. "The Union was saved," Keith said, "but we knew the war was far from done."[1] Malinda would tell a friend that "a lot of people at home [Watauga and Caldwell Counties] were going Yankee at the news."[2]

The Blalocks' old regiment, the 26th, had been ravaged at Gettysburg, and even though the couple would not have hesitated to blast away at relatives in gray, Keith encountered a pang of sadness upon learning that two of the Coffey boys had died on the Pennsylvania battlefield. "They were good men even if they were Secessionists," he remembered.[3]

What young James B. Moore went through from July 1 to July 3, 1863, at Gettysburg would not only scar him physically and emotionally, but would also stoke his hatred of the Blalocks to a new fury once he learned of "their murderous raids'" with their gang of Tories and escaped Union prisoners at home in Watauga and Caldwell Counties.[4] On the last day of June 1863, Moore, the "Coffey boys—Cleveland, John, Jones, Ninevah, Thomas, and William"—Jackson Gragg, and other men whom Keith and Malinda had known for most of their lives piled into camp alongside a creek flanking the turnpike that led to the little Pennsylvania farm community.[5] "All worn out and broke down" from a forced march "at the double-quick," they arose to reveille at five in the morning of July 1, 1863, gnawed a breakfast of hardtack and cooked but cold bacon, and began to march toward Gettysburg in a hunt "for badly needed shoes there."[6] As Moore would record, "We walked straight into Hell."[7]

Emerging from a swirling morning mist, Moore and the Coffeys forded Marsh Creek some three-and-a-half miles west of the town and ran straight into the federal cavalry of General John Buford. The 26th's brigade and another formed a line of battle near the road, and three lines of skirmishers went forward, the federal cavalry firing and retreating as the 26th and its brother regiments pushed up the road.

By early afternoon, Company F and the 26th had been forced by heavy Union cannonades and infantry fire to fall back in good order to Herr Ridge.

Moore and his Watauga and Caldwell friends endured relentless federal fire throughout the early afternoon, taking cover as best they could in a strip of thin woods fronting McPherson's Ridge. In shifts, Moore and the Coffeys were among details sent to the rear to fill and refill the company's canteen in the creek. Lieutenant John Holloway, whom Keith had known in the local schoolhouse, strode up and down the company's position, clapping the shoulders of his neighbors, offering words of encouragement for the coming ordeal. To the company's north, the Watauga and Caldwell men could see Confederate General Richard Ewell's corps moving out in perfect order against the Union positions on Oak Ridge. According to a Watauga soldier, "Never was grander sight beheld . . . the lines extended more than a mile, all directly visible to us."[8] Moore and his mess-mates knew their turn was coming.

The order for Company F and the 26th arrived around 2:30 in the afternoon. Robert E. Lee had ordered General A. P. Hill to commit the North Carolinians against the strong Union force dug in along McPherson's Woods.

To Moore, the Coffeys, and the rest, "the order came at a most inopportune time"—they had watched for the past two hours as the federal troops had prepared their defenses in and around the distant tree line, and recognized "the desperateness of the charge that lay ahead."[9]

James Moore would never forget the scene. All along the North Carolinians' line, the call to "attention" pealed. The troops sprang to their feet and fixed bayonets. Then, the order to advance was barked by the officers on horseback. The regimental flags hung limply in the sultry air; the 26th, anchoring the brigade's left flank, moved out in unison with the 11th, the 47th, and the 52nd North Carolina Regiments.

Hearts pounding, many throats dry, Company F followed the blue and white regimental colors, carried by Sergeant Jefferson B. Mansfield. The long lines advanced "in beautiful style, at the quick time," and as they waded into the wheat field, the Union troops opened fire from the woods.[10] Several men of Company F toppled into the golden sheaves and disappeared from sight. Most of the early federal volleys, however, whined over the rebels' heads.

Approaching Willoughby Run, Company F and the rest of the North Carolinians began to return fire, more and more of the Confederates now falling dead or wounded. Thomas and Ninevah Coffey went down in the sheets of federal Minie balls and blasts of shells and canister shot belched by James H. Cooper's Pennsylvania battery.

At the line's left, Company F spilled through gaps in briars and underbrush to cross the creek and push forward. They reformed their line with the rest of the regiment on the opposite bank of Willoughby Run and advanced. Now, the Union fire poured "as thick as hailstones in a storm" into the mountain boys.[11] But they surged at the Yankees, "came on with rapid strides, yelling like demons," and broke across the first line of federal defenders.[12]

Moore and those still around him pressed halfway up a hill and closed to within twenty yards of Michigan and Indiana men. Screams and moans rising everywhere along the hill, piles of butchered men strewn across the grass, rebel Lieutenant T. J. Cureton looked to his right "and saw no more than three men where Company F had been."[13]

One of the trio, Sergeant J. T. C. Hood, would recall: "In the open field the federals got a better range, and volleys of deadly missiles were sent into our ranks which mowed us down like wheat before the sickle."[14]

Writhing amid the carnage was James Moore, his thigh torn clean open by a Minie ball. All of the Coffey boys lay dead, as did Jackson Gragg.

Of the more than eight hundred men who marched with Keith and Malinda's former regiment into the action at Gettysburg on July 1, 1863, 734 were killed, wounded, or captured. All ninety-three men of Company F had been hit; one of the Blalocks' old officers, Captain Romulus M. Tuttle, wrote: "It was, indeed, a fateful field for Company F, for, in the engagement that followed, every officer and every man of it bled or died from wounds received."[15]

As the casualty lists reached Watauga and Caldwell Counties a week after the Battle of Gettysburg, hatred of the Blalocks among families whose sons had been killed or maimed on the Pennsylvania slaughter ground exploded. That the couple had "deserted and profaned our [the Confederate] cause"[16] led the Moores, the Greens, the Boyds, and the Coffey step-uncles to grimly promise each other that they would "kill the obnoxious Unionist Keith Blalock."[17]

Throughout the Blue Ridge, William, Reuben, and McCaleb Coffey and many zealous rebels brooded that "only the hand of Providence could now save the Cause."[18] Others, however, turned their sorrow and rage against unionists and deserters, and the fighting in the mountains soon entered an even more savage phase. The scenario suited Keith and Malinda, for with General Ambrose Burnside poised to strike in east Tennessee, George Kirk intended to "raise the ante in North Carolina."[19]

Tensions in Keith and Malinda's haunts continued to swell in the late summer of 1863, and many neighbors who had once deemed the couple traitors and bushwhackers began to view them differently as the Home Guard literally kidnapped men and packed them off to the front and as Confederate cavalry stationed in the region behaved, in a Watauga farmer's words, "worse than the Yankee raiders."[20] The rebels burned out unionist families and ran them off their blazing farms and homes to Tennessee and Kentucky, where a Union officer wrote about the women and children's woes and the wives' desire for revenge: "I heard them repeat over and over to their children the names of men which they were never to forget, and whom they were to kill when they had sufficient strength to hold a rifle. These women, who had been driven from their homes by the most savage warfare our country has been cursed with, knew what war was, and they impressed me as living wholly to revenge their wrongs."[21]

Keith and Malinda also had their own list of names.

One Watauga man who was not among those on the Blalocks' personal litany was a farmer named John Walker. A boyhood friend of Keith and a man determined to fight for neither side and to remain on his land, Walker put together a clever scheme to trick local Confederates. He joined the Home Guard at Camp Mast, and like the unit's other men, spent two-weeks' rotation on duty and two weeks at home working his farm every month. During his first return from camp, he visited several unionist neighbors, including Levi Coffey, a distant relative of Keith's stepfather. Coffey, at Walker's behest, slipped into the mountains with a request for Keith: Walker wanted to borrow a federal uniform. When Keith and Malinda learned the reason, they handed Coffey the garb.

Walker, at his farm, fashioned several fake wooden rifles, presented them to several farmers and their wives who were all in on the plot, and awaited Coffey. As soon as Coffey returned from the Blalocks' hideout, Walker set his plan into action.

Just after twilight on a Sunday, when several Confederate neighbors were passing in front of Walker's home, more than a dozen riders emerged from the woods behind Walker's home. Several dismounted, ran into the house, dragged Walker out with his hands bound, hoisted him on a horse, and galloped back to the woods, his wife and children screaming for help.

As neighbors gaped at the lanky Union officer and his "guerrillas" in the semidarkness, they "knew" that Keith and Malinda Blalock had struck again and feared what they might do to poor John Walker.

Walker, haggard and filthy, stumbled into Camp Mast a month later with a tale of how the Blalocks had turned him over to a party of Union cavalry to "enlist" him in the federal ranks. An officer, Walker asserted, had believed the prisoner unfit to serve, had written out a parole paper for him, and had released him. Now, Walker handed the document—forged, of course—to Major Bingham. Bingham studied it for several moments and then told Walker that he must, "as a gentleman honor-bound," honor the parole's terms that he not take up arms for a year.[22]

Walker's friends always believed that Keith Blalock had forged the papers, a contention he never denied. But Walker's confidence that the war would end before his parole expired would prove misplaced. In a Confederate uniform, Walker was soon to play a key role in the lives of Keith Blalock and Austin Coffey.

Confederate cavalry from Virginia had driven thousands of "broken-down mounts" into western North Carolina throughout the first half of 1863 and set them loose to forage at will.[23] In Watauga, already hard hit by drought, depleted crops, and a loss of manpower to both the rebel and Yankee sides, the roaming horses drew comparisons to "locusts."[24]

For the Blalocks and their partisan company, the horses proved useful in two ways. The raiders would steal, Keith noted, "the healthiest-looking ones" to replace their own worn-out mounts.[25] He added that the mere sight of Confederate riders turning horses loose on locals' land helped turn neutral folk into unionists. "The Secessionist cavalry [were] worse than Yankee raiders," Keith opined, neglecting to mention that he, of course, was one of those "raiders."[26]

Many Watauga families had reason to share Keith's contention about the Confederate regulars. They not only drove the horses onto any tract in the county, but also behaved more like an occupying army than "our own boys."[27] An elderly local farmer wrote that the cavalrymen were "frequently breaking open granaries, drinking . . . insulting citizens, and making themselves a terror to the whole population."[28]

Foolishly, the soldiers made little distinction between families holding Union or Confederate views. Quartermasters would ride up to unionist Austin Coffey's home or his secessionist neighbors' farms alike, demand several bushels of corn, and offer two dollars per bushel of virtually worthless Confederate bills. If a farmer balked at "the deal," the soldiers broke open every crib of corn he owned and scattered it on the ground for their horses. Those who accepted the offer were handed "a written order on someone who they . . . [said was] coming on behind to pay him."[29] If that "someone" did show up, which was rare, the already enraged farmer found that the chit was for only $1.50 per bushel.

To the further anger of mountain families, the Confederate cavalry never bothered prominent rebel sympathizers such as William and Reuben Coffey. Keith claimed that his step-uncles never sold a bushel of anything to the cause they espoused, and assisted gray-clad soldiers who "plundered and drove off cattle, pocketing the receipts while they were supposedly arresting deserters."[30]

Keith would wryly note that even his old commander, Governor Zeb Vance, railed against the Confederate cavalry, whose depredations he branded "intolerable, damnable, and not to be borne!"[31]

Vance wrote: "If God Almighty had yet in store another plague—worse than all others which he intended to have let loose on the Egyptians in case Pharaoh still hardened his heart, I am sure it must have been a regiment or so of half-armed, half-disciplined Confederate cavalry! . . . Cannot officers be reduced to the ranks for permitting this? Cannot a few men be shot for perpetrating these outrages, as an example? Unless something can be done, I shall be compelled in some sections to call out my militia and levy actual war against them."[32]

Vance, naturally, never sent the ill-armed militia against the regulars, but Keith and Malinda did not anger anyone except loyal Confederates by ambushing the cavalry in narrow passes throughout the mountains. "We knocked more than a few of them down," Keith said.[33] But any good will that the couple's guerrilla actions against the cavalry and the Home Guard might have sparked among neutral folk evaporated each time "Keith, Malinda, and their desperadoes" galloped up to a farm, ransacked it, and set home and barns ablaze.[34] With the couple and their riders likely to materialize anywhere from the Watauga River to the Globe Valley, nestled beneath the Grandfather in Caldwell County, Confederate loyalists feared to walk or ride more than a few miles from their homes. In their fields or at their supper tables, locals kept their rifles close at hand.

Keith claimed that he never raided a farm or homestead where unionists lived. As proof, he would offer the testimony of friends who ran safe houses for his unit and for the men that he piloted through the lines. Malinda told a relative that she and Keith "always knew where our friends were," friends such as her second cousins, who lived near the Watauga River and operated a safe haven for the Blalocks and their men.[35]

While Keith and Malinda left unionists alone, "neutrals," along with rebels, constituted fair game. On an August 1862 evening, the Blalocks and a handful of their company burst from the woods and across a cornfield to the MacTier farm in Caldwell. One of the family's daughters, then fourteen, would remember: "The Blalocks were in full Yankee uniform, and her [Malinda's] hair was short as a boy's. They pointed short rifles [Spencers] at my Father, who was no Confederate. Keith Blalock told us to turn over our corn and bacon. We did, but they burned our barn despite it. Uniforms or not, they seemed nothing but bushwhackers to me."[36]

Finding that the combination of Confederate cavalry and Bingham's militiamen, better armed and disciplined than most Home Guard contingents, made operations "a bit too hot" in Watauga County in August 1863, Keith and Malinda launched most of their raids into Caldwell County, especially the farms of the Globe Valley.[37] They swooped down at night from Blowing Rock or the Grandfather, burning, looting, and gunning down several of Caldwell's Home Guards whose muskets and hunting rifles proved no match for Spencers. The Blalocks and their men grew so emboldened that they targeted several Confederate officers on leave and killed them in their own homes.

A Confederate officer in Caldwell County felt so overmatched by Keith and Malinda's weaponry that he struck an unofficial truce with the guerrillas. After the war, the man revealed that, at nightfall, in 1863–64, he and his men had often sipped whiskey, eaten, and "fraternized" with the unionists. "At night," he wrote, "I am generally out with the boys [Keith's company]. Of course, they know enough to peek out of my sight during the day, which makes it exceedingly difficult for me to catch them."[38]

Another rebel officer whose cavalry took losses in several hit-and-run forays by the Blalocks' company wrote of them: "They are not only determined to kill in avoiding apprehension (having just put to death yet another of our enrolling officers), but their esprit de corps extends to killing in revenge . . . so far they have had no trouble for subsistence. While the disaffected feed them out of sympathy, the loyal do so from fear."[39]

Partly out of fear of Keith and partly out of common blood, the Coffey step-uncles struck an unofficial deal of their own with Bingham and Confederate regulars: Austin Coffey was to be left alone even though he harbored Keith and Malinda frequently. Keith and Malinda, in turn, refrained from burning out William, Reuben, and McCaleb Coffey. All understood, however, that away from the Coffeys' homes, no quarter would be given among the Blalocks and the step-uncles. For the moment, Austin Coffey and Keith's mother remained safe on his land.

Keith and Malinda's ability to slip in and out of Austin Coffey's house seemingly at will perplexed the Home Guard, who, on Bingham's order, watched the dwelling twenty-four hours a day whenever a hint that the couple had come down the mountain drifted to Camp Mast. The Confederates, suspecting that the partisan husband and wife sneaked into the house from the thick woods flanking its rear, thrashed among the trunks, gnarled branches, and thickets dozens of times, but found no footprints—aside from their own—or other signs that Keith and Malinda had visited.

On several occasions, Bingham's men had descended upon the house at night and had politely but firmly insisted that Coffey and his wife allow them to search the two-story house and its cellar. Each time, the rebels, hoping to find the Blalocks cringing somewhere inside, stomped away empty-handed.

The locals would not discover the secret for years. Long after the war, Keith reportedly revealed it to Murray Coffey: "They [Austin Coffey and Keith] knew of a narrow tunnel that started a hundred yards or so away in the woods and ran underneath the house. No one else knew of it, and Keith and Austin never knew whether it was an old Cherokee tunnel or a mining shaft. They cut a passage into the cellar and built a false piece of floor that fooled the Rebels every time."[40]

Eluding capture and harassing Home Guards, regulars, and Confederate loyalists alike, Keith, with Malinda alongside, was waging Kirk's guerrilla war in the mountains every bit as effectively as Kirk had envisioned. With equal skill, Keith also carried out his other mission: to pilot recruits for the 10th Michigan Cavalry and another gathering federal regiment, the 2nd North Carolina, to east Tennessee and transfer them to fellow pilot Daniel Ellis and other scouts for the final grueling trek to Union encampments.

There were times, too, when Malinda piloted deserters and unionists to Tennessee without Keith, her knowledge of the terrain and the "railway" as keen as her husband's. Except for her guerrilla comrades, "who were in on the secret," few of the desperate men she guided to Schull's Cove ever realized that the small, wiry figure cradling a Spencer was anyone else but a scout named "Sam."[41]

When Keith and Malinda turned over the refugees to the Tennessee scouts, the couple also handed them the men's signed recruitment papers for the 10th, which was assembling at Grand Rapids, Michigan, or for the 2nd Mounted, which was forming just across the Kentucky border. Colonel Thaddeus Foote, formerly of the 6th Michigan Cavalry, mentioned Keith Blalock's effectiveness in helping to round out the new regiment's ranks in several war department reports composed soon after July 4, 1863, when the unit's official recruitment commenced.

George Kirk took a decidedly personal satisfaction in the Blalocks' piloting and ambush skills, their success confirming the federal officer's assessment of Keith as a valuable guerrilla asset. Kirk himself was a rising force in the east Tennessee theater of operations, and his success in setting up a network of unionist irregulars throughout the Great Smokies and the Blue Ridge had earned him a major's insignia by August 1863. Throughout the year, he had led dozens of raids himself into North Carolina.

Kirk shared with Keith a willingness to cut down any rebel he encountered. He also advocated the Shermanesque approach to war—to destroy civilian morale by stealing every horse, pig, cow, and chicken in sight, by torching every rebel home possible, and by literally bringing the war to every Confederate porch in the region. In Keith Blalock, Kirk had found an apt pupil. Kirk planned to include him in the most daring and the largest-scale operation the Tennessean had yet devised—the war's deepest federal incursion to date into western North Carolina.

Kirk's plan accelerated with the dramatic news that Union General Ambrose Burnside's troops had taken Knoxville on September 2, 1863. Only the Great Smoky Mountains separated western North Carolina from the federal forces. In the adjoining Blue Ridge, Keith and Malinda plotted a signature strike to conclude their "tense, violent season" in Caldwell County before joining Kirk in Knoxville.[42] Their target was personal: the Moores.

CHAPTER ELEVEN
A Bloody Reunion

S HORTLY after dawn on or around September 1, 1863, Carroll Moore rose for breakfast at his large farmhouse in the Globe Valley. He joined his nephews Patterson, Jesse, Jade, and William Moore, all of them teens, too young for conscription but serving with their uncle in the Home Guard. Major Bingham had assigned the youths as bodyguards to Carroll Moore, whose verbal threats against Austin Coffey had reached Keith Blalock.

Also sitting at the table was Carroll's son James, shipped home from the 26th after the Union ball at Gettysburg had shattered his left thighbone and permanently crippled him. James's Enfield, which he had been allowed to take home, was braced with his wooden crutch against his chair. His father's and the cousins' rifles rested similarly alongside them.

As soon as they finished breakfast, the Moores planned to ride up to Blowing Rock, where Jesse had spied Keith and Malinda's current camp and had sneaked away before Keith's pickets saw him. The Moores intended to follow the same hunting path Jesse had taken, to wait for darkness, and to ambush Keith and Malinda as they slept.

The feud between the Blalocks and the Moores had reached the verge of an even bloodier stage, for several weeks earlier, the Blalocks had led a raid against the farmhouse, only to discover that Carroll Moore was away. "I was visiting my cousin Daniel," Moore said, "and the Blalocks leading a party of fifteen or sixteen men including a Lieutenant James Hartwell [one of Kirk's men] came to my house, compelling my wife to open the door, and commenced robbing and plundering. The same party had robbed that night Daniel Moore and Job Moore, both of them my cousins, taking among other things a couple of mules from Daniel and one from Job."[1]

Of all the Moores, none wanted both Blalocks dead more than James, who had not yet arrived in the valley the first time the Blalocks attacked his parents' home. Still seething at Keith and Malinda's stunts in the 26th and, in his mind, their turning deserters and traitors, and now at the news that the couple had ransacked the home and had terrorized his mother, James planned to ride out with his father and cousins to settle all of his and his family's accounts with Keith and Malinda. Despite his wound, he had already joined the Home Guard and relished the imminent "bloody reunion with the Blalocks."[2]

As the Moores ate, their hunting dogs started barking at the far edge of their fields where the woods led to the Grandfather. The men paid little attention to the distant noise, figuring the hounds had bounded upon a rabbit or some other animal.

At the forest's edge, a dozen crouching figures—eleven men and a woman—emerged and fanned out in a wide arc, the dogs scattering. The band worked their way quickly to a rail fence some fifty yards from the farmhouse and took up positions on all four sides of the building. Keith, Malinda, and their men braced their Spencers on the rails, trained them on Carroll Moore's downstairs windows, and waited for Keith's order to open fire.

One of the Moore cousins had bragged about their impending ambush several days earlier, and from the Blalock's network of unionist informants in Caldwell County, the news had filtered back to Keith. He had decided to attack the Moores first.

From the kitchen table, James Moore happened to look out an open window—and spied the figures arrayed behind the fence. He bellowed the alarm just as the first cracks of fire from the Spencers echoed outside.

The Moores dove to the floor, grabbed their weapons, and crawled nearer to the windows, keeping their heads down. The Yankees' bullets whistled through the windows and crashed into walls and furniture. The Moores could not even lift their heads, let alone return fire.

With the instincts honed on battlefields from New Bern to Gettysburg, James Moore realized his family's only hope was to cut down Keith, Malinda, or both. He positioned himself on his knees alongside the kitchen window, angled himself for a view of the fence, and picked out a blue-uniformed target with his Enfield. He squeezed the trigger, and his British-made musket roared. His target crumpled behind the fence rails. Moore reloaded quickly and pumped a second ball into the prone figure.

Suddenly the partisans' fire slackened, then fell away. The Moores saw their foes scampering across the fields and back into the forest. Malinda was able to run away despite the two wounds in her right arm.

The Moores and "a neighbor boy" who, hearing the shots, had grabbed a rifle and had scampered to "some cover where he was laying out near the house"[3] opened fire on Blalock's gang as they tore for the woods. Outnumbered, the Moores did not pursue the guerrillas.

The moment Malinda was hit, Keith ordered the retreat. As he and his company fled, Malinda still holding her Spencer with her good arm, Keith had glimpsed James Moore's visage through the window.

A quick inspection of Malinda's wounds showed that the balls had clipped her forearm and shoulder but had missed any bone. They fashioned a makeshift sling and climbed back up the Grandfather. "We were scouting our way to Knoxville to join up with Kirk," Keith contended.[4]

Down in the Moore farmhouse, Carroll Moore thrashed on the floor, a Spencer round having blown his left calf and shin apart. He would survive, but would use a crutch the rest of his life. James Moore swore additional revenge against Keith and Malinda, and Keith said he would never pause until he "put a bullet in Moore's brain."[5]

Both men would have their chance. Meanwhile, the Moores took steps to protect Carroll and his wife. Carroll Moore later said that "James, returned home from the war, organized a small party consisting besides himself of three boys, one of them his brother, and two the sons of my cousin Daniel Moore for the purpose of guarding our own houses whenever there was no body of Home Guards in the neighborhood."[6]

With rebels all over the Grandfather and the Globe scanning the forests and crags for any hint of the Blalocks and their men, James Moore and his party moved to defend whichever Moore homes and farms lay nearest to the most recent alleged sighting of Keith and Malinda, and "staid [*sic*] around at different houses for some weeks thereafter."[7]

James and Carroll Moore, who was bedridden for over a month from his wound, were determined that when Keith and Malinda struck again, they would wade into murderous fire. Few in the Globe Valley or on Grandfather Mountain doubted that the Blalocks would return to Carroll Moore's home. The only mystery of the imminent clash was the date.

CHAPTER TWELVE
Hard Men All

W HEN Keith and Malinda reached Knoxville in mid-September 1863, the city teemed with federal troops who had marched triumphantly into the former Confederate bastion two weeks earlier. A Union soldier whom they had helped pilot to safety described the feeling of relief that the first sight of the city and the federal encampment evoked: "There was the park of army-wagons. There was the tented field. There were federal soldiers on parade. We stood a moment in silence and looked congratulations at each other. We did not fall down and give up the ghost; we did not go into ecstasies. We did not hug each other; we simply felt good and went on."[1]

Keith and Malinda went first to a hospital tent where a surgeon examined Malinda's wounds and assured her that her arm was neither infected nor permanently disabled. But another medical condition, one she had just discovered, would prevent her from scouting or from fighting with Keith until next spring. Malinda was pregnant with the couple's first child.

The Blalocks found a Knoxville woman whose husband was also serving with Kirk, with whom Malinda would stay during the pregnancy, safely within Union lines.

With Malinda "settled in," Keith reported to Kirk's encampment just outside the city, where the Tennessean was organizing six to eight hundred recruits as the 2nd North Carolina Mounted Infantry.[2] Many of the men greeted Keith with back slaps and outstretched hands, for he had piloted them out of North Carolina and away from Confederate conscription parties. "They all asked him how Sam was," Murray Coffey relates. "'Shot up a bit, but getting better,' Keith told them."[3]

Now, for the first time, Kirk revealed his bold gambit to Keith: The major was going to lead his regiment into North Carolina and dig in there. The mission's chief goal was to prove that Union troops could penetrate so deeply into Confederate territory that the Richmond government would be compelled to siphon off troops to safeguard its rear.

The military stakes in east Tennessee were high. The French Broad River, coursing from Tennessee to Asheville, North Carolina, and beyond, divided

North Carolina lengthwise. If the Union army decided to launch a full-bore offensive through the Blue Ridge passes that Keith and other scouts knew so well, Robert E. Lee's supply lines into Virginia would be severed. And the Union forces in the west would link up with those in eastern North Carolina to virtually cut the Confederacy in half. General Ulysses S. Grant, not yet arrived in eastern Tennessee but planning a December 1863 inspection of Union troops there, was in fact mulling a strike through the mountains.

George Kirk knew nothing yet about Grant's consideration of an offensive into North Carolina, but did realize the importance of east Tennessee and North Carolina for Lee's Army of Northern Virginia. Itching to launch the largest federal strike at that juncture into western North Carolina, Kirk greeted Keith Blalock warmly and assigned him a key reconnaissance mission: Keith, Joseph Franklin, and several other scout captains were ordered to slip back into the mountains and locate the best route for eight hundred men to ride or march to Warm Springs, North Carolina. The scouts would have to work fast, for Kirk had scheduled his raid for late October.

Kirk had judiciously chosen Warm Springs, which was tucked close to the French Broad River. The sudden appearance of federal cavalry pounding up to the town was calculated by Kirk to stoke Confederate fears that an offensive to cut the state in two loomed.

Embarking on "a scout" without Malinda alongside for the first time in many months, Keith slipped across the Great Smokies into Madison County with a handful of his ablest men, including Malinda's cousin Adolphus Pritchard.[4] They snaked on horseback up and down barely visible trails through "the blue and secretive valleys" of "Bloody Madison."[5]

The county had earned its sobriquet because of the bitter and brutal divisions between a small cadre of wealthy "slave-ocrats" whom the bulk of Madison's poor farmers despised as blue-blooded tyrants to blacks and hard-scrabble whites alike. Gentlemen-farmers—"damned Secesh"—and poor mountaineers and farmers—"black-hearted Lincolnites"—battled each other throughout the county, site to some of the mountain war's worst atrocities. "Hillbillies fighting high-falutin slavers" was soldiers' assessment of Bloody Madison.[6]

Keeping to the deepest woods possible, Keith and his fellow scouts mapped out a twisting route barely wide enough for horses at many spots, but just big enough, as Kirk noted, and always under cover of brush and foliage. The scouts also discovered that between the state line and Warm Springs, the closest Confederate unit was a battalion of regular mounted infantry dispatched to Marshall, sixteen miles away, by General Robert B. Vance, the brother of Zeb and commander of the newly created Western Military District of North Carolina.

Keith and his men returned from the slopes above Warm Springs to the

Great Smokies and sent word to Kirk that they had marked a trail. Then they waited for the first hint of a large dust cloud down in the valleys to the east.

✣

In the last week of October 1863, eight hundred riders, a flag-bearer holding a tasseled stars and stripes and a burly, mustachioed major in the vanguard, rode into the Great Smokies. As twilight gave way to nightfall near the North Carolina border, Keith and two other scouts stood atop a boulder at the edge of a narrow defile, watching the double-columned, blue-coated horsemen's approach.

As the Union troops reached the pass, Keith and his comrades clambered down to greet George Kirk and the 2nd Mounted. Comprised of men from every county in western North Carolina and east Tennessee, the former were eager for a fight on their home soil. Keith would pilot them there.

One of Kirk's aides handed Keith a letter from Malinda, who wrote that she was in good health but wished she could "have gone [to Warm Springs] with the boys."[7]

Meanwhile, the "boys" rode into the pass and clattered toward the forests of Madison. A cavalryman described the scene: "We were obliged to lead our horses, single file, up the terribly rocky and steep trail, horses falling, men stumbling and swearing the entire length of the line. We were dripping with perspiration . . . not daring to discard our overcoats for fear of delay or surprise. Such was the intense darkness of the forest that we were not able to see our hands before our faces. . . . We pressed onward along the crest for a number of miles, and long before the break of day began the descent.

"The mountaineer scouts lighted their long pine torches and led the column down the trail single file. The men bumped against the horses, and the horses bumped against the men. As we moved down the wild mountain trail, I thought the column resembled an immense serpent, with every vertebra in its back in violent action, winding its way into the darkness of the forest."[8]

Exertion led the men to drain their canteens quickly, and wherever an icy stream of spring water coursed between rock along the trail, the soldiers darted from the line to refill them.

✣

On October 29, 1863, the heavy tread of cavalry horses and the ring of spurs and riders' accoutrements broke the predawn calm of the hamlet of Warm Springs. Residents rattled from sleep figured that a large contingent of Confederate cavalry was riding through on the way to east Tennessee. As people peered out their windows, however, they gaped. "The Yankees had come out of nowhere," a man wrote. "The brazen Kirk and his scout Blalock were out front."[9]

Kirk deployed his men along a wooded ridge overlooking a "tourist hotel" and its outbuildings, which his men occupied. The only possible approach to the federals' positions was an acute angle of the town's sole road. Anyone attempting to dislodge Kirk and his men could not even see them until they turned that corner. And when they did, Spencers and muskets would sweep the route from three sides. When the invaders began to dig in along the ridge, townspeople locked their doors and shuttered their windows. Kirk apparently planned to stay awhile.

By nightfall, news reached Major John Woodfin, commander of the mounted rebel battalion in Marshal, that Yankee cavalry had taken Warm Springs. No one seemed to know just how many Union troops had materialized up the road.

John Woodfin, a courtly, well-respected Asheville attorney who was a former law instructor and a longtime friend of Governor Zeb Vance, assumed the federal force could not number more that fifty to a hundred men. He simply did not believe that a force anywhere near the strength of Kirk's regiment could have ridden into the county without attracting someone's attention. If anything, he decided, an overconfident band of partisans in Union garb had terrified locals into thinking the raiders were federal regulars.

Despite the major's bars on his shoulders, Woodfin's experience with war was hunting down guerrillas and deserters. He had shown his mettle in several fierce actions against partisans in the county, but he had never encountered a foe as well-trained and as well-disciplined as Kirk's men. Chances were that if someone had told Woodfin that it was George Kirk who held Warm Springs, Woodfin, well aware of the Tennessean's formidable reputation, would have waited for reinforcements.

At the battalion's encampment that evening, Woodfin cantered to the parade ground, ramrod-straight atop his huge black cavalry charger, Prince Hal. He barked the order to "mount up" and 150 troops climbed into their saddles and formed up "double-file."[10] Unlike many Home Guard units, Woodfin's men were well-equipped, but their repeating pistols and carbines were no match for the 2nd North Carolina Mounted's waiting Spencers, muskets, rifle-guns, and Colt revolvers.

After a hard ride to the outskirts of Warm Springs, which the Confederates reached just after daybreak, Woodfin, riding at the head of his men, raised his gloved hand. His men halted.

The rebels had reached the hard angle shielding Kirk's men and their positions from view. With several of his staff officers, Woodfin rode away from the road's bend and along the bank of the French Broad River until they came to a wooden span bridge, reined in their mounts, and scanned the ridges ahead and the hotel beneath them.

In an outbuilding near the hotel, Keith Blalock and other men selected by Kirk for their sharp-shooting prowess crouched behind windows and waited.

For several more minutes, Woodfin and his aides peered through field glasses at the ridgeline. Then, he waved his riders through the bend and led his aides across the bridge.

Keith and his companions held their fire as Woodfin and his staff rode within a few yards of the outbuilding. On the ridges and in the hotel, the rest of Kirk's men waited for the bulk of the Confederate battalion to clear the road's angle.

Spencers suddenly opened up, and sheets of rounds tore into the Confederates within seconds. Woodfin was blown from the saddle and killed instantly.

It was over in just a few minutes, the rebels shattered by Kirk's firepower and leaving riders crumpled inertly or writhing in the road and near the bridge. A bugler blared the retreat—but the battalion already clattered away in full flight.

The "Battle of Warm Springs" had ended as quickly as it had broken out. Not long after Woodfin's broken unit raced into Marshall with the news that "thousands" of Yankees held the high ground at Warm Springs, shock quickly coursed to Asheville and on to the capital, Raleigh, 250 miles away.

Governor Vance immediately sent orders that the 64th North Carolina march from east Tennessee and up the French Broad River Valley, and he dispatched several cavalry battalions to Warm Springs. Alarmed that the Union force there was the vanguard of an offensive into North Carolina, Vance took the train to Morganton, hopped aboard a horse there, and rode "hell-bent-for-leather" to Marshall to take command of the Confederate forces converging on the town.[11]

While Vance made his way westward, a small contingent of Asheville's most prominent citizens rode to Warm Springs with a flag of truce to ask Kirk's permission to remove the bodies of Woodfin and the other Confederate dead. Given the Union officer's reputation, the civilians displayed a great deal of nerve.

They rounded the blind corner beneath their white flag and discovered no sign of the Yankees—just their lethal handiwork scattered in the road and in front of the hotel. Kirk, Keith, and the 2nd North Carolina had slipped away during the night along the return trail Keith and the other pilots had scouted. They were headed to Greeneville, Tennessee.

To the fury of Woodfin's Asheville friends and his former student, Vance, Kirk's men had stripped the officer's body of all valuables, right down to his boots, and had left him half-naked where he had fallen. Kirk had not only dealt the governor a personal loss, but had also proven that Union troops could reach out and strike the French Broad River region in force. As Keith rode back into the Great Smokies with his comrades, Jefferson Davis's government was about to commit troops needed elsewhere to western North Carolina and east Tennessee. Kirk's raid had reaped its desired purpose.

Of his part in the brief but bloody engagement at Warm Springs, Keith would tell a Union official that he "helped scout the way and beat Woodfin's boys."[12]

To a Coffey relative, Keith added: "Malinda was sorry she missed the fight."[13]

CHAPTER THIRTEEN
Scouting and Raiding
for the Union

A S 1863 came to a close, Confederate hopes in east Tennessee and western North Carolina dwindled. General James "Pete" Longstreet, reluctantly dispatched by Robert E. Lee to drive Burnside westward, had besieged Knoxville in the fall but had failed to recapture the city. In December 1863, Longstreet ordered his army into winter quarters at Greeneville, Tennessee.

"We were a might pleased that the Secesh gave up the battle [of Knoxville]," wrote Malinda. "I wanted to have my infant in peace."[1]

"Peace" was likely the furthest thing from Malinda's thoughts, which an acquaintance, Nancy Lennon, noted were "all with getting back to scout with Keith."[2]

Keith visited Malinda in Knoxville whenever he could, but Kirk was keeping him busy in the Smokies and the Blue Ridge, where "I [Keith] kept the federals informed about conditions under the Grandfather."[3] And with Kirk's martial fortunes continuing to rise, Keith's value as "a trusted lieutenant" likewise soared.

In December 1863, Keith received an official dispatch addressed to "W. M. Blaylock [sic] Mountaineer Scout and captain."[4] The brief letter, written by Lieutenant Frederick A. Field, of the 10th Michigan Cavalry, informed Keith that the regiment would arrive in east Tennessee by March 1864 and would need mountain guides to "go a scouting" for the regiment.[5] Keith, with Kirk's assent, would soon put his skills to work for both the Michigan regiment and Kirk's outfit. Malinda planned to join him.

As Keith and his guerrilla company, up to thirty men, ranged back and forth from Tennessee to North Carolina in the late fall and early winter, they reported that conditions for the Confederate army were deteriorating in the region and were ripe for "a Federal plucking."[6]

After Longstreet gave up the siege of Knoxville and went into winter quarters, he wrote General Robert Vance a letter "requesting him to put his troops at Newport [East Tennessee]."[7] Longstreet's request had a twofold purpose: He believed that if Vance moved from North Carolina into Tennessee, he could still "give protection to his own district . . . at Warm Springs, . . . and at the same time guard [Longstreet's] left in Tennessee and protect in a measure . . . foraging wagons."[8]

Vance, traumatized by Kirk's raid on Warm Springs and the prospect that the Yankee officer would strike up the French Broad River Valley again, vacillated throughout December. Keith informed federal officers that, in the mountain counties, battered by a particularly harsh winter and still reeling from crop failures and conscription, ever-swelling numbers of neutralists were, in Keith's words, "turning Yankee in sympathies"[9] because of the "foraging parties" Longstreet turned loose in Watauga, Caldwell, Ashe, Wilkes, and Catawba Counties.[10]

Keith reported that Longstreet's hungry, sullen soldiers were bullying the locals, whether loyalists, neutralists, or unionists, even more harshly than the Confederate cavalry of the previous winter. They requisitioned—"stole," according to Keith—every horse, mule, pig, cow, and chicken they could find, insulting women and beating up any local farmer or mountaineer whose attitude struck them as "unpatriotic."[11] For McCaleb, William, and Reuben Coffey, the Greens, and the Moores, the "pass" extended them as fellow Confederates by the cavalry during the past winter meant nothing to Longstreet's men, who cleaned out the step-uncles' corn cribs and barns and tossed the quartermasters' worthless chits at the men, leaving them only a few horses for Home Guard duty. Upon hearing that a courtly Virginia officer had derided Reuben Coffey to his face as "a mountain churl," Keith would say to Murray Coffey, "Served that Secesh right."[12]

Irate with the Confederate army, worried that Keith might go back on his word to leave his step-uncles' property alone, Reuben Coffey and his daughter, Millie, moved to a large cabin he owned alongside Meat Camp Creek, in Ashe County, near an old log mill used as a primitive meat-packing house by local hunters and the source of the creek's name. Despite his anger at Longstreet's men, Coffey still rode two weeks each month with Bingham's Home Guard and boasted that he would kill Keith and Malinda the moment he saw them. To Murray Coffey, Keith said: "If he'd [Reuben] seen me, he'd have turned tail."[13]

Throughout December 1863 and early January 1864, Keith's scouting duties superseded but did not halt the raids—or robberies, as James Moore labeled them—into the Globe Valley that had made the Blalocks "the terror of the region."[14] Keith usually tracked Confederate activities during those months with just a few handpicked mountaineers and sharpshooters, including Malinda's cousin Adolphus, a Georgian Confederate deserter named Edmund Ivy, Levi Coffey, and another rebel deserter, James Gardner.

Keith, Jim Hartley, Lewis Banner, and fellow unionist scouts reported that rebel deserters were eagerly joining local outliers. Hard-pressed mountain families and the Home Guard were finding it increasingly difficult to distinguish among unionist guerrillas, deserters with their Confederate army weapons, and genuine outlaws. In the eyes of the Moores, "The Blalocks were traitors, deserters, and criminals."[15]

Confederate soldiers and Home Guards in western North Carolina soon devised several ploys intended to lure "the Blalocks and other notorious Tories and traitors" out of their hideouts and into the open, where the rebels could seize or cut down the partisans, preferably the latter as far as the couple's enemies were concerned.[16] The gambits were fashioned by local Confederates as the deteriorating situation in the mountains made apprehension and punishment of unionists and escaped federal soldiers and conscription of deserters, shirkers, and outliers ever higher priorities. As Confederate regulars and Home Guards who combed the Blue Ridge for their quarry and their prey slipped farther up the heavily wooded slopes, the hunters' frustration grew and sparked a plan to "make Unionists come out of the hill."[17] The rebels had decided that a canny way to force local fugitives out of their hiding places was "running at the men's families."[18]

In several instances, Confederates employed a new and controversial tactic to pry men from the hills. The rebels rounded up the families of the men and threw them in jail. "Women as well as children were taken and they were held without food," wrote a local. "Then word was sent out that whenever the men decided to give themselves up, their families would be released. Most of them came in."[19]

When Governor Zeb Vance heard of the measure, he immediately ordered it to stop. If Major Bingham had dared imprison Keith Blalock's stepfather and mother, he would have undoubtedly gotten a reaction from Keith, but not the desired result. The Watauga Home Guard believed that only one measure—execution—could stop the Blalocks.

The Confederate troops and militia also attempted to infiltrate mountain guerrilla companies like that of the Blalocks by "planting" fake Union escapees. Posing as men who had broken out of the prison camp at Salisbury, the actors, looking properly dirty and weary from their "ordeal," materialized at mountain cabins where, as rebels suspected or knew outright, unionists lived.

Although some of the families could size up a plant quickly, the tangled loyalties of the region, a glib tongue, and some good acting sometimes fooled people. The fakes would then ask for food, shelter, and, most importantly for the Confederates' purposes, pilots to take them through the mountains and to Yankee lines.

Several times, unionist scouts did show up to guide the "prisoner," only to find that the man's real comrades, Home Guards or Confederate soldiers, had been watching nearby. The scouts and any unionist men in the cabins were hauled off in chains or ropes.

Keith and Malinda never fell for the ruse, in part because they had honed a keen sense of who was "Secesh" and who was union, in equal part because the couple's network of informants and allies in Watauga and Caldwell Counties proved equally shrewd in determining real escapees from frauds.

As an escaped federal from Salisbury recorded, a unionist family who was part of the Blalock's operation proved wary of his appearance. J. V. Hadley and two other Union soldiers had escaped from Salisbury, had been chased by rebel soldiers into the Blue Ridge foothills before losing them in huge laurel thickets, and were so desperately hungry that Hadley climbed down to a small farm and began digging up cabbages.

Suddenly, three women appeared at the edge of the patch, and Hadley, terrified that they would run to alert the Confederate soldiers, waved at them. "Hello girls," he called. "Don't be frightened—we won't hurt you."

"Who are you?" called out one of the young women.

"We are soldiers."

"What kind of soldiers?"

Hadley hesitated a moment and then replied: "Confederate soldiers, of course."

Peering at him with obvious suspicion, the woman retorted, "Well, you ought to be engaged in better business [than stealing cabbages]."

Hadley countered: "What better business can we be at?"

"Picking huckleberries."

"Why, I believe you're a Yankee," Hadley said.

"No, I ain't," she said. "But I'm no Secesh."

Hadley, careful in choosing his words, asked: "How's that, not a Yankee and not a Secesh? What are you?"

"I believe in tendin' to my own business and lettin' other people alone."

"But would you have the Yankees overrun the South, steal our Negroes, and rob us of our property?"

"Yes," the girl retorted, "if you don't quit this fightin' and killin'. You all fetched on this war. Fir [*sic*] a few niggers you've driven this country to war and forced men into the army to fight for you who don't want to go, and you've got the whole country in such a plight that there's nothing goin' on but huntin' and killin', huntin' and killin, all the time."[20]

Hadley, gambling that she was a unionist, revealed that he and his companions were escaped federal soldiers and needed food, cover, and a mountain pilot. At the same moment, the young women had decided that Hadley was really a fleeing Union prisoner of war. She helped the three men, but, typically amid the gnarled loyalties of the mountain populace, she led the men to a cave nearby and sneaked food and water to them for several days because "her landlord was a loyal Rebel and because the neighbors were Rebels too."[21] The young woman was a practiced hand at subterfuge: her brother was a Confederate deserter who had been hiding without detection in the mountains with his sister's help for a year and a half.

Hadley and fellow federal prisoners relied upon the Blalocks and other pilots to "pass them through the lines," and Keith always contended that he had taken Hadley and the other two soldiers from another pilot near Blowing Rock and had led them down the trails to Crab Orchard, Tennessee.[22] "In nearly every trip we [the Blalocks] made over into North Carolina," Keith would state, "we returned with more or less escaped prisoners, refugees, and recruits who had learned of my movements from the Union men along the way at whose houses I was in from time to time and in the habit of stopping or calling for entertainment [dinner] and information."[23]

Fortunately for rebels posing as fleeing prisoners, they never found themselves in the position of trying to gull the fearsome guerrilla and scout. Keith and Malinda's "Union men and women" proved capable of sniffing out a fraudulent escapee long before the word was sent to the Blalocks.

Keith and other federal guerrillas employed their own ways of punishing militia and Confederate soldiers for harassing and brutalizing unionists' families. Characteristic of mountain warfare, the retaliation proved an ambuscade. One of Keith's men, Joseph Webb, described one such "mission": "With William Blalock, we went over onto the Elk in Johnson County to whip out [attack] a Rebel picket belonging to Vaughn's regiment [Confederate cavalry] in that locality."[24]

On the way back from the raid, an incident further illuminated the almost claustrophobic nature of the war in the mountains. "We returned to the Crab Orchard [Tennessee], but not until Hartley, Blalock, and party had taken a couple of horses from two Union men by the name of Jim Campbell and Burt Dugger, which they had stolen according to their own statements from some Rebel soldiers a few days previously.

"Hartley and Blalock told them that they [the raiders] had the authority to steal horses and to turn them over to the Federal Army."[25]

Horse-theft—"commandeering"—was an officially sanctioned activity for federal troops and scouts and Confederate regulars and militia alike. To people who could only fume helplessly as Yankees or rebels led off horses, the difference between either side was negligible.

The Northern press, including *Harper's Weekly,* lionized the deeds of the mountain pilots and partisans, portraying the Keith Blalocks as "romantic" patriots, yet part bandits who robbed "rich Confederates."[26] Portrayed throughout the Union as "guardian angels" for escaped Union prisoners, the guerrillas were revered from afar; however, to the loyal Confederates and the neutralists of the Blue Ridge, the sight of Keith Blalock, as well as his wife, in "full federal regalia, armed with a Spencer and a Colt," was something entirely different and entirely menacing.[27] Keith and the other "romantic" partisans could—and did—kill as suited both their survival and their own personal reasons.

As the brutal winter of 1863-64 dragged on, a Watauga native ten years old and all too acquainted with the raids of both sides at the time would remember: "Hit [*sic*] was awful for the folks in the mountains, whichever [unionists or Confederates] came through. They stripped the beds, cleaned anything they wanted out of the houses, robbed the bee gums, and drove off the cattle and hogs, and of course they took the horses. Anything that could travel."[28]

In early January 1864, Keith Blalock was one of several scouts tracking the sudden increase in activity of General Robert Vance's troops in North Carolina. Vance finally believed that he could comply with Longstreet's directive to strike in east Tennessee. When Vance set out with about twelve hundred troops, including cavalry and artillery, along a trail that his engineers had hacked through the mountains, Keith trailed them, watching from various hiding spots amid the crags and woods as the Confederates lugged their ordnance with oxen to the crests of the Smokies.

Keith and other mountaineers doubted, in their reports, that Vance's men could continue farther, the descent into Tennessee possible only by a narrow mule path. But the rebels took the cannons apart and lugged the barrels, carriages, wheels, axles, rigging, and ammunition down the pass. The soldiers' hands torn apart by the rough artillery ropes and harnesses, the barrels ringing against jagged rock, the troops lurched into east Tennessee. Ice storms and powerful gusts battered both Keith and the troops he stalked.

Finally, on or around January 10, Vance's force reached the foothills of the Smokies and put the cannons back together. Mulling his next move, Vance made a mistake by dividing his command. With false intelligence provided to him by local men who were part of Keith and Kirk's network of spies and informants, Vance was convinced that no federal troops, just unionist guerrillas, lay ahead of him.

Vance ordered the bulk of his force, including artillery, toward Gatlinburg, Tennessee, on January 12, 1864, and led about two hundred men toward Sevierville, Tennessee, planning to disrupt federal supply lines to Knoxville.

Vance's riders spotted a Union supply train of twenty-eight wagons creaking with food, blankets, shoes, and other provisions that Longstreet's men needed desperately. The Confederate cavalry pounced and seized the wagon train, and if Vance had turned back with his haul, he would have had "a splendid little victory" and would have alarmed the Union commanders about their vulnerability in the mountain passes.[29] Buoyed by his success, however, Vance chose not to hook up, as intended, with the rest of his force at Schultze's Mill, on Cosby's Creek, Tennessee. Instead, he moved westward in hopes of seizing other Union supply trains despite being slowed down by the vehicles he had already captured.

Keith and other guerrillas' harassment soon convinced Vance to turn back for Cosby Creek, but not soon enough. Shortly after the Confederate commander captured the federal supplies, Keith and his comrades felled trees and rolled boulders into the path of the rebels and sniped at the column from ridges as it strained to clear the obstacles from the road. As the partisans' Spencers dogged Vance's men every step of the way, several scouts rode to the camp of the 15th Pennsylvania Cavalry with word of Vance's predicament. The regiment's commander, Colonel William Palmer, ordered his men to saddle up at 3 A.M. on January 14 and rode hard to the east.

With Keith and other unionists continuing to pick off riders and to block the road, Vance debated whether to turn north and deliver the wagons to Longstreet or to turn back to North Carolina. He chose the latter, but at that moment Palmer's cavalry was closing fast.

The 15th Pennsylvania's scouts caught up with the wagon train near the banks of Cosby Creek on January 15, 1864, and the rest of the Union cavalry reached the ridges flanking the creek shortly after nightfall. Below them, the exhausted Confederates lurched to a halt, unhitched the oxen, and started the cooking fires. The rebels' smoke wafting upward in the frigid, still air, Palmer's riders hid in the woods covering one of the ridges and waited for the dawn.

On a nearby rise, Keith and several of his men, all aware that Palmer's troops would strike at sunrise, bedded down on the frost-tinged forest floor and waited or dozed. Having scouted Vance's progress, launched several ambuscades, and helped slow down the wagon train, Keith and his band had done their work. Now, they would watch the final results. "They [Vance's men] had no idea that the 15th was there and that they had no chance," Keith told Murray Coffey. "I told Malinda later that with Vance's boys out of the way, we could attack the Secessionists at home easier—us against them and the guardsmen [Home Guard]."[30]

The Confederate camp stirred shortly before daybreak, men pushing themselves out of their frozen blanket-rolls and lining up in front of the mess-fires for a tin of corn mush and a bit of captured federal bacon. From his perch, Keith scanned the ensuing action.

"All this time," a Pennsylvania sergeant would record, "our command was standing on the rise of the descent to Cosby's Creek, watching all these maneuvers. The Confederate vedettes had gone down for . . . [their breakfast], leaving no one on lookout. We could plainly see the wagons coming up the stream, and those in front going into camp, when the order for the charge was given. With a yell such as the mountains have never heard before or since, our command fell upon the Confederates in the center, forcing them up and down the stream in direst confusion, with little or no resistance.

"The fight, to the best of my recollection, lasted but five minutes, several of the Confederates being killed or wounded. But a great surprise was in store for us. With a little squad of men we were moving among the wounded and dead, and I was taking a revolver from the pocket of a Confederate officer, when one of the men called my attention to General Vance, and a squad of men, consisting of two aid[es] and orderlies, advancing toward us. I was soon in the saddle and demanded their surrender."[31]

Vance, fuming, blamed his disaster in part upon the failure of Lieutenant Colonel James L. Henry to arrive with the bulk of the Confederate force at the creek as Vance had ordered. He also wrote of the role that Keith Blalock and other Unionists had played in the defeat by salting Vance's operation with informants who delivered false intelligence to the rebels. Vance would charge: "Believing that most of my command was down the creek [according to "traitorous local scouts"], I turned there, but soon after found my mistake. Nearly the whole of the command was *up* the creek."[32]

Amazingly, nearly two-thirds of Vance's men climbed into their saddles and galloped headlong out of the trap and back to North Carolina, where Keith and Malinda would face them again. But the Confederate incursion from western North Carolina into east Tennessee was, for all purposes, finished, a disaster for the Confederate army. Robert Vance would spend the war's duration in a Union prison, assigning blame for the defeat and seeking for decades to clear his name.

Keith Blalock relieved a Confederate cavalry officer of two repeating "horse pistols" [Colts], one for Malinda, eager to rejoin her husband, and one for himself.[33]

On April 8, 1864, with Keith away on "a scout" in Watauga and Caldwell Counties, Malinda delivered the couple's first child, a boy she named Columbus F. Blalock. Keith returned to Knoxville long enough to see his son and to carry him, with Malinda back at his side, to her relatives in Carter County. The couple's joy was tempered by the grim news they had learned from a Tennessee unionist scout. Confederate cavalrymen had killed—executed, according to rebel sources; murdered, said Union neighbors—Malinda's cousin Thomas Pritchard in late January 1864.

On December 1, 1863, a company of Confederate cavalry rode into Eliza-bethtown, Tennessee, near the border of western North Carolina. A captain whose haggard, goateed visage was that of a hardened guerrilla, R. C. Bozen, born and raised in Grayson County, Virginia, espoused the Confederate cause with a fury and considered any Southerner, unionist or neutralist, who did not share his loyalty to the cause his enemy and a traitor.

Bozen was a fearless and resourceful cavalryman; even one of his sworn enemies remarked that the Virginian was "pugnacious and redoubtable."[34] But, as with so many others swept up in the brutal mountain war of shifting loyalties, bushwhacking, and murder, Bozen had scores to settle—in his case, any deserter making his way across the mountains toward Union lines, any unionist scout, and any man, woman, or child aiding either of them.

Bozen and his men terrorized families from the Watauga River to the Smokies, committing a string of atrocities that mountain unionists matched ambush for ambush and hanging for hanging. Even in such an arena of crimes and retaliation, however, Bozen stood out for his ruthlessness. A Carter County man charged that Bozen's "command was composed of men whom he had collected together in Grayson County, and who, as well as their leader, seemed to be entirely destitute of human feeling."[35]

Bozen and his riders had been ordered by Longstreet to round up con-scripts, but locals contended that while Bozen's men "remained in Carter County, they appeared to have no desire whatever to engage in any other business but that of murdering Union men, and plundering their houses, rob-bing their families of what little provision they might have to keep them from starving."[36]

Again, it must be pointed out that unionist bands preyed upon rebel homes with equal cruelty. Still, the crimes of Bozen and his company led a Carter County man to pen the following verse:

> *Bozen's rouges prowl about in dark nights;*
> *Killing and stealing they call Southern rights;*
> *They rob our houses, they plunder and press,*
> *And frequently they take a lady's fine dress,*
> *And it's hard time.*[37]

In Watauga, Caldwell, and Burke Counties, the same doggerel could have ap-plied to Keith and Malinda Blalock, with "Northern rights" replacing "Southern."

Thomas Pritchard, in his twenties, had been scouting for the Union in east Tennessee for more than a year; numerous times Keith and Malinda had turned over to Pritchard escaped federal prisoners of war from Salisbury, de-serters, and recruits for both Kirk and the 10th Michigan Cavalry.

When Bozen's men showed up in January 1864, Pritchard had gone into hiding in the mountains, "endeavoring to keep out of the way of the Rebel soldiers."[38] Two Confederate scouts who lived along the Watauga River soon discovered his hideout and went straight to Bozen with the information.

Bozen and his company seized Pritchard and tossed him into a cold, tiny cell in the Elizabethtown jail, where he was beaten and languished for several days. Finally, three of Bozen's men dragged Pritchard from his cell in the morning, bound his hands behind his back, and, as the soldiers rode behind him, forced him to walk a mile or so from Elizabethtown. A Union scout wrote about what transpired once they reached the woods: "They took him into a small thicket of bushes about one hundred yards off the main road, and shot him through the head, breast, and bowels. One of these fiends then took up a large club and struck him across the forehead, crushing his head perfectly flat. They then left him and rode on up the road, laughing and talking as if the bloody tragedy in which they had just been participating had afforded them the most pleasant and agreeable diversion.

"He was killed about twelve o'clock in the day, and his mangled body remained where he had been killed until about twelve o'clock on the next day, when his aged mother, accompanied by a few friends, removed the body of her murdered son, in order to bestow upon it the last sad rites of parental affection."[39]

Not long after hearing the news of her cousin's murder, Malinda rode eastward with Keith, back to their own corner of the war. Then Malinda soon cut her hair short again, put on a federal tunic, and rode away with Keith to join Colonel Kirk in the Shelton Laurel region, in Madison County. Malinda and Keith would visit the child when they slipped in and out of east Tennessee.

To a relative, Keith would say: "Kirk had a big raid going, and we [Keith and Malinda] were part of it."[40]

Kirk was planning the most daring and most dangerous raid of the mountain war to date.

KEITH AND MALINDA reached Shelton Laurel in the third week of April 1864 with a dozen other scouts. They met with Kirk, who welcomed "Sam" back, commented that he was looking a bit pale, and inquired about "his" wounds. "I told him I was fit, ready to ride and scout," Malinda said.[1]

To the couple's and Kirk's disappointment, General William Tecumseh Sherman had convinced Ulysses S. Grant that a massive offensive through the mountains of North Carolina posed physical and logistical nightmares for a large army. Grant himself rode with aides into the Smokies and Blue Ridge passes and realized that a resourceful Confederate general could mount a bloody defense with minimal forces. In describing the terrain to a Michigan cavalry officer, Keith Blalock noted that "it is a lot worse than any map shows."[2]

Sherman favored stripping east Tennessee of anything that Union troops could carry and leaving western North Carolina to selected cavalry units and guerrilla companies. While Kirk, the Blalocks, and other unionists were ready to comply and unleash a war within a war bound by no conventional military restraints, a Union offensive was in the offing—just not yet.

Keith and Malinda, as well as every other scout and pilot in the region, knew how thin the Confederate forces were, especially after Vance's debacle. Following Vance's capture, the Confederate Congress had appointed Colonel John B. Palmer the new commander of the Western District of North Carolina; he inherited an impossible task. To defend 250 miles of mountains, he had the depleted 62nd and 64th North Carolina Regiments, both of them beset by desertion. Along with those undependable regulars, Palmer could look to about 250 cavalrymen led by slow-moving, unsteady James Henry.

Palmer lamented to Richmond that he would have to place even more reliance on Home Guard units. Though exceptions such as Bingham's two Watauga companies existed, most of the militia had degenerated to even lower levels than before, a polyglot of teenage boys, elderly men, and a few wounded veterans ill-equipped, badly led, and ready to buckle when ambushed by unionists and bushwhackers.

For Keith and Malinda's mission of scouting for Kirk and unleashing a new series of hit-and-run raids against rebels' homes, small detachments of Confederate regulars, and Home Guards, their home county had never offered such bloody opportunities.

The couple reached one of their old hideouts near Blowing Rock in late April and found not only their informants, but also neighbors fed up with the depredations of Confederate cavalry, eager to point the way to rebel encampments ripe for ambush. On several occasions in the spring of 1864, Keith, Malinda, and other scouts operating in bands as few as five and as many as one hundred in number and comprised of unionists, rebel deserters, and outright robbers, sneaked up on bivouacked Confederates and cut their throats as they slept. The guerrillas picked off cavalrymen in passes, and, "adding to Keith and Malinda's fame or notoriety, depending on where one stood on the war," looted and burned dozens of farms and lodges under the Grandfather.[3]

In the Globe Valley, a farmer whose sons had marched off with Confederate regiments, but who was a neutralist wrote of his and his neighbors' fear of the Blalocks and their company: "We never go to bed without thinking that they may come before morning."[4]

Watauga farmer Rufus Patterson wrote that "the Blalocks, Robbers, and Bushwhackers became more violent . . . and we will soon be ruled by Bushwhackers—Tories and Yankees."[5]

Every night in the spring and summer of 1864, the Moores and Greens, as well as William, Rueben, and McCaleb Coffey slept with the proverbial "one eye open," their weapons at hand, every window and door covered and locked. Every hoofbeat echoing from sundown to sunrise evoked alarm among the rebel families around the Grandfather and Blowing Rock. "They [the Blalocks' many enemies] all knew we were coming for them," Keith said. "But only Malinda and me [*sic*] knew when."[6]

To torment his step-uncles and other foes further, Keith would constantly plant rumors, through his web of informants and "neutralists," that "tonight was the one" in which he Malinda, and "the Blalock men" would attack the Coffeys, the Greens, or the Moores.[7] The purported targets would stay awake all evening, peering into the darkness and listening for footsteps or horses. When dawn broke with no sign of Keith and Malinda, their duped enemies were enraged. Hiram Crisp, a friend of the Moores and the Greens, wrote: "The Blalocks wore those federal uniforms as an excuse to bushwhack their neighbors."[8]

"We only went after Secessionists who were looking to kill us first," Keith claimed.[9]

George Kirk, who never balked at terrorizing civilians espousing Confederate sympathies, allowed Keith and Malinda full latitude in their vendettas, so long as they carried out his April and May 1864 directives: to recruit more men for his ranks, to harass Confederate regulars and Home Guards, and to apprise Kirk of any rebel activity in the mountains.

Keith and Malinda piloted at least thirty-three unionists to Tennessee passes from where other scouts led them to Strawberry Plains, near Knoxville. Keith noted a typical "rescue" of Union prisoners from Salisbury by him, Malinda, and their men: "I took with us [through the mountains] about forty-five men, escaped prisoners, eight of them officers, and also a few refugees and a few recruits. I had a list of these officers in a memorandum book and remember the names of Captain Minney of a Pennsylvania regiment and a Captain Goodyear of an Illinois regiment; also of a Captain Wilson and a Lieutenant Velford of New York regiments, some of whom fell in with [Keith] near Lenoir and others near the Grandfather Mountain."[10]

Kirk needed every man the Blalocks and his other guerrillas could send him, for he was organizing the 3rd North Carolina Mounted Infantry, a new regiment.

On February 13, 1864, Major-General John M. Schofield had issued Special Order No. 44:

> *Authority is hereby granted to Major G.W. Kirk, of the Second North Carolina Mounted Infantry, to raise a regiment of troops in the eastern front of Tennessee and the western part of North Carolina. The regiment will be organized as infantry and will be mustered into the service of the United States to serve for three years, unless sooner discharged. The regiment will rendezvous as soon as practicable at headquarters Department of the Ohio, or other place here to be hereinafter designated, to be mustered into service. The commanding officer is authorized to mount his regiment, or such portion of it as may from time to time be necessary, upon private or captured horses. This regiment will be known as the Third Regiment of North Carolina Mounted Infantry.*
>
> *By Command of Major-General Schofield*[11]

In his reference to "private or captured" horses, Schofield literally gave Kirk and his operatives license to take any horse they came across in Tennessee and North Carolina. Kirk and the Blalocks took full advantage of the directive, which led Confederate and neutralist families, wincing or cursing as the raiders took horses away, to brand the unionists as not only bushwhackers, but also horse thieves.

The Blalocks' company mounted several ambushes in which they tricked Confederate cavalry under General J. C. Vaughn's command into dismounting and pursuing several partisans into the woods. As the rebels gave chase, the rest of Blalocks' men scampered to the riderless cavalry horses, killed or chased off any guards, and galloped off with their new mounts, slated for the 3rd Mounted Infantry.

After the Blalock band had carried out several such successful attacks, Vaughn ordered his officers to ride out in groups of fifty or more to discourage the partisan units from their "thievery."[12] The Blalocks responded by linking their dozen or so men with similarly sized companies led by pilots such as Jim Hartley and by hitting the rebels in Watauga and Caldwell even harder.

By now, in the fourth spring of the war, locals viewed the Blalocks and the Confederates with equal fear and weariness. "Truth was," Keith related, "people were going to lose their horses and corn to either the Rebels or us."[13]

No matter what side families were on, about all they could do against marauding unionists and Confederates was to hide provisions and an animal or two and hope that when riders approached, they would leave homes standing. "At least we didn't carry off men against their will to the Union army," Keith would offer.[14]

In that one respect, he was right. Todd R. Caldwell, a Morganton man and friend of Austin Coffey, complained that conscription parties remained relentless: "Men professing to be impressing agents from Longstreet's army and elsewhere are getting to be as thick in this community as leaves here in Vallambrosa."[15]

Also proving the truth of Keith Blalock's view of ongoing "impressment gangs," Lieutenant J. C. Wills, of the 33rd North Carolina Infantry, charged that growing disloyalty to the Confederacy in the mountain counties was due in large part to the conduct of "Vaughn's command having passed through recently and pillaged the county as they went."[16]

Wills wrote of the cavalrymen's misconduct at the same time that Keith and Malinda were riding back to the Grandfather to add to their rebel neighbors' misery. "In crossing the Blue Ridge, on my way here, on the 16th [April]," Wills wrote, "I met Gen. V. [Vaughn] and two or three other officers (of his staff, I presume). Half a mile behind him I met some half doz. of his soldiers, and I continued to meet them in squads, of from two to twenty, all the way to this place (Boone)—stragling [*sic*] along without the shadow of organization and discipline. In this manner they continued to come for ten days. The whole command (some seventeen or eighteen hundred men) just disbanded, and turned loose, to pillage the inhabitants, and thoroughly did they perform their work. It was not merely stealing but open and above board highway robbery. They would enter houses violently breaking open every door, and helping themselves to what suited their various fancies—not provisions only, but, everything, from horses down to ladies' breast pins."[17]

The Moores, the Coffey brothers, and the Greens returned from two weeks' duty with Bingham's Home Guards to find that Vaughn's men had visited the loyalists' homes, leaving corn cribs, liquor cabinets, barns, kitchens, bureau drawers, trunks, and chests in empty disarray. Many times, the Blalock band swooped down on rebel families' farms only to find that Confederate cavalry had ransacked the sites first. At several such farms near Boone and in the Globe Valley, Keith and Malinda committed the final depredation: they set the houses and outbuildings ablaze.

Described as "an outlier chieftain" by James Moore, Keith and his men pinned down Bingham's men to such a degree that when General John W. McElroy, the Home Guard commander for western North Carolina, issued a call for units to join him at Mars Hill, few could spare even a handful of men.[18] Bingham replied: "Respectfully, Sir, it is impossible for me to part with one of my companies at present . . . owing to the presence of the Blaylocks [sic], Hartley, and their outlaw friends in Burke, Caldwell, and Watauga."[19]

A letter in April 1864 from McElroy to Governor Zeb Vance details the immense problems that Kirk, the Blalocks, and other unionist raiders posed for the Home Guard companies in the mountains:

> *The county has gone up. It has got to be impossible to get any man out there [for the Home Guards] unless he is dragged out, with but very few exceptions. There was but a small guard there [Burnsville, Yancey County] and the citizens all ran on the first approach of the Tories. I have 100 men here [Mars Hill, Madison County] to guard against Kirk . . . and cannot reduce the force; and to call out any more home guards at this time is only certain destruction to the country eventually. In fact, it seems to me, that there is a determination of the people in the county generally to do no more service to the cause. Swarms of men liable to conscription are gone to the Tories or to the Yankees—some men that you have no idea of [informants posing as rebels or neutralists and working for Kirk and Blalock] while many others are fleeing [to] the Blue Ridge for refuge . . . that discourages those who are left behind, and men [are] conscripted and cleaned out as [if] raked with a fine-toothed comb; and if any are left; if they are called upon to do a little home guard service, they at once apply for a writ of habeas corpus and get off . . . if something is not done immediately for this country, we will all be ruined, for the home guards now will not do to depend on.[20]*

McElroy's dismal words prompted Governor Vance to appeal to Confederate Secretary of War James A. Seddon with a near-desperate request: "I beg again to call to your earnest attention the importance of suspending the execution of the conscription law in the mountain counties of North Carolina. They are filled with tories and deserters, burning, robbing, and murdering. They [the counties] have been robbed and eaten out by Longstreet's command, and have lost their corps by being in the field nearly all the time trying to drive back the enemy. Now that Longstreet's command is removed and all of East Tennessee is in Union hands, their condition will also be altogether wretched, and hundreds will go to the enemy for protection and bread."[21]

Even the wives of loyal Confederate soldiers beseeched their husbands to desert because their families were in dire condition. A young private of the 26th who deserted and was seized by the Home Guard offered a letter from his spouse in defense of his action: "My Dear Edward [Cooper], I have always been proud of you, and since your connection with the Confederate Army I have been prouder that ever before. I would not have you do anything wrong for the world, but before God, Edward, unless you come home, we must die. Last night I was arrested by Eddie's crying. I called, 'what's the matter, Eddie?' and he said, 'oh, Mama, I'm so hungry.' And Lucy, Edward, your darling Lucy, she never complains, but she is growing thinned and Edward, unless you come home we must die."[22]

Edward Cooper was put in front of a firing squad for desertion.

By 1864, even many Confederate loyalists in the mountains were nearly as angry at the government in Raleigh and in Richmond as at the Blalocks and other unionists. The *North Carolina Weekly Standard* ran an editorial about the conditions for Confederate families in the mountains and wondered: "How Are Soldiers Wives to Get Bread?"[23]

In the *North Carolina Weekly Standard,* a Blue Ridge loyalist wrote to the editor: "Will you be so kind, Mr. Editor, as to inform Jeff Davis and his Destructives, that after they take the next draw of men from this mountain region, if they please, as an act of *great* and *special* mercy be so gracious as to call out a *few,* just a few of their exempted pets . . . to knock the women and children of the mountains in the head, to put them out of their misery."[24]

Exacerbating tensions in the Blalocks' home counties even further, the precious commodity of salt was "hoarded by the loyal Rebels and kept from the hands of poor rural mountaineers suspected of Union sympathies . . . this tactic is designed to punish [unionists] and also to drive the deserters from their hideouts into the towns."[25] The measure also prodded desperate and angry men into the bands of Keith Blalock and Jim Hartley.

Around the Grandfather and down in the Globe Valley, Keith and Malinda and "Kirk's man Hartley" continued to exploit the deteriorating and violent scenario, raiding almost at will.[26] "They [the Blalocks] became so brazen that they attacked farms in the daylight. They had not done so before," Bingham would write.[27]

Keith and Malinda's trust in their friends and spies eventually led the pair into overconfidence. Bingham, too, had "people up there" [Blowing Rock and the Grandfather][28]; on the upper slopes of the Grandfather, one of them, a man named Farthing, whom Keith and Malinda derided as "a Secesh bushwhacker," had smelled something few locals had encountered since the war's early days—real coffee.[29] In the mountains, only Union troops or Confederates lucky enough to have found it on Yankee prisoners or corpses generally got to gulp coffee.

Farthing trailed the aroma and discovered a small band sitting around a campfire and sipping from tin cups—federal cups. Two of them, in blue tunics, he immediately recognized.

Within hours, Bingham sent out word that both companies of the Watauga Home Guard were to report to Camp Mast. He also requested and received fifty of Henry's Confederate cavalrymen to assault the hideout of Keith and Malinda Blalock.

🐍

On a moonless night in late May 1864, 150 men rode out of Camp Mast and up the lower trails of the Grandfather. They halted halfway up, dismounted, hid their horses, and followed Farthing up a hunter's path on foot.

Around two in the morning Edmund Ivy ran shouting into the clearing to alert the Blalocks and "their squad" that the woods below were full of soldiers and guards.[30] Jarred from sleep near the campfire, Keith and Malinda grabbed their Spencers, led their horses behind a jumbled mass of boulders, and took up firing positions.

As sheets of rebel fire lit up the woods in front of the clearing, the guerrillas instantly realized how badly outnumbered they were. They returned fire for a minute or two, clambered atop their horses, skidded up a rock-strewn trail, and vanished.

Keith and Malinda fled "clear back to Tennessee with a souvenir" of the ambush: a ball had ripped away a chunk of Keith's left hand.[31] One of the Blalocks' band, M. E. Paul, a cousin of Keith, wrote that "we were on scouting duty with a squad of men when we got in a fight with Capt. Bingham's company of N.C. Militia and Confederates."[32]

Keith gave a more accurate assessment of the action: "Bingham nearly got us—me and Malinda were lucky that time."[33]

Although the Blalocks had "high-tailed" from the near-ambush too quickly to identify individual guards' faces, Jim Hartley and Harrison Church would tell Keith that all of his old foes had fired at the couple on the Grandfather. If Keith had ever considered a rapprochement with his step-uncles, any such thoughts evaporated soon after the rebel bullet pierced his hand; if

William, Reuben, and McCaleb Coffey thought that they had chased Keith and Malinda away for good this time, they were mistaken. The Coffeys, the Moores, and the Greens would face the couple and their Spencers again.

At the federal camp at Strawberry Plains, Keith and Malinda plotted their revenge.

"Wherever things led," Malinda told her cousin Adolphus, "I'd be at his [Keith's] side."[34]

Bingham would soon regret that the Blalocks had slipped away yet again.

CHAPTER FIFTEEN
Enlisted in the U.S. Service

L ATE in May 1864, Keith, Malinda, and three of their mountain comrades galloped into the sprawling federal encampment and navigated the rows of canvas tents until they reached those of George Kirk's 3rd North Carolina Mounted. Keith reported to Kirk that, aside from a small detachment of Confederate artillery and Bingham's and Walton's Home Guard companies, no large Confederate force currently operated around Blowing Rock and the Grandfather.

That intelligence, combined with the reports of Kirk's other mountain pilots, indicated that the only rebel force of consequence at the moment between Knoxville and Morganton, North Carolina, was several hundred troops at nearby Camp Vance. Kirk intended to launch a surprise strike at the Confederate base and to burn a key bridge over the Yadkin River. His commander, General Schofield, had sanctioned the raid, but was unaware that Kirk, once he reached Camp Vance, had a second set of startling objectives.

Keith and Malinda, in her customary guise as Sam, first learned just how ambitious Kirk's scheme was when they discovered that the officer intended to bring along a Tennessee railroad engineer. At the depot in Morganton, Kirk planned to steal a locomotive, pack several cars with troops, hurtle down the tracks to Salisbury, attack the Confederate prison camp there, and free the thousands of federal prisoners. He figured that he could load them onto the train, make a dash for Morganton, and pilot them all to Tennessee. Even for George W. Kirk, the plan's audacity was striking, and if Schofield had known what his subordinate was plotting, the general would likely have called off the raid on Camp Vance.

As Kirk readied the final details for his departure date, June 13, 1864, Keith met with Colonel Luther Trowbridge, commander of the 10th Michigan Cavalry. Noting Keith's and Malinda's value as scouts and guerrillas for Kirk and their success in piloting recruits to the 10th and to the 2nd and 3rd North Carolina Volunteers, Trowbridge asked Keith to sign on as "a recruiting officer and captain of scouts for the Michigan regiment."[1] If he accepted, Keith would be granted full latitude in selecting his scout company from his own men—Edmund Ivy, Levi Coffey, and other mountaineers—and from men he had piloted to sign the enlistment paper of the 10th.

Although Keith and Malinda had planned on accompanying Kirk on his assault against Camp Vance, the prospect of joining the 10th made a great deal of sense to the couple. First of all, the unit would be in the vanguard of Union troops sweeping at some point into North Carolina, affording Keith and Malinda the opportunity to be "a regular unit's" eyes and ears on their home soil. Keith's mention of the 10th as "regular army" reflected his conviction that if he were affiliated with a bona fide cavalry regiment as opposed to Kirk's operation, he would have an easier time filing for the pension the U.S. War Department would undoubtedly provide all who had fought in the Union army.[2] Keith, wrongly, as it turned out, was concerned that if he could list only his guerrilla activities as proof of his service, some Washington bureaucrat would insist upon documentation—specifically, an enlistment paper rather than just scouting or recruiting notices. "Malinda and I talked it all over," he said, "and I figured it would be better for us if we had the 10th next to our names instead of scouting for Colonel Kirk."[3]

Keith and Malinda also decided something else: Malinda would never pass the federal Army's physical. "They weren't as desperate as the Secessionists for any old body," Malinda recalled. "And the Tenth's surgeon who fixed Keith's hand [Assistant Surgeon W. D. Scott] wouldn't be fooled by 'Sam.'"[4] Sam could, however, still serve the regiment and wear its uniform as an "unattached" scout in Keith's company.[5]

On June 1, 1864, Keith strode to the tent of Lieutenant Frederick Field, a bull-necked, gregarious man who had struck up a friendship with Keith and "Sam." When Keith announced his desire to enlist in the 10th as "an officially attached scout and recruiting officer," Fields produced a paper for his own unit, Company D.[6]

In firm handwriting, Keith signed his second muster roll, but this time he did so willingly:

"*I, William Blalock, born in Yancey in the State of North Carolina, aged Twenty-Six Years and by occupation a Farmer Do Hereby Acknowledge to have volunteered this First day of June 1864, to serve as a Soldier in the Army of the United States of America for the period of Three Years.*"[7]

Keith would note: "My stepfather would be real proud that I took the Union's oath because this oath meant everything to us. We were Union men."[8]

With Field witnessing, Keith officially took the oath of the cause that he had already been serving since the fall of 1862:

"I, William Blalock, do solemnly swear, that I will bear true faith and allegiance to the United States of America, and that I will serve them honestly and faithfully against all their enemies. . . ."[9]

Fields and Keith then walked over to one of the 10th's medical tents, where Surgeon Scott "minutely inspected the Volunteer, William Blalock."[10] He found the strapping, blue-eyed, light-brown-haired scout "entirely sober and able-bodied," the examination confirming Keith's and Malinda's decision that "Sam" could not have passed medical muster for the 10th.[11]

Keith would soon number "S. M. Blalock, Edmund Ivy, Adolphus Pritchard, and Levi Coffey" as riders with "W. M. Blalock's Scout Company, 10th Mich. Cavalry, June 1864, Strawberry Plains."[12]

When Keith received his new blue uniform, so too did Malinda, as independent Union scouts were allowed and as she and Keith had done before, while in Kirk's service. With the full assent of Trowbridge and Field, Keith would "go a scouting" for the regiment in east Tennessee and North Carolina with few if any restrictions on his movements in the field.[13] His new commanders needed men who knew the mountains, and were willing to turn Keith Blalock loose, with Malinda and his old gang alongside, for his proven ability to garner intelligence and bedevil the Confederates. If, on scouts, the Blalocks happened to settle their vendettas with rebel neighbors, no matter how savagely, Colonel Trowbridge did not care. For the 10th and the other federal regiments in the upper east Tennessee theater of operations would soon carry the concept of "total war"[14] into western North Carolina.

Keith would write that he enlisted in the 10th "with the understanding that I was to be employed as a scout in keeping the army . . . informed as to the number and location and movements of the enemy in Western North Carolina, a district of country with which [I] was well acquainted, having been born and raised [there].[15]

"Having received notice as to the information that was desired," Keith stated, "I would proceed in the most cautious manner possible to obtain the same from Union men who lived in and near the locality of the enemy's forces, traveling through the mountains by day and night and stopping with the Union men here and there, of which there were a number who could be confided in to the fullest extent.

"[I] would deliver the same [intelligence] to my company officers, who would report it to General Stoneman, and when the information was deemed of much importance"—'as was not infrequently the case,' one of Keith's superiors wrote—"I would be taken in person to the General for particular inquiry."[16] Keith was not merely bragging; Captain Minihan confirmed that the lanky mountaineer and Stoneman, the polished West Pointer, met often and that the cavalry commander trusted Keith's information.

Keith Blalock in his only
known photograph, taken
circa 1870. His wounded eye
and hand are just visible.
*William Eury Appalachian History
Collection, Applachian State
University*

Malinda "Sam" Blalock in
a photo taken some twenty
years after the Civil War.
*Southern Historical Collections,
University of North Carolina,
Chapel Hill*

A unionist guerrilla in the North Carolina mountains. Union scout Daniel Ellis drew the picture, and its subject bears a striking resemblance to Ellis's comrade, Keith Blalock.

Thrilling Adventures of
Daniel Ellis

Confederate general and North Carolina Governor Zebulon Vance, to whom Malinda Blalock revealed her gender while in the service of the 26th North Carolina.

Southern Historical Collection,
University of North Carolina,
Chapel Hill

Unionist guides—
"pilots"—taking escaped
federal prisoners of war
and unionist civilians
over the Blue Ridge
Mountains to safety.
*Harper's Weekly/Library of
Congress*

Unionist guerrillas
battling Confederate
cavalry in the mountains.
*Harper's Weekly/Library of
Congress*

A bloody clash in the
mountains between rebel
and Yankee guerrillas.
*Thrilling Adventures of
Daniel Ellis*

Linville Falls, North Carolina. Keith and Colonel George Kirk's men passed here on their way to raid Morganton.
Library of Congress

A band of Confederate deserters and "outliers" similar to the Blalocks' "gang" on Grandfather Mountain, North Carolina.
Harper's Weekly/Library of Congress

"War in the Mountains."

Harper's Weekly/Library of Congress

Captain R. C. Bozen, who murdered Malinda's cousin Thomas Pritchard, with his men hunting and killing unionists in east Tennessee.

Thrilling Adventures of Daniel Ellis

A unionist scout fleeing Confederate cavalrymen in the North Carolina/Tennessee mountains.
Thrilling Adventures of Daniel Ellis

Stoneman's raiders, his "Cossacks," on the prowl in the North Carolina mountains. Slung behind their shoulders are Spencer rifles, the Blalocks' weapon of choice.
Harper's Weekly/Library of Congress

A typically brutal and up-close scene of the war in the mountains. The Blalocks knew such action well.
Thrilling Adventures of Daniel Ellis

Union General George Stoneman. The Blalocks served with his cavalry raiders in the mountains in the war's final year.

Library of Congress

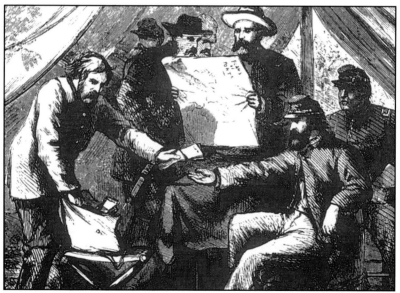

A Union scout delivers intelligence to his commanders. Keith Blalock personally reported in this manner to General Stoneman.

Thrilling Adventures of Daniel Ellis

"The Grandfather in Profile." Grandfather Mountain, where the Blalocks operated throughout the Civil War.

Harper's Weekly/Library of Congress

Keith and Malinda's mountain lodge, near Linville Falls, North Carolina, in 1875. This sketch was drawn by their friend, Shepherd Dugger.

War Trails of the Blue Ridge

"I enlisted in the U.S. service," said Keith, "and Malinda was right there too."[17]

✦

Although news reached Watauga and Caldwell Counties that Keith Blalock had joined the 10th Michigan Cavalry as a scout and a recruiting officer, his many enemies throughout the region refused either to believe or accept that Blalock ever acted on any authority except his own. Joseph Webb, who lived alongside Wilson's Creek, in Mitchell County, North Carolina, "was acquainted with Keith Blalock and his wife for several years before the war and had visited them from time to time at their house near the top of the Grandfather Mountain some seven or eight miles distant."[18] Even though Webb told neighbors rebel or Yankee that he "saw Blalock in the latter part of 1864, and he was leaving for Tennessee for the purpose of enlisting in the Union Army," the Moores, among many local Confederates, refused to believe that Blalock would take orders from anyone.[19]

When several neutral people said that they had heard that Keith had joined the 10th, Jesse Moore replied that he "believes nothing about Blalock's enlistment in the Union Army."[20] The rebel added that he did not "grant for a moment that Keith or Malinda ever scouted for anyone but themselves."[21] George Kirk and the Union prisoners whom the Blalocks had piloted to safety proved otherwise.

Another neighbor, Langston L. Estes, a unionist who had recently returned from a dangerous trip to visit relatives near Strawberry Plains, Tennessee, told neighbors in the Globe Valley that not only had he seen Keith "in a Yankee uniform and armed with a Spencer rifle and a Navy revolver," but also that he had spoken to him.[22] "He told me straight that he had been to the Union army and had enlisted in the 10th Michigan Cavalry to scout and recruit," Estes said.[23]

Still, Mrs. McCaleb Coffey chided that "Blalock was *said* to have enlisted in the Union Army not long after he and his gang had been accused of stealing cattle in Watauga County" and that she refused to accept "any knowledge or information as to Blalock acting as a scout.[24]

"I refuse to hear anything of the kind," she said.[25]

On the other hand, Mrs. Austin Coffey boasted: "I am the mother of William Blalock, who was a soldier in the 10th Michigan Cavalry and proud [that] he went away to the Union Army in May 1864."[26]

✦

The regiment that the Blalocks now served had fought a brilliant and bloody action against Confederate General A. E. "Mudwall" Jackson near Carter's Station, Tennessee, in late April 1864 and had acquitted itself with equal effectiveness at Powder Spring Gap, on April 28; at Dandridge, May 18; and at Greeneville, on May 29. With Trowbridge and his staff planning to send out "detachments of the regiment ... to engage in scouting and pursuing small bands of rebels in East Tennessee and the North Carolina passes" throughout the summer and fall, the Blalocks had arrived at a propitious moment for the 10th to use their brutal skills.[27]

On June 13, 1864, Keith, with Malinda, rode out of Strawberry Plains on the couple's first scouting mission for the 10th. Their destinations were Mitchell County and then a foray into Burke, Caldwell, and Watauga to check on rebel activities, especially at Camp Mast. Rumors that detachments of Confederate cavalry were assembling there had reached Schofield's headquarters.

Keith and Malinda did not depart with just Ivy and Pritchard. "We rode out with Kirk and two hundred of his men," Keith would say.[28]

The Blalocks had found a way to participate in "Kirk's Raid."

Chapter Sixteen
Look at the Damned Fools!

~

G EORGE W. KIRK'S force was composed of handpicked, hard-bitten veterans of his 2nd and 3rd North Carolina Mounted Infantry; men who could fight either as conventional troops or as resourceful guerrillas. Estimates of the raiders' strength varied, Keith Blalock putting it at 200, another of Kirk's men claiming 236, and a third source claiming only 130.

What was never in dispute was the unit's firepower. Kirk had made certain that most men carried a Spencer, repeating pistols, and ample ammunition.

According to Keith, their route "passed through Crab Orchard, [Tennessee], and went up Chucky River, passing through Limestone Cove, and crossing the mountains at Miller's Gap, two miles from Montezuma [North Carolina], then called Bull Scrape."[1] At Miller's Gap, the men dismounted and proceeded on foot, laden with blankets, rations, ammunition, and their weapons. Kirk planned to steal new horses at Camp Vance.

An old friend of Keith met the column near Montezuma, selected as Kirk's guide to the Confederate stronghold. Joseph V. Franklin, born and raised near Linville Falls, had grown up with Keith, knew Malinda well, and "knew the country like a book."[2] He led them to a pine thicket, where the troops camped near the home of unionist David Ellis.

Franklin had chosen the route well, guiding the band undetected through the mountains until they reached the Linville River, whose waters Keith and Franklin had swwm and fished in their youth. Kirk drove his men relentlessly deeper and deeper behind Confederate lines.

On June 27, 1864, Keith, Malinda, and the others halted "for a blow [breath]" at Upper Creek, within sight of the main road to Morganton.[3] Then Kirk ordered everyone back on his feet "just at dark," and the column marched all night the twelve miles to Morganton.[4]

At daybreak, Franklin wrote, "we got to the conscript camp [Camp Vance] at Berry's Mill Pond, just above what was then the terminus of the Western North Carolina railroad."[5]

From the cover of a wooded ridge, Keith and Malinda, clutching their

Spencers, stared down at the Confederate encampment, rows of rough-hewn log huts spread across a five-acre clearing crossed by two springs. The camp was one of dozens established by the North Carolina legislature in the fall of 1861 and scattered from Morganton to the Piedmont. At first, Camp Vance had been a bona fide training camp for recruits bound for the battlefields of the eastern coast and later those of Tennessee, Virginia, Maryland, and Pennsylvania. Conditions in the camp had deteriorated by the spring and early summer of 1864, garrisoned by soldiers who, with the exception of their officers, were conscripts and wanted nothing more than to go home.

Although several West Pointers had run the camp in its early days with the characteristic spit and polish of many academy men, those days were a distant memory; now, the sanitation and living conditions ranged from abysmal to "worse than an unkempt barnyard."[6] Just several weeks prior to Kirk's arrival in the ridges above Camp Vance, a rebel conscript had written of life in the squalid "bastion": "Paw, I want you to hire me a substitute if you can, for I would not stay her fore [*sic*] all that I ever expect to be worth in this world."[7]

The federal raiders had arrived too late to catch the rebels sleeping in their quarters—the shrill notes of reveille reverberated in the warm morning air.

From the cabins, about three hundred soldiers, many of them unwilling conscripts, and officers stumbled blearily to the parade ground for assembly and, next, breakfast. Their weapons were stacked in front of the cabins, and aside from officers wearing side arms, few men were armed. Major McClean, the camp commander, was absent that morning, and in his place was a green lieutenant named Bullock.

As Keith and Malinda, crouching next to Franklin, and Kirk's men aimed at the gray-uniformed figures forming for the morning muster, Kirk and two of his officers strode under a white flag down the ridge and into the midst of the stunned Confederates and demanded their immediate surrender.

Bullock asked for a few minutes either to consider his plight or else to attempt resistance, and Kirk returned to the ridge. Not long afterward some of the rebels broke toward the stands of muskets, grabbed their weapons, and sent a few ragged volleys of Minie balls screeching at the trees above the camp.

Kirk's men countered with withering blasts, ten conscripts and one officer killed in the fusillade of copper-sheathed Spencer bullets, and "an unknown number" sprawled wounded across the clearing.[8] The Confederates hastily showed a white flag.

For over a century, many Confederate accounts of the action would claim that none of the rebels had opened fire and that Kirk and his men had cut down ten conscripts and an officer in what seemed nothing less than cold-blooded butchery. But archaeologists digging at the old site of Camp Vance in 1970 dug up piles of spent Minie balls that proved that the garrison had indeed put up some kind of a stand. Kirk's Spencers, of course, had quickly carried the fight.

Kirk's casualties were two dead and five men slightly wounded. Kirk himself was hit in the arm, but not seriously, "losing the only blood that he lost during the war."[9] The Blalocks and their comrades soon tied the prisoners' hands, placed the captives under guard, and burned the camp to the ground—the hospital the only building spared the flames.

The federals' day of ambush and looting had just begun. They pushed into Morganton, burning three thousand bushels of corn and over two tons of military supplies in a warehouse. At the railroad depot, Keith and Malinda helped destroy a locomotive and four cars because a scout had ridden up to Kirk and warned him that rebel troops were rushing to Morganton from three directions.

The news of Kirk's strike traveled faster than the raiders anticipated. A family named Lowdermilk living on the outskirts of Camp Vance dashed down the road into Morganton and "gave the alarm."[10]

A group of fifty men gathered in the center of town and started for the camp, sending "two scouts" ahead.[11] Kirk had dispatched pickets along the road, and they opened fire on the pair rushing up the road from the town. Both the scouts and the pickets turned and ran, the latter shouting to Kirk that they had been "found out."[12]

Reluctantly, Kirk abandoned his scheme to rush down the tracks and liberate the Union prisoners at Salisbury. Keith and Malinda, who had guided dozens of escapees from Salisbury over the Grandfather, were as disappointed as Kirk and Franklin that the rescue mission had fallen apart: "We intended to release the federal prisoners confined there, arm them, and bring them back with us; but the news of our coming had gone on ahead of us, and we gave it out."[13]

With fires engulfing the depot, commissary buildings, and Camp Vance, casting an eerie glow that could be seen miles away, Keith and Malinda did their part to herd 279 Confederate prisoners back toward Tennessee. But the column would not march off unimpeded. Fourteen miles from Morganton at 3 P.M. on June 29, 1864, they ran headlong into sixty-five Confederates under the command of Colonel George Loven. Kirk quickly determined that the rebels' faces—youths and old men—spelled inexperience, and, employing a ruthless tactic Keith later described as "crafty," the Union officer placed twenty of his prisoners as a human screen in front of his men.[14]

Keith and Malinda, astride two of the forty-eight horses Kirk had seized at Camp Vance and Morganton, dismounted with the other riders, scrambled behind a picket fence that marked property actually belonging to Colonel Loven, and braced their Spencers' barrels along the fence.

One of the Confederates described the action: "Kirk formed a line of battle, putting fifteen or twenty prisoners taken from Camp Vance in front. About fifty of our men fired on Kirk's men, killing one prisoner, B. A. Bowles . . . who was about thirty years of age, and wounding also a boy of seventeen years of age another one of Kirk's prisoners.

"We then retreated, but Kirk retained his position for ten minutes after we had gone. When we fired on them, I heard Kirk shout: 'Look at the damned fools, shooting their own men,' referring to the Camp Vance prisoners whom he had so placed as to receive our fire."[15]

As the Confederates realized they had fired on their own men and as the Blalocks and the rest poured fire back at them, Loven's troops fled.

Keith and Malinda remounted their horses and galloped around the fence across Israel Beck's field, up a cut through the woods, and onto a trail. The Union troops on foot followed with the prisoners and "mules loaded down with all the best wearing apparel they could gather up through the country, and all the bedding they could find, all of which they had packed into bed ticks from which the feathers and straw had been emptied."[16]

Of the skirmish on Loven's land and Kirk's ruthless tactic, Keith would offer that "no one but real soldiers had any business fighting Kirk. . . . [H]e would do anything he had to do."[17]

With the certain knowledge that every Confederate unit in the region was seeking to cut his escape, Kirk pushed his men even harder until he halted twenty-one miles northwest of Morganton. He set up camp behind a low ridge that commanded the single road along which the Confederates could approach.

At daybreak, Keith and Malinda awoke as pickets ran into camp and shouted a warning that rebels were advancing up the road. Kirk ordered his men to take up firing positions on the ridge and behind trees to enfilade the oncoming column, leaving guards with the prisoners.

Through a thick dense fog, Keith and Malinda squinted at the road, wide enough only for two or three men to squeeze through at a time. Keith spied the features of old enemy Colonel Thomas G. Walton, from whom Keith had escaped in 1862.

Though told by pickets that up to twelve hundred Confederate regulars, Home Guards, and even prison guards rushed up from Salisbury were coming on, Keith and Malinda had little to fear. To their ambush-trained eyes, their perch was perfect for Spencers to turn the pass below into a body-choked bottleneck. They opened up at Kirk's order on the rebel vanguard.

Several riders pitched from their saddles to the road, and the advance files wavered, then buckled.

Joseph Franklin, near Keith and Malinda as always during Kirk's Raid, recalled that from where the trio fired, it was obvious that the rebels could not recover. Colonel Walton quickly came to the same assessment: "Only a few were in the advance when they came upon Kirk's camp, as they were scattered for a mile or more along the road down the mountain; and having no room in which to form except the narrow cart-way that was enfiladed by the enemy, they retired."[18]

Later that day, Keith and Malinda parted with Kirk, who would return unmolested to Knoxville, using the Winding Stairs road. "He hated to lose us," Malinda wrote to a friend, "but he knew we had to go a scouting for the Michigan men."[19]

Turning directly north, their saddlebags packed with bacon and hardtack they had taken from the Morganton warehouses, Keith and Malinda rode into Caldwell County and toward the Grandfather. Word that they had taken part in Kirk's stunning raid would precede them. Their enemies were waiting.

The audacity of Kirk's Raid shocked Confederate authorities from Raleigh to Richmond. He had penetrated seventy-five miles into rebel territory without detection and had ripped apart the forces sent out against him. In Knoxville, he was feted by citizens and fellow officers alike from the moment he marched his 132 prisoners and mules laden with rebel bounty into Strawberry Plains. Forty of the prisoners actually enlisted as recruits in Kirk's regiments, a development confirming to Schofield and Sherman just how divided were loyalties in the mountains.

Kirk, in the *Knoxville Whig* and several other Tennessee newspapers, singled out his scouts, among them the Blalocks, for their skill and bravery throughout the raid. General Sherman sent Kirk a congratulatory telegram on his exploit, but warned him to refrain from taking such unsupported risks so deep in Confederate territory. Schofield personally expressed similar words to Kirk.

Although both generals issued caveats to Kirk and pointed out that he had not completed his most important objective, to destroy the Yadkin River Bridge, they realized the demoralizing effect the officer's bold move had upon the Confederate troops and civilians throughout the mountain counties. The impact that Kirk, the Blalocks, and every man who had raided Camp Vance with them had upon the South echoed in an official Confederate report concerning the raid. Written by Captain C. N. Allen, who rode into the gutted Camp Vance on June 29, 1864, the day after Kirk struck, the communiqué railed against his band as largely composed of recruits like the Blalocks, "deserters and tories from Tennessee and Western North Carolina."[20] Allen pointed out: "All of them were armed magnificently, the most of them with Spencer repeating rifles. They released some recusant conscripts and deserters from the guard-house here and armed them immediately."[21]

Two of those "magnificently armed tories," Keith and Malinda Blalock, toted a half-dozen extra Spencers, paid for by Kirk, and ammunition for friends along the Grandfather.

CHAPTER SEVENTEEN
As You Deserve, Damn You!

D URING the month of July and the month of August [1864],
"detachments of the Regiment [10th Michigan Cavalry] were
constantly engaged in scouting and [in] hunting small bands of
Rebels in East Tennessee and North Carolina," stated the regimental record.[1]

Two of those scouts, Keith and Malinda Blalock, slipped back onto the
Grandfather. To a war department official, Keith would say that "in the latter part of August [1864] following his enlistment, he left the command [the
10th Michigan Cavalry] at Strawberry Plains to gather what information he
could concerning the forces of the enemy on the Western North Carolina
Railroad, and particularly in the neighborhood of Camp Vance [Morganton,
North Carolina]."[2]

Joseph Webb, a neighbor who saw Keith and Malinda fording Wilson's
Creek and heading toward Blowing Rock, wrote: "[The Blalocks] returned
home the following August [1864] in Yankee uniform, armed with a Spencer
rifle and a Navy revolver on a scouting and foraging expedition."[3]

The Blalocks quickly found that Kirk's hard-hitting raid had so heartened
local unionists that some even dared to return to their homes. The Blalocks'
informant Levi Coffey was among the men returning to and working their
acreage in defiance of Bingham's Home Guard companies. The strategy of
banding together in groups large enough to fight pitched actions against the
Confederates in the mountains—the same tactic Keith and Malinda had used
two years earlier on the Grandfather—had taken hold in a far deadlier way
in the Blue Ridge in the summer of 1864. With rumors rampant that a Union
army would soon storm into Watauga County, Levi Coffey and other men in
Keith and Malinda's network were willing to hold their ground with a simple and savage approach: "When the rebels let us alone, we let them alone;
when they come out to hunt us, we hunt them! They know that we are in
earnest. . . . At night, we sleep in the bush. When we go home by day, our
children stand out picket. They or our wives bring food to us in the woods.
When the Home Guards are coming out, some of their [unionists] members
usually inform us beforehand; then we collect twenty or thirty men, find the

best ground we can, and, if they discover us, we fight them. But a number of skirmishes have taught them to be very wary about attacking us."[4]

A sort of mystique had covered the Blalocks, Jim Hartley, and Harrison Church for the unionists and outliers around Blowing Rock and the Grandfather. Viewing the scouts and pilots as valiant foes of the Confederacy, local unionists eagerly answered the Blalocks' summons when the couple wanted to bushwhack rebel soldiers or raid an especially well-defended farm in the last summer of the war. To Confederate families and to neutral neighbors, however, the Blalocks were bloody-minded brigands. As always in the mountains, the truth lay somewhere in between, muddied by partisan passions, personal feuds, and a genuine devotion to the Union or the Confederacy.

Keith and Malinda tended to their scouting mission, assessing the state of Bingham's and Walton's guards and tracking bands of Vaughn's cavalry that still materialized in the western counties. But they also roamed with old comrades and new recruits all over the Globe Valley, where they left a trail of fire, smoke, and dead Home Guards gunned down in what the Blalocks called war and the region's Confederates deemed cold-blooded murder. An escaped Salisbury prisoner aptly described the Blalocks' band and the other men fighting in the mountains: "We had been wont to regard bushwhackers of either side with unrefined horror."[5]

In the summer and fall of 1864, Keith, Malinda, and the rugged men who raided under the couple's command were, like every band of guerrillas in the Blue Ridge and the Smokies, "walking arsenals."[6] A Union correspondent wrote: "Each had a trusty rifle, one or two Navy revolvers, a great Bowie knife, haversack, and canteen. Their manners were quiet, their faces honest. . . . Ordinarily very quiet and rational, whenever the war was spoken of, their eyes emitted that peculiar glare which I had observed, years before, in Kansas, and which seems inseparable from the hunted man."[7]

As Keith and Malinda, both "arrogantly going about in federal uniforms, his that of an officer," rampaged with their men, sometimes in bands as small as five, other times with fifty or more, throughout the Grandfather and the Globe, rebels and families desperately claiming that they were neutrals developed a crude alarm system in Watauga County.[8] They kept a horn at hand, and the moment someone spotted the Blalocks riding out of morning mists or the dark slopes, it would echo for miles. But after nearly two years of hit-and-run ambushes and raids, the Blalocks and their comrades would gallop up to a rebel's home or farm, loot it, burn every structure to the ground as the family gaped helplessly, and ride off with "anything worth stealing."[9]

Seventeen-year-old Leonidas L. Green, whose father, Robert, had been bushwhacked and shot by Keith, never forgot a sudden sighting of Keith and Malinda in the late summer of 1864. "I saw Keith Blalock and his men near

Blowing Rock," Green wrote. "He was in full Yankee uniform, braid and all, with knee-high cavalry boots. His wife, Malinda, was with them, and she also wore a uniform and boots. Their faces were darkened by the elements, and everyone of their group was heavily armed. I was fixing a fence, and they rode on past."[10]

The teenager, a member of Bingham's guards, would soon encounter the Blalocks again, and on that occasion, they would not leave him alone. If they had then known that Green already rode with Bingham, the youth would have "been found in the woods with a hole in his head."[11]

The Blalocks' company, as well as those of scouts Harrison Church and Jim Hartley, all of them labeled bushwhackers and "lawless bands" by Bingham, now ambushed Home Guards at every opportunity.[12] From behind rocks and trees and from perches above the trails, Keith, Malinda, and their scouts poured fusillades into detachments of militia, the cracks of Spencers and the screams of men and mounts piercing the mountain passes. Guards unfortunate enough to be seized while riding or walking alone were often discovered days, weeks, and even months later by neighbors, a single shot to the forehead testifying to their fate. Near the Watauga River in summer 1864, unionist partisans—the Blalocks, according to several locals, Hartley's men, according to others—kidnapped a rebel guerrilla leader and dragged him deep into the woods. His family found his rotting remains several weeks later; his skull had been bashed in, his body riddled with twenty-one bullets in the chest area alone.

Several of Keith's enemies believed that he was not responsible for that particular killing. "Blalock always took credit for men he killed, but never boasted about this one," said L. L. Green.[13]

Although the Blalocks' many enemies would assert that Malinda had executed men in cold blood, Keith adamantly maintained that she "never shot an unarmed man."[14] There was never any reason to ask him if he had ever executed a Home Guard or a rebel bushwhacker, for he would not hesitate to pull the trigger of his Spencer, his Sharp's, or his Colt on them, as several episodes would soon reveal. When asked how such executions were acts of war, Keith offered an answer that unionists and Confederates alike terrorizing the Blue Ridge understood: "We all tried to do to them before they did to us."[15]

Malinda concurred, "We did what needed doing for the Union."[16]

"For personal retribution and satisfaction," Jesse Moore said.[17]

In equal sanguinary measure throughout the Blue Ridge and the Smokies, militia and rebel bushwhackers, as well as marauding Confederate cavalry and infantry detachments, hanged or shot escaped Union prisoners, outliers, and especially enemy partisans who stumbled into Confederate hands. The Blalocks and other unionists often came across the grisly handiwork of their foes. Whenever Keith and Malinda found a corpse in the remains of a blue uniform that identified an escapee from Salisbury who had blundered into a squad of militia or bushwhackers, the couple cut him down from the tree where he had been hanged. Sometimes they found remains in a heap beneath a noose—the body had been decaying there so long that it had literally slid from the rope.

Fellow scout and Blalock friend Dan Ellis recounted a grisly incident relating both the violence of the mountain war and the hatred Keith and Malinda encountered from, as well as dealt out to, loyal Confederates of the Appalachians. Shortly after Ellis had happened upon the remains of three unionists hanged from a tree, a young woman came up the trail.

"Why were those men killed?" Ellis asked her.

"They were a parcel of Lincolnites that our boys captured at that spring while they were getting water," she replied.

"That is a horrible sight, madam. Is that the way that the Lincolnites are disposed of when they are so unfortunate as to be captured?"

"Yes, they receive no mercy whatever from our boys. If you will go down the road about one hundred yards you will find a parcel of them that were captured here a short time ago, and were shot immediately, and were thrown behind an old log, and covered up with leaves and chunks."

"How does it happen that so many men are captured in this neighborhood?"

"Why, there is a company of soldiers stationed on Clinch River, and they have selected the best hunters in the country to watch the roads and mountain paths to catch men who are making their way through the lines."

"Well, that is the most diabolical sight that I have ever witnessed in my life."

"Oh, that is not a strange sight to me, by any means. I have seen the hat and shoes taken off many Lincolnites, and have seen them kneel to pray before being shot."

"And did it cause you no emotions of pity to witness such a spectacle?"

"No, none whatever. That is the very way that men ought to be treated whenever they are caught running away to Old Abe. All of them ought to be killed."

"But do you think that the poor men whom you have seen murdered so unceremoniously were really guilty of any crime for which they deserved to be killed?"

"Yes, I have no sympathy for them whatever. I believe it is perfectly right to kill them whenever they are caught. I have a husband and two brothers in the Southern army, and every man who is unwilling to fight for the Southern Confederacy, who may be caught in the act of running off to Kentucky, ought to be hung or shot."[18]

Although Ellis's unabashed Union bias filled his words, Keith would attest to the truth of such scenes that he and Malinda found during the guerrilla warfare in the mountains, a theater of operations in which little or no quarter was given or expected by either side. If they were taken alive by rebel scouts or bushwhackers, a noose or a single bullet to the head would likely be the least of what Keith and Malinda would face.

In Carter County, a corner of east Tennessee that the Blalocks often slipped in and out of on their scouts for both Kirk and the 10th Michigan, the couple had to exercise constant wariness of a local Confederate guerrilla named Captain Wilcher. The Blalocks and every unionist operating in the mountains had heard of the fate of eleven men who had been captured by Wilcher's band while trying to reach federal lines. Wilcher and his men had slowly cut several of the prisoners apart with bayonets; the rest they clubbed to death with rifle butts. For a final bit of "sport," four of the partisans spread-eagled the last prisoner, an old man, on the ground, and held him down; then, Wilcher and the rest took turns dropping rocks on the man's head until his skull was crushed.

Crimes such as Wilcher's bred retaliation by the Blalocks, Hartley, Kirk, and other unionists in an ever-quickening spiral of violence.

Bingham responded to the Blalocks' ambushes by issuing orders that Home Guards reporting to camp for their two-week shifts travel in groups of not less than fifteen and that those departing Camp Mast ride home in similarly sized detachments. On their farms, rebels, like their unionist counterparts, posted children as lookouts and raced to escape routes at the first cry that the Blalocks or other guerrillas were coming.

To hamper the Blalocks' raids into the valleys, Bingham sent his men on sweeps of mountain trails at various hours of the day and night. Across the mountain passes a lethal game of cat-and-mouse reached a new level of fury, Keith and Malinda pitting their knowledge of the terrain and their gift for ambush against Bingham's equal feel for the region and his tenacity. "We wanted Major Bingham as bad as he wanted us. We even visited his house [near Lenoir, Caldwell County] a few times, but he wasn't there, just his wife [Nancy] and a few Guards he always posted there. We matched a few shots with them, but nothing came of that."[19]

A Coffey relative would remark that "Keith and Malinda never burned Mrs. Bingham out on account they feared the Major would go after Keith's mother and Austin Coffey."[20]

Despite Keith's constant urgings that his stepfather and his mother let him pilot them to safety through the so-called "mountain underground railway," they refused to budge, Coffey confident that the respect that even his rebel neighbors harbored toward him constituted a form of protection. Murray Coffey, however, would say: "Keith worried all the time about them and made sure that word reached every Rebel around that he would kill anyone who moved on them [his parents]."[21]

As the leaves of the Blue Ridge forests turned with a glorious blaze of hues, heralding fall 1864, no one had bothered Austin Coffey except when Vaughn's cavalry had handed him a worthless receipt, had emptied his corn crib, and had "requisitioned" his mules and two horses, leaving only a stooped plow horse. Coffey's position remained adamant: he and his wife were among those who "would not attempt the uncertain journey to our [federal] lines."[22]

In the final week of August 1864, William and Reuben visited their brother Austin to deliver a message: anyone found harboring an escaped Union prisoner, a guerrilla, or a bushwhacker would be arrested or worse. No one, no matter how well liked and respected, was safe. And as the war turned against the Confederacy in the mountains and on every distant front, violence against unionists surged to its highest levels and sparked retaliation that was equally harsh.

A federal prisoner who had escaped from Salisbury wrote of the hardships pro-Union families endured in Watauga and Caldwell Counties: "During our whole journey we encountered only one house inhabited by White Unionists which had never been plundered by the Home Guard or Rebel guerrillas. Almost every loyal family had given to the cause some of its nearest and dearest. We are told so frequently—'My father was killed in those woods' or 'The guerrillas shot my brother in that ravine' that, finally, these tragedies made little impression on us."[23]

The Blalocks took revenge "in kind" whenever their friends' farms were raided. "They [Keith and Malinda] put fear in Rebels around the Grandfather. . . . If you hurt one of theirs, you knew they were coming for you and yours."[24]

"Few Rebel homes and farms could feel completely safe from them, whose definition of Rebel was anyone who had something worth stealing," wrote L. L. Green.[25]

On August 28, 1864, Keith, Malinda, and fifteen assorted scouts and outliers swept down from the Grandfather and burned out Benjamin Green, brother of Robert and a lieutenant in Bingham's Home Guards. "It was the Blalocks surely," wrote one of the Greens. "They took everything that wasn't nailed down and ordered their man Levi Coffey to set fire to the house and barn."[26]

By nightfall, Benjamin Green and eighteen men of the Home Guards had saddled up and were riding up the Grandfather. One of their informants had provided the news that Levi Coffey, rather than head with the Blalocks to one of their hideouts, had opted to spend the night at the house of Mrs. Adelaide Fox, one of the couple's spies since 1862. "Women always found Levi pretty [term used in the Blue Ridge of the era for both a good-looking woman and man]," Malinda said. "Ben Green was not the only man who had ever wanted to kill Levi."[27]

When Green and the militia neared the Fox cabin, overlooking present-day Foscoe, they dismounted and formed a firing line behind a fence. No more than fifty yards from the sturdy two-story structure, they opened up without warning.

Coffey rolled out of a bed on the second floor—he was not alone, according to locals—as Minie balls ripped into the walls and through the windows. Coffey leaped clad only in a nightshirt through a shattered rear window and raced for the nearby woods. Seconds later Adelaide Fox followed wearing next to nothing. She vanished into the forest unscathed but a rebel's pistol ball ripped into Coffey's shoulder and sent him sprawling. Somehow he staggered back to his feet, reached the woods, and, with Green and his men rushing across the yard and crashing into the thicket, ran, crawled, and climbed up the slopes to safety.

Coffey reached the Blalocks' lair near Blowing Rock, where they patched up his shoulder. "I'd had enough of the Greens," Keith would tell Murray Coffey, "and after what they did to Levi we wanted to hit them right away. Remember that I could have killed one of them [Robert], but spared him."[28]

The Blalocks and their band quickly planned just the sort of action that, on October 17, 1862, had led General William T. Sherman to write: "You know full well that on your side guerrillas or partisan rangers commit acts which you would not sanction, and that small detachments of our men commit acts of individual revenge, leaving no trace whereby we can fix responsibility. . . . If we allow the passions of our men to get full command, then indeed will this war become a reproach to the names of liberty and civilization."[29]

In the mountains, the Blalocks' own code, their belief that they were justified to embark upon missions of "individual revenge" whenever those actions had some relation, however limited, to the war, emitted a brutal but tradition-steeped force that neither Sherman nor any other commander in the east Tennessee and western North Carolina districts could curb. War and vengeance were one and the same in the mountain war, a personal war.

A few thousand feet down the crags from Blowing Rock, Benjamin Green's brother Lott lived in one of the county's finest homes, a rambling stone-walled lodge that served equally well as a home or a small fortress. A Home Guard lieutenant with a reputation for beating unionist prisoners just short of death, Lott Green made a particularly inviting target for the Blalocks.

Choosing a quick strike rather than a raid in force, Keith cobbled together a compact squad of six men and one woman. As he had when bushwhacking Robert Green, Keith selected a Sharp's rifle to settle his grudge.

The Blalock band climbed down an old, overgrown Cherokee path from Blowing Rock as soon as night came. By late evening, the Blalocks, Sampson Calloway, Edmund Ivy, Ben Gardner, Adolphus Pritchard, and Levi Coffey (his shoulder patched up and painful), sneaked out of the woods, darted across the front yard, knelt on the grass a few yards from the long porch, and aimed their rifles at the front door and the two large windows flanking it. Keith then motioned for his band to stay in place, strode onto the porch, and knocked.

Green, expecting a doctor that night for an unspecified visit, pulled open the heavy white-oak door to find Keith glowering at him and his band "armed to the teeth" just a few paces away.[30] Green slammed the door shut and bolted it.

Keith bellowed for Green and any other man inside to surrender. Someone behind the door shouted: "What treatment will you give us?"[31] The voice did not belong to Lott Green.

Keith, who had not seen any horses tied to the hitching posts adjoining the porch, hesitated for a few moments. "He knew something was wrong," wrote L. L. Green, who crouched with an Enfield near one of the windows. "It was Keith and his band that had strolled into an ambush. And we knew the treatment they would give us—so we gave it to them first."[32]

Again, the man asked what terms Keith would accord them. Now he recognized the voice—that of Home Guard Henry Henley, Green's brother-in-law.

Keith retorted: "As you deserve, damn you!"[33]

As a small firing port in the window suddenly flew open and Henley slid his Enfield's barrel through it, Keith dove behind a small stone wall. Henley fired, and Sampson Calloway shrieked as he was knocked backwards. He writhed in the grass, clutching his side.

From the windows Lott Green, his brother Joseph, and L. L. Green blasted away at the dark figures spread across the lawn as Henley waited for Keith to stir behind the wall. Keith yelled for covering fire, and Malinda, Coffey, and everyone except the moaning Calloway poured Spencer fire at the windows, scattering the guards from their perches. Keith squeezed off several rounds at the door and then raced back toward the woods. His comrades followed him, Ivy grabbing Calloway's arm and dragging him to the cover of a laurel thicket. As Keith and the rest regrouped, a bugle call blared from the house. In the distance another horn pealed.

"We knew that Bingham and his boys would arrive soon, so we got out of there in a hurry," Keith later said.[34]

As the Blalocks and their men clambered on foot up the mountain, the Greens and Henley rushed from the house. "They had fled already," L. L.

Green would write, "and even though we did not find any dead, we did spy a blood trail. About this time, Captain J. W. Councill and eighteen more guards rode up. When we told him it was the Blalocks and they only had a small part of their squad with them, Councill ordered us to give chase."[35]

The officer divided his men into two groups, one dismounted detachment to follow the blood stains, the other to ride up a main trail and hopefully get behind the Blalocks before they could choose a higher piece of ground from which their repeating rifles could hold off a force three or four times their pursuers' strength.

The Blalocks and their men thrashed through thickets and tangled stands of pines, slowed down by the moaning Calloway. Just over a mile up the slopes from Green's house, they broke into the cabin of Keith's old friend John Walker, who, fortunately for his own safety, was not at home; if he had been caught aiding the Blalocks, the Home Guard would have arrested or executed him.

As Malinda cleaned out Calloway's wound, a gaping hole along his rib cage, and bound it with strips they tore from Walker's bedsheets, Keith, Coffey, Ivy, Pritchard, and Gardner peered through the windows, listening for any sounds of approaching guards.

Benjamin Green and nine other rebels tracked Calloway's bloodstains to the cabin, pitch-black, with no signs of anyone inside it. One of the guards crawled nearly to the front door, then back to the others to report that the blood trail ended at the stoop. Green and his men surrounded the cabin. Henley, perhaps grabbing Calloway's Spencer where he had dropped it at the Greens' and a haversack full of ammunition, now worked his way to a rail fence near the back door. The fence surrounded Walker's cabin, and that of a neighbor, Mrs. Medie Walker McHaarg, Walker's sister.

Keith picked up Calloway from the blood-sodden bed and shouted to Mrs. McHaarg to open the gate in front of her house. Uncertain who was calling her, she pulled it open nonetheless, and the Blalocks and their men rushed out the front door and cut left to the gate and the woods behind and snapped off shots at two guards stationed near it. The pair scattered as the Spencers crackled. The other eight rebels blasted away at the fleeing unionists, the muskets' and rifles' flashes illuminating the darkness.

With Calloway in Keith's arms, the Blalocks slipped through the gate and into the forest, Coffey, Pritchard, and Gardner right behind them. Edmund Ivy reached the gate last, and as he dashed through it, Henley chased after him, stopped, and emptied several rounds into Ivy's head and back. The Georgian, Keith and Malinda's friend and comrade of nearly two years, was dead before he hit the ground.

The Blalock band kept running and lost their guards by leading them into a blind gorge. "The Blalocks' luck was as good as their skill," L. L. Green would say of the melee at Walker's cabin. "If they had waited even a second longer [to run away], we would have killed them all."[36]

Keith had not escaped the action unscathed. A ricocheting Minie ball had cracked his left wrist; despite the pain, he had not dropped Calloway. The Blalocks left Calloway at a safe house hidden a mile or two above Shull's Mill.

Keith's report of the action claimed that he, Malinda, and his men had been "suddenly set upon by a squad of Rebel footmen and horse who were scouting through the mountains on the lookout for escaped prisoners, Union scouts and refugees, and just as [I] turned, they fired a volley at me at a distance of not over twenty steps and wounded the left arm, the ball entering the arm about four inches below the elbow and coming out in the knuckle of the fore finger, involving the wrist joint in its course, some of the bones of which subsequently worked out. We dodged into the bushes and escaped. This shooting occurred on the 30th of August (on or about), not far from, about 3 miles, the Grandfather Mountain, and not so far from the house of my stepfather Austin Coffey."[37]

Having deposited Calloway with unionist friends, Keith and Malinda "lay in the brush the night following [my] being wounded . . . and on the following day saw and talked with James Gragg, who passed near the spot.[38]

"We remained in the woods until the morning of the third day, when we got near to my mother's [Mrs. Coffey's] house, some four or five miles distant and remained concealed in the laurel under a cliff near the house, some two or three days until we got word to Lewis Banner's on the Elk, some 10 or 12 miles distant. Then, a party of some 15 to 20 men [union] and among them Samuel Banner and Little Charlie Hughes came and took us away."[39]

The one who "got word" to fellow unionists was Malinda, who stole along the trails, watching for any sign of Bingham's Home Guards, who were "all over the mountains searching for her husband."[40] William Voncannon, a tough, twenty-four-year-old Banner's Elk resident who had forged a formidable reputation as one of Kirk's guerrilla leaders and as an officer in the 3rd North Carolina Mounted Regiment, said "that about the first of September 1864, Mrs. Blalock, the wife of William Blalock, with whom I was well-acquainted and had lived on the Eastern slope of the Grandfather mountain," had hiked "about fifteen miles and brought word to the Union people living on the Elk [the Banners] that her husband had been wounded in the arm by the Rebel Home Guard and that he needed us to come over and give him a safe escort out of the country."[41]

With Malinda showing the way, Voncannon led "a party of about seven of my men and went with her and found him near his mother's house [Mrs.

Austin Coffey's], with his left arm badly wounded. We brought him through the Elk Valley."[42]

While Keith had "laid out the night he was shot, and the following day" in the laurel thicket, propped against the cliff, he spoke with several friends who sneaked food and water to him.[43] They risked their own lives if spotted by "a squad of Bingham's Home Guards who were in search for him."[44]

Mrs. Martha Coffey, married to one of Austin's cousins and the sister of unionist Jesse Gragg, was returning "from huckleberrying with her friend Mary Curtis, and when near Austin Coffey's house we met up with him [Keith] in the woods."[45] According to Mrs. Coffey, Keith "showed them his arm which was badly shot and told them that it had been done the evening before by the home guards that had come upon him."[46]

He told them that "he was waiting around in the woods for Malinda to return with his friends."[47]

"We went to the house [Austin Coffey's] and got Keith something to eat," Martha Coffey would recall. "He told us that he was scouting and recruiting for the Union Army, and he wore some blue clothes with yellow stripes on the sleeves of his coat."[48]

Inside the house, Keith's mother peered out the windows for the Home Guard, worried that her son, whom she described as "waylaid and shot and concealed within a few hundred yards of his old home," would be hauled from the thicket by the rebels before "a party of his friends could come over from the Elk and take him out of the country."[49]

Keith's mother and stepfather did not relax until Voncannon and his Spencer-toting men showed up and spirited Keith out of his hiding place and onto the trails toward Banner's Elk. But over the next few weeks, as word that Keith had hidden out within sight of his parents' house and under the literal noses of Home Guards pounding up and down the nearby road reached Confederate neighbors, they grumbled that Austin Coffey should be arrested for aiding his stepson. Several men were willing to do more than that to "Old Austin."

❧

Safely away from Bingham's men, Keith would remember: "We stopped the first night with William Voncannon on the Elk, next down to Lewis Banner's house."[50]

At Banner's farm, Keith and Malinda mounted two horses provided by "Uncle Lewis," and "the next day we [the Blalocks] reached Daniel Stouts' in the Crab Orchard, Carter County, Tennessee," where the couple remained "some two or three weeks afterward while Keith healed up."[51]

Joseph Webb visited with Keith at "the house of Mrs. Stouts in the Crab Orchard," and "I [Webb] was told by him that some of Bingham's rebel home guards had been lying in wait for him and fired upon and gave him the bad wound in the arm from which he was then suffering."[52] Keith bragged about having escaped the rebels yet again, but the colorful story left far less of an impression upon the visitor than the wound, Webb later recounting that "the ball had torn up everything near the elbow and all the way down past the wrist and on the back of the hand."[53]

According to Webb, he had warned Keith and Malinda, "on the same morning of the day before [Keith] was shot," that they were "running in danger by staying about home where the Rebels were likely to run in on them and kill them at any moment."[54] Keith had replied that he "intended returning to his command at once," obviously not wanting to reveal his other plans regarding the Greens.[55]

In hindsight, Keith and Malinda would have done well to have listened to Webb's warning.

When Keith did ride out to rejoin his regiment, he traveled only at night because of the rebel bushwhackers infesting east Tennessee, and worked his way west until he hooked up with a detachment of the 10th's scouts and "then got back to my command which was still at Strawberry Plains."[56] Malinda waited at the Stouts' home for his return.

"Things had gotten a little too hot at home," Malinda wrote, "but we did not stay away very long."[57]

The couple's rebel neighbors and the Home Guards were furious that they had nearly "done for Blalock," only to have him slip away once more.[58] Jesse Moore wrote of his disappointment that "Bingham's Home Guards had fired upon him [Keith] and wounded him, but he escaped out of their hands and left the country."[59]

Carroll Moore similarly lamented that the "Home Guards shot and wounded Blalock but that he lived to disappear from the neighborhood for a while."[60]

To Mrs. McCaleb Coffey, "that lot of his [Keith's] friends who took him over to Tennessee" had cheated her from seeing her unionist relative dragged in front of a firing squad or stretched from a noose.[61]

࿓

In a 10th Regiment report, Captain James Minihan wrote: "William Blalock was wounded in the left wrist while in the discharge of his duty a Scouting Upper East Tennessee Division in action [against] rebel scouts in ambush Aug. 30, 1864."[62]

By the time 10th surgeon Thomas Shaw cleaned Keith's wound and attempted to reset the bone, the wrist had begun to heal crookedly. Slowly, Keith would lose flexibility and strength in his hand and forearm. But the wound would not stop him from either conducting his scouting and recruiting duties or his and Malinda's private war against their Confederate neighbors. With the Confederacy's war degenerating into a desperate struggle just to hold on in the latter part of 1864, Keith and Malinda would seize the chance to settle all of their old scores in Watauga and Caldwell Counties.

Mrs. McCaleb Coffey stated: "Before leaving [the county], Blalock declared that they intended to kill William Coffey, Carroll Moore, Lott Estes, and Robert Green, all of them quiet and peaceable citizens and none of them belonging to the army [Confederate]."[63]

To citizens throughout the mountains, Mrs. Coffey's description of Keith Blalock's enemies was correct—if one was a Confederate.

CHAPTER EIGHTEEN
Deplorable Condition

I N late July 1864, as the Blalocks were terrorizing their rebel neighbors, Zebulon Vance was reelected governor of North Carolina, defeating controversial newspaper editor and so-called "peace candidate" W. W. Holden.[1] The final tallies arrived on August 4, Vance trouncing his foe, whom many North Carolinians considered a unionist traitor, 57,873 to 14,432. Vance's triumph quelled Richmond's fear that Holden would take the state out of the Confederacy.

One of Vance's first proclamations of his new term was a promise that every deserter who returned voluntarily would garner only "nominal punishment."[2] Despite Richmond's praise of Vance's "wise and timely" measure, desertions mounted in the fall of 1864, and the mountain counties became even more flooded with rebels "gone over the hill."[3] In Watauga and Caldwell Counties, Bingham grumbled that every available conscript was already a soldier in a gray uniform, a deserter in hiding, or, in Keith Blalock's case, "gone off to wear Yankee uniforms."[4]

Bent upon hunting down deserters and outliers who ignored Governor Vance's amnesty, Bingham authorized the Home Guard to employ every imaginable effort to track down deserters and shirkers alike. The guards of Watauga County would use the order as a blanket excuse for atrocities in the fall of 1864 and into the new year. Again, Austin Coffey's brother McCaleb warned him to stay away from Keith and Malinda and any other known scouts and unionists. Austin Coffey ignored the "advice."

Across the border in east Tennessee, Coffey's stepson and Malinda rode on several scouts for the 10th in October 1864. Keith's wrist, the ulna bone severely swollen and jutting at an odd angle, did not prevent him from using his Spencer in several sharp skirmishes with Confederate cavalry near Strawberry Plains. In one especially hot action northeast of Knoxville, Keith and Malinda galloped among several scouting companies of the 10th and the 13th Tennessee (U.S.) Cavalry when they encountered a few hundred Confederate cavalry from General John C. Breckenridge's battered army. The Blalocks and the other riders of the 10th in the vanguard opened up at half-pistol range with their Spencers, the road filling with dead and wounded. But the rebels regrouped and charged the 10th, only to find the Tennesseans materializing on the attackers' flank. The Confederates retreated in good order to the northeast, the skirmishing continuing until nightfall.

Throughout most of November and early December 1864, the 10th was billeted at Strawberry Plains, and Keith and Malinda made a few quick rides to the passes of the Blue Ridge and the Smokies to reconnoiter Confederate defenses in the region. Rumors were rife in the 10th that something big was in the works, likely an offensive thrust at the rebels. No one outside Schofield's and General George Stoneman's inner circle, however, knew yet where and when that strike would come. Keith and Malinda's service was about to become entwined with that of Stoneman, a forty-two-year-old West Pointer with a military reputation in tatters and an ache to redeem himself before the war ended.

Keith and Malinda had seen the haggard, handsome Stoneman on numerous occasions at Strawberry Plains and Knoxville. Six foot four, sporting a thick black beard, and known for his fearlessness under fire, George Stoneman was just the sort of man Keith Blalock admired on first sight—a man who would fight.

In 1863, when Keith and Malinda had been making a regional name for themselves with Kirk, George Stoneman had made front-page headlines in the Union's newspapers. None of those headlines was laudatory. He had garnered public attention first during the Chancellorsville campaign. His commander, General "Fighting Joe" Hooker, had sent Stoneman and some ten thousand Army of the Potomac cavalrymen in a daring strike to disrupt Robert E. Lee's communications and supply lines with the bulk of Hooker's total mounted force.

Stoneman and his corps tore up miles of railroad track radiating from Richmond and sent alarm rippling from the Confederate capital to Lee's headquarters. Lee sagely chose not to chase Stoneman and to focus on Hooker's army—now without cavalry support. Even worse for "Fighting Joe," one of Stoneman's columns was so preoccupied by fear of rebel cavalry hitting the Union flanks that the blue-uniformed riders accomplished next to nothing. Stoneman's so-called "First Raid" was at best a nuisance to Lee, at worst a failure in force.

Although the raid had proven a tactical error by Hooker, the blame fell squarely on Stoneman, who was excoriated in the papers for lack of initiative and was soon jettisoned to a post shuffling papers at the war department in Washington.

Eventually, Stoneman wrangled a field command again, this time with General William T. Sherman. During the action between Sherman and Confederate General Joseph E. Johnston, Sherman unleashed his fiery march on Atlanta, while Stoneman's cavalry, though far better armed and fed than the rebel riders, was beaten in every major engagement. Sherman lost so much confidence in his cavalry regiments that he often employed them as dismounted infantry.

In the summer of 1864, Sherman gambled that his cavalry could take advantage of what he viewed as a prime chance to sever Confederate General John B. Hood's only serviceable supply line and force him to abandon besieged Atlanta without a pitched battle. Sherman handed Stoneman and General Edward McCook the military opportunity of their careers to date. McCook, with 3,500 cavalry, and Stoneman, with 6,500, were ordered to converge on and destroy Lovejoy Station and force Hood to deliver Atlanta to Sherman's rapacious "bummers."[5]

Stoneman presented an even more ambitious strike to Sherman: the New York-born cavalryman argued that once Lovejoy Station was invested, he could gallop down to Macon, Georgia, and liberate the starving, disease-wracked horde of Union prisoners of war at the infamous Andersonville. With graphic newspaper and magazine stories of the prison camp having enraged the North, Sherman grasped the emotional and morale-lifting effects that Andersonville's fall could have at home as the Union geared up for the final bloody year of war. With the warning to Stoneman that he must take care of Lovejoy Station before turning to Andersonville, Sherman sanctioned Stoneman's gambit.

On July 26, 1864, Stoneman and his cavalry thundered toward their main objective: Hood's supply depot. But Stoneman, deciding that McCook's column could take Lovejoy Station alone, pounded straight at Andersonville. Rebel cavalry commander Joe Wheeler, with ten thousand hard-riding, veteran troops, pounced in turn on the divided Union cavalry. Not only did Stoneman's riders fail to take the depot, but they also were routed near Macon. Even worse, two thousand federal cavalrymen were killed or captured, the prisoners including Stoneman and seven hundred of his column. Adding the final indignity to Stoneman's debacle, he was seized by Home Guards, not Confederate regulars.

Fortunately for Stoneman, he was handed back to the Union army in a prisoner exchange, sparing him the horrors of incarceration at his intended target, Andersonville. He returned to Sherman, however, in near-abject disgrace. Few believed that after the disastrous end of "Stoneman's Second Raid," he would ever receive another chance to lead troopers into action. In the fall of 1864, shortly after the chagrined Stoneman was shipped back to the federal army, he was assigned to east Tennessee seemingly to ride out the war's duration in ignominy.

One high-ranking Union general still believed in Stoneman's abilities. General John Schofield was convinced that Stoneman's boldness was perfectly suited for the brutal hit-and-run action of east Tennessee and western North

Carolina. He listened with interest when Stoneman almost sheepishly submitted a plan to his commander for a cavalry raid-in-force against several key rebel outposts in the theater from southwestern Virginia to the mountains of western North Carolina.

Stoneman had chosen a timely moment to submit his plan. In December 1864, Hood had ruined his redoubtable Confederate Army of the Tennessee in assaults against the federal lines in the Franklin-Nashville campaign. Sherman was raging through Georgia and planning to strike the Carolinas. In coastal North Carolina, the Confederacy was soon to lose Wilmington, the South's final link to European supplies. Lee's once-vaunted army, wracked by desertion and battered by Grant's hammer blows ever closer to Richmond, hung on valiantly, but he and his staff knew that the war was lost. With rebel supply lines shrinking, rail lines and depots in North Carolina and western Virginia were a vital link to Lee.

Stoneman's plan tied in beautifully to the overall strategy of the federal army's impending campaigns in 1865. First, the disgraced cavalry commander wanted to hurl a large mountain force into southwestern Virginia to destroy one of the Confederacy's most vital remaining stretches of tracks, the line between Bristol and Wytheville. That objective accomplished, he proposed to veer off to Saltville, also in western Virginia, to destroy the South's last significant saltworks. Without salt as a curing agent, tons of meat would rot long before it reached Lee's troops and the civilians in Richmond.

In the third step of his plan, the part that would require the special skills of the Blalocks and other mountain-savvy guides, Stoneman wanted to turn south into the Blue Ridge of North Carolina, pour down the passes, burst into Watauga and Caldwell Counties, and smash his way to the prison camp in Salisbury to free the 10,000 Union captives and destroy the huge munitions and provisions depot there. To Keith and Malinda, who had helped so many Salisbury escapees over the mountains, the bold proposal would have deep appeal. The prospect of destroying the rebel supplies at Salisbury enticed Sherman, who planned to invade the state and did not want the cache waiting for Johnson or Lee if they retreated to North Carolina—a very real prospect.

Stoneman affixed a personal side to Schofield with the plan: "I hope you will not disapprove . . . as I think we can see very important results from [the plan's] execution. I owe the Southern Confederacy a debt I am very anxious to liquidate, and this offers a propitious occasion."[6]

Unknown to Sherman, Schofield had received a telegram from Secretary of War Edwin Stanton, who ordered that Stoneman be relieved of any future commands in east Tennessee. Schofield pretended that he had never actually read the directive: He had decided to give Stoneman one last chance for military redemption. On a far less grandiose but brutal scale, Schofield's action dictated the war that the Blalocks and their friend George W. Kirk would fight. For if the first two steps of Stoneman's mission proved successful, the assault into western North Carolina would depend in large measure upon those scouts who knew the Blue Ridge. No one possessed more familiarity with the Watauga passes than a pair already scouting for the 10th Michigan.

Stoneman received marching orders from Schofield, who risked his own career by ignoring Stanton's dictate, on December 6, 1864. He told the cavalry commander that if successful at Saltville, he would lead the strike into western North Carolina whenever the moment arrived.

That same day, the 10th was ordered to Knoxville and told they would ride out on December 10. At nightfall of December 6, the regiment's scouts set out in detachments of as few as six riders and as large as fifty. The smallest units galloped out ahead of the others and began scouting the route to Saltville. Keith, Malinda, and four comrades who had learned their martial trade under Kirk headed toward Virginia on Captain James Minihan's order.

Along the route, the Blalocks and other scouts sneaked past small bands of Confederate raider John Morgan's shattered, "once terrible men," no longer much of a factor since their leader's death in September 1864.[7] The scouts reconnoitered the road through Bristol, Tennessee, and across the Virginia line to Abingden, where they spotted a small force of Confederate troops. The individual bands of scouts converged in the wooded perimeter above Saltville to find General Breckenridge with a force of only twelve hundred rebels. Working their way back, the Blalocks met up with Stoneman's 5,500 riders surging to western Virginia and joined them.

At the sight of Stoneman's approaching column, Morgan's former men put up a brief and uninspired fight and melted away. The scouts, riding ahead once again, drove off a few companies of rebel scouts Breckenridge had sent to assess Stoneman's strength. A few blasts from the Spencers of the Blalocks and their comrades sent the rebels racing back to Saltville with the grim news that several regiments of Michiganders and Tennesseans were on the move straight at the railway and the mines.

Stoneman suddenly surged at Marion, only twenty miles from Saltville, which compelled Breckenridge to retreat there and to defend the crucial lead works and those at nearby Wytheville. He quick-marched his troops and skirmished with Stoneman's cavalry throughout December 18, but only with half of the Union force.

Keith and Malinda galloped with some 2,500 other troopers to Saltville and pounded into the undefended town that same afternoon. The couple helped start the business of gutting the saltworks and was joined by the rest of the expedition on December 19. Breckenridge, outnumbered, outgunned, and outmaneuvered, could do nothing as the 10th Michigan and Stoneman's other regiments took two days to knock Saltville out of the war for good. On the way back to Knoxville, the raiders also destroyed critical miles of track.

The tracks could be repaired at some point, though every day that trains could not ferry supplies toward Virginia was a trial for the Confederacy. But the destruction of the saltworks constituted a disaster not only for the rebel troops, but also for civilians from the Blue Ridge to Richmond. Along the coast, people could at least attempt to extract brine from seawater as a curing agent for meat. Even so, the battered Confederacy's demand for salt far outstripped the ability to deliver it. A long, hungry winter loomed for Southerners.

In the Blalocks' home counties, the ruin of the saltworks would arguably hit people harder than anywhere else in the Confederacy. Locals, unable to preserve meat, would have to rely on game they downed and cooked as soon as possible, and hunting in the snow and ice of the mountains was a grueling task. Even if a family wanted to slaughter a pig, they would have to track it to the hog pens high up on the Grandfather and the surrounding crags, as most people had either lost all of their livestock to Yankee or rebel raiders and were forced to hunt wild pigs. Faced by that harsh prospect, loyalists and unionists alike throughout the mountains harbored even greater resentment against the few local families whose Confederate connections had enabled them to stockpile modest reserves of salt. On the shelves of the region's general stores, none could be had.

With the mission against the saltworks a complete success, only the loss of many horses that would have to be replaced concerned the Union army's department of upper east Tennessee and Western North Carolina. Stoneman won the accolades he had so long craved and could now pour his energy into the coming federal knife-thrust into western North Carolina.

While the ebullient Union cavalrymen clattered back to Knoxville, Keith and Malinda headed down the Blue Ridge to Blowing Rock and the Grandfather. They were dispatched by Captain Minihan to go "a scouting to report on events under the Grandfather" for Stoneman.[8] They were also coming back for blood. Keith decided that the time was right to settle all accounts with the Greens, the Moores, and William, Reuben, and McCaleb Coffey.

The Blalocks reached Blowing Rock as a late-December blizzard lashed the Blue Ridge. On the other side of the mountains, a storm of a different and even deadlier sort was taking shape in and around Knoxville, and in Watauga and Caldwell Counties; the return of the Blalocks foreshadowed its fury.

PART FOUR

A Grim Cycle

CHAPTER NINETEEN
Dead in the Sawdust

I N a hunting lodge concealed by a thicket on one of the Grandfather's steepest slopes, Keith and Malinda gathered some familiar faces—Levi Coffey, Adolphus Pritchard, and Joseph Franklin—as well as a dozen unionists who had ridden with the couple, Kirk, and Jim Hartley. Keith wore a dark blue, double-breasted officer's frock coat, with canary-yellow stripes adorning his trousers' seams; Malinda wore a sky-blue greatcoat with a yellow-flanneled cape that she could pull over her head in the snow and rain. The new uniforms would be local unionists' and Confederates' first glimpse of the thousands more of Stoneman's troopers to follow. A rebel would claim that in the flamboyant garb, the 10th Michigan looked "as much Cossacks as soldiers."[1]

Keith recorded that in December 1864 he "made those trips as a scout into Western North Carolina without meeting with any mishaps" and that "in early January 1865, [I] set out on a fourth scout and went as far as Ikord's Station [Camp Vance], then the terminus of the Western North Carolina railroad, and picked up what information I could concerning the enemy, having with me a dozen men and returning with a dozen more [recruits] who had joined me for the purpose of going through the lines of the Union Army."[2]

In late December 1864, David Moore ran into Keith and Malinda, who, Moore would state, "had returned here," and he "remembers to have remarked to Blalock that his arm healed up the quickest (although it was not completely healed then) of any wound he had ever seen that was as bad as it was.[3]

"I had heard from time to time of his [Keith's] being back around the county with a squad of something like a dozen or twenty men under him, which he kept pretty close in the mountains and which he used for their mutual protection against the home guards, who were arresting all Union men and killing all Union soldiers, especially escaped prisoners, they could lay hands on."[4]

Moore also recounted that in early January 1865, "the Blalocks came to my house with a squad of sixteen men along in the Winter before the War closed, and had dinner prepared for them," risking retaliation from local rebels.

"[Moore] admonished Blalock of the danger that he was incurring by appearing in the neighborhood with a force under him, as they were liable to be attacked at any moment by a superior force of the home guards, who were patrolling the county almost continually. To which Blalock replied that he was born and raised in the county and that he was not going to be run out of it, but was determined to defend himself in it."[5]

As they ate, Keith "inquired of [Moore] if I knew where the guard was stationed that had been raised in the neighborhood to take the place for home defense of the Rebels, and bragged how he had helped when a gang of the Rebel Home Guards had been driven out of the settlement previously."[6]

Moore replied that he "could not help much as the Guard referred to did not have any regular stopping place, but was first at one place and then at another."[7]

Keith did not "state what his intentions were in respect to the Guards in question, whether he designed attempting their capture or not or what else he expected to do with his men."[8]

Moore's account of that dinner with the Blalocks also revealed a rift that had divided the Moore family. "Blalock had with him at the house one Judson Moore, brother to Carroll Moore, who was in command of the Guard in question," Moore wrote. "I heard Blalock say to him that if he (Judson) would go to his brother and tell him that if he and his men would lay down their arms, that he [Keith] wouldn't hurt nor molest one of them; but Judson declined to carry the message, saying that he wouldn't do it."[9] If he had, his brother would likely have had him arrested on the spot. And neither did Carroll Moore believe that Keith, who had sworn to kill them, would not "hurt or molest them."[10]

The Blalocks left David Moore's home "about dark with the intention of going to Madison Estes' house about two-and-a-half miles further up the creek to meet up with Lieutenant James Hartley, who had his men with him."[11]

Also encountering the Blalocks "in the following Winter [1864-1865]" was Joseph Webb, who recalled that "the first time I met up with Blalock, after he returned, was after Christmas 1864.[12]

"Blalock's bad wound was pretty well healed," Webb stated. "He had a squad of men under him at Rich's [a unionist] on John's River, some seven or eight miles from my own home. I went over there to see what it all meant, and not finding him [Keith] at Rich's, I followed on to David Moore's in the same neighborhood, where I found him and a party of some fifteen or sixteen men under him, all of them armed and some four of them in federal uniform."[13]

Later, Webb remembered that he had actually seen the Blalocks "about three weeks before this."[14] Webb related that "Blalock then had a squad of about the same number with him, and they had got together on the Joe White's Mountain to lay plans for bushwhacking the Rebel home guards that were expected to pass that way very shortly."[15]

Webb continued: "I learned from them that some kind of adventure in reference to a rebel guard in the neighborhood was to be taken soon, but the precise nature of it was not fully made known to me, and in the next few weeks, we learned what that was."[16]

With a bit of prescience Webb added, "Keith appeared to still have a grudge against [William] Coffey."[17]

By the end of December 1864, Keith's and Malinda's enemies had also heard that the couple had slipped back around the Grandfather. According to Jesse Moore, "The first I learned or heard of the Blalocks' being back in the neighborhood after having been wounded in the arm was around the 25th of December, at which time I was at Camp Vance with a company of Home Guards, and there got word that Blalock and a party under him were raiding up and down the Globe settlement stealing stock and plundering houses. I returned home."[18]

Moore's father, Carroll, also noted that "Blalock had disappeared from the neighborhood for awhile, but near or about the first of the year [1865], within a day or two of that time at the farthest, Blalock was back with a party of some fifteen or sixteen men."[19]

Brazenly, Keith stole down to Austin Coffey's house to visit his parents, and his mother remembered that he "arrived in company with a couple of Union soldiers by the name of George Perkins and William Blackwell, and was in Yankee uniform at the time. Higher up the mountain, my son had a squad of men under him."[20]

Keith had selected Perkins and Blackwell for a special and murderous purpose.

As Keith outlined his plans for January 1865, they seemed, in fact, more appropriate for rampaging bushwhackers than for soldiers. Having gathered intelligence through his still-intact web of informants, Keith had already sent a scout back to Knoxville with the news that Confederate forces were stretched thin throughout the mountain counties, with no more than two thousand assorted infantry and cavalry, along with Home Guard units of varying reliability and skill. Now in command was General James G. Martin, a veteran West Pointer who, in August 1864, had been Lee's personal choice to replace the sacked John B. Palmer. A hard disciplinarian and a cool head under fire, the forty-five-year-old Martin was called "Old One-Wing" by his men in reference to his having lost his right arm on a battlefield in the Mexican War battle of Churubusco. From his headquarters at Morganton, he was determined to raise new recruits, destroy the hated Kirk, and eliminate as many unionist guerrillas, outright bushwhackers, and federal scouts in the mountains as possible before contending with the prospect of a federal on-slaught through the Blue Ridge in early spring 1865.

In Watauga and Caldwell, William and Reuben Coffey had burned out dozens of unionist farms and had helped round up outliers and escaped Union prisoners with increased fervor, advocating a scorched earth policy if and when the Yankees invaded. To Keith and his fellow scout Dan Ellis, every action that the Confederate Coffeys and other rebels in the region took against unionists constituted an atrocity; however, the rebel loyalists believed more than ever that the Blalocks and any other unionists were traitors who had to be wiped out. Both camps understood, and with his step-uncles still swearing to kill both him and his wife, Keith Blalock wanted to strike first, before his uncles knew that he had returned to the Grandfather.

In early January 1865, one of the worst winters that locals had ever ex-perienced cloaked the Blue Ridge in deep snow and unleashed ice storms driven by winds that could reach over one hundred miles an hour or more on the highest slopes. Military activities, whether scouting missions or raids by either side, nearly ceased as each day brought more snow and gusts. No one would have figured Keith and Malinda to raid in sometimes knee-high snow and even deeper drifts; for horses, the trails were sometimes impassa-ble. The Blalocks decided otherwise.

On January 9 or 10, 1865, Keith, Malinda, George Perkins, and Bill Blackwell rode to McCaleb Coffey's house late in the evening, a light snow-fall muffling their approach. They reined in a short distance from the front porch.

Mrs. McCaleb Coffey recalled: "The Blalocks came to our house long after dark, and Blalock [Keith] called my husband to the door and threatened to kill him. He was not home.

"The other two men, who I learned later were called George Perkins and Bill Blackwell, from Tennessee, were then strangers to me. All were in Yan-kee uniform."[21]

She stated that "they did not come into the house, but before leaving, Blalock again declared that they intended to kill William Coffey, Carroll Moore, Lott Estes, and Robert Green."[22]

Mrs. McCaleb Coffey would soon discover just how fortunate she and her husband had been on that frigid evening.

✦

Eleven riders galloped into the yard of Reuben Coffey on the frigid but clear early morning of January 12, 1864. Six wore blue uniforms, the others heavy homespun woolen coats.

A man in a federal greatcoat dismounted and walked through the snow to the front door. Cradling a Sharp's rifle, he knocked.

Polly Coffey opened the door to find Keith Blalock on the stoop, demanding that her husband show himself. Despite the woman's insistence that Reuben had left a few hours earlier and would not return until that night, Keith pushed past her and whistled for several of his men to come inside for a search of the house. After ransacking the house with no sign of his step-uncle, Keith led his men back to the horses, sent all except George Perkins and William Blackwell back to the mountains, remounted, and rode the mile and a half to the long, slope-roofed farmhouse of William Coffey.

Again, a heavy knock rang like a gunshot through the chill air, and, again, a white-haired woman answered the door. Sixty-one-year-old Annie Boone Coffey, a direct descendant of the legendary Daniel Boone, now faced her glaring step-nephew. She did not need to be told what he intended.

From her saddle, Malinda stared down at the older woman whose home the couple had visited often before the war. Malinda had never before ridden onto the property with a Spencer in her hands.

One of Keith's men suddenly shouted and pointed at a figure stumbling through a snow-blanketed field toward the woods. Within seconds Keith had climbed back on his horse, and the trio closed on sixty-two-year-old William Coffey, hatless, coatless, and shivering from the cold and fear alike.

They forced him to trudge half a mile at gunpoint until they reached James Gragg's ramshackle sawmill, next to a frozen creek.

They kicked open the door, shoved the gray-haired, gray-bearded Confederate inside, and crowded in after him. One of the men forced Coffey to sit on a scarred wooden bench. James Gragg, who had just been getting ready to head home to his nearby cabin, stared in silence at the Blalocks and at Coffey, who "rocked back and forth with his arms wrapped around his knees."[23]

Out of "deference" to Austin Coffey, Keith had decided not to shoot the prisoner, but instead gestured to one of the others, a local unionist named Perkins.[24] As Gragg could do nothing except gape, Perkins darted behind Coffey, pointed a Colt pistol inches from his skull, and blew a hole in the back of his head.

Without a word, according Gragg, "the Blalocks and their bushwhackers just left quick and left me with Old William bleeding and dead in the sawdust."[25]

"To Keith and Malinda," Murray Coffey would remark, "William was a Home Guard and would have done the same if he had caught them first. William's crowd didn't see things that way. They called Keith and Malinda bushwhackers, murderers, and worse."[26]

The killing of William Coffey shocked locals, even though such executions or cold-blooded murder, depending on one's Yankee or rebel leanings, had proven all too common throughout the war in the mountains. Confederate neighbors deemed the deed an atrocity and charged that Keith had expressly brought Perkins and Blackwell into the county as a personal "execution squad."[27]

Jesse Moore said that "of all Blalock's depredations, this was one of the worst."[28]

"William Coffey," Moore wrote, "who was murdered by George Perkins and a Bill Blackwell in 1865, whom Blalock had brought in from Tennessee for that purpose, had come into the neighborhood with them and had been present at the killing."[29]

Adding another rebel voice to the valid charge that Keith had ordered the old man's death, Carroll Moore railed that "Blalock was accountable for the murder of William Coffey, against whom he [Keith] always had a spite, and this had caused his murder."[30]

Even Joseph Webb, friendly with Keith and Malinda, was unnerved by the killing and tried to shift much of the blame from Keith to the man who had actually pulled the trigger. "I met with him [Keith] at the house of Anne Woodruff, about five miles from the Blalocks' old house," Webb stated, "and there were with him George Perkins and William Blackwell, and Perkins told me that he and he alone had killed the old man William Coffey about an hour before that. Blalock was present but did not know what Perkins was about. Blalock remarked that he would not have done it as that was no way to treat prisoners, that he ought to have taken him through to the Union Army and treated him according to the Rules of War."[31]

Despite Webb's highly dubious "case" that Keith had not known that Perkins was going to shoot Coffey and despite any remote possibility that Keith might have suffered a momentary pang of conscience at the sight of the elderly man lying on the floor of Gragg's mill, the Blalocks and their men were not operating under the "rules of war." They were fighting under their own brutal rules of war—ones matched with equal savagery by their enemies.

Still, Webb strove to "clean up" Keith's reputation and culpability. "Perkins again told me that no one except himself shot the old man, and he [Perkins] himself had shot him with Jones Coffey's pistol that he had captured the night before."[32]

Even Webb acknowledged that Keith's "grudge against Coffey" was well-known in the region, but in a last-ditch attempt to temper Keith's role in the murder, offered that it should be remembered that "outsiders" had killed Coffey. "Perkins and Blackwell were strangers to me and had never been in the settlement before, so far as I knew or heard of."[33]

Jesse Moore aptly summed up the opinion of the local Confederates with his charge that even though "the shooting had been done as was said by

Perkins, who was from the Crab Orchard, over in Tennessee, it was in Blalock's revenge for William Coffey's having scouted the Home Guards the way to his [Keith's] house."[34]

Mary Curtis, who had fed Keith as he had hid in the laurel thicket near Austin Coffey's house, did not absolve him in the murder, stating that William Coffey had been killed by three men—Perkins, Blackwell, and Keith.

Understandably, as well as predictably, Keith's mother said that Perkins and Blackwell had acted on their own. She understood fully the increased dangers descending upon her own husband in the aftermath of his brother's murder.

Keith had given the order, and everyone in the region knew it. McCaleb and Rueben Coffey secreted themselves in remote cabins where they could only hope that Keith did not find them.

The Blalocks had settled one score, and next on their list were the Moores.

Bingham's men, including the Moores and the Greens, searched the lower trails and forests of the Grandfather and Blowing Rock, but because of reports that Kirk and six hundred men had been spotted near the border, did not dare explore the higher ridges, where Keith, Malinda, and their men were hiding. Even if the guards had found them, the only way in passed through a narrow gorge that the scouts' Spencers would have turned into a killing ground.

Their efforts to catch the Blalocks yielding nothing, the local Home Guard, now joined by Confederate regulars from Colonel A. C. Avery's 17th Battalion, devised another way to retaliate against the Blalocks, a personal brand of retribution by now so common in the mountains.

CHAPTER TWENTY
Blood in the Orchard

AS the news that the Blalocks' band had executed William Coffey spread from the Grandfather to the Globe Valley, local Confederates took precautions against the couple's next raid, wherever it might unfold. It would come quickly.

On January 6, 1865, according to Keith, he and Malinda "stopped overnight at the house of Madison Estes, on the John's River, where we met up with Lieutenant Jim Hartley, of the 3rd North Carolina Mounted Infantry, who had with him some fifty or sixty men that he had picked up in Wilkes County [North Carolina] whom he was taking through the lines as recruits for his regiment, the most of them being armed."[1]

Keith went on: "We heard it reported that there was a force of about four hundred of the Rawley [sic] Guard in the Globe Valley with their headquarters at the house of Carroll Moore, some two miles farther down the river.

"We discussed my taking with me a party of just twenty or so men from my own and Hartley's party for the purpose of making a reconnaissance to ascertain the truth of the report that I might communicate the fact to General Stoneman's command, as it was further reported that the force of Rebels was moving in the direction of the Union lines."[2]

David Moore, who stopped in briefly at Estes's house that night, recalled that "Lieutenant Hartley and Blalock talked a long time about the chance of surprising and capturing the guard that we had just been told was camping at Carroll Moore's farm."[3]

Chief among the points Keith and Hartley hashed out was how to proceed if, indeed, up to four hundred Confederates were deployed in and around Moore's house, barns, and fields. The two scouts' combined companies numbered no more than eighty men.

Malinda, too, listened intently, for she intended to take part in the action if her husband and Hartley decided to make a move of any sort.

Keith wondered whether a bushwhacking of the rebels—if they marched into the passes of the Blue Ridge—might not offer the best option. But Hartley, the more he mulled their choices over, was inclined to launch a hit-and-run attack at Moore's farm, "knock down as many as we could," and retreat back into the mountains.[4]

Joseph Webb, now one of Keith and Malinda's men, also recalled the details of that meeting in Estes's house:

> *After dark of January 6, 1865, I went with the Blalocks and their party to the house, where we remained overnight.*
>
> *There was stopping at Estes's that night Lieutenant James Hartley, a famed scout and recruiting officer who had with him a number of men including two Rebel deserters that had met up with him.*
>
> *For a long time Blalock and Lieutenant Hartley consulted together between themselves as to what should be done in reference to a neighborhood guard unit that was known to be spending the night at the house of Carroll Moore a mile or so below us near the river.[5]*

As Keith and Hartley went on talking, most of the men rolled up in blankets either in the house or the barn and tried to sleep. They were rousted from sleep an hour or so before dawn by Keith and Hartley, "who told us to make ready for movement," Webb wrote.[6]

Grabbing his Spencer, Webb "heard Lieutenant Hartley say to Blalock that he [Hartley] wanted him to capture or kill the guards if possible and to bring him all the horses for General Stoneman's boys and, for himself, particularly a pony that belonged to one of Mr. Moore's daughters."[7]

Hartley, running a fever and a rough-edged cough, according to Webb, "did not go with us, on account that he was not well and did not want to expose himself to the night air."[8]

Twenty-year-old Langston L. Estes, a tow-headed, muscular mountaineer and the son of Madison Estes, was about to see his first action with a guerrilla band. "I had come in home that night from Mulberry Creek with Lieutenant James Hartley," the young man would say, "and with us was a veteran of Kirk's named Carpenter. Blalock was there, both he and his wife, him in full Yankee uniform, his Missus in a blue coat and a cape with a yellow stripe, with fifteen of Blalock's men, six of whom wore federal uniforms and all of who were heavily armed. They came to my father's house, where they remained until about an hour before daybreak."[9]

Mrs. McCaleb Coffey mirrored the viewpoint of the region's rebels with her assessment of the Blalocks' band, whether clad in federal blue or mountain homespun: "He [Keith] got a gang of the worst kind of men under him, and among them Joe Webb and Joe Coffey, son of Enoch [a cousin of Keith's stepfather]."[10] Of course, Keith and Malinda would have rendered a similar opinion of the militia that McCaleb, Reuben, and William Coffey had served so often.

Now, opting to strike that militia, Hartley told Keith, "I want you to come down and take the Guards and everything that Moore has."[11]

Mustering in Estes' snow-covered yard, Keith, with Malinda, led his fifteen and two of Hartley's most experienced guerrillas and set out in a biting wind down a twisting, laurel-shrouded path, the first gray streaks of dawn piercing the dark sky. Langston Estes would write: "Our purpose at the time was of whipping out the Guards."[12] No one in the company knew yet whether there were four, forty, or four hundred rebels at Carroll Moore's farm.

As Keith took his band down the trail, he had no way of knowing that the Moores were expecting him. On the previous evening, thirty-eight-year-old Jesse Moore, Carroll's brother and the namesake of one of Carroll's boys, had warily scouted several trails leading to the Moore farm and had spotted a small figure disappearing into a brush-lined ridge ahead of him. His rifle cocked, Jesse stalked the figure, uncertain if it was a man or an animal. For a moment, he thought of turning back, afraid that it might be a unionist bushwhacker. But he worked his way closer to see it was a woman. Peering at her from a thicket twenty yards away, he recognized Malinda Blalock. He continued to stalk her.

"I saw Blalock's wife going up the river [the John's River] toward Madison Estes's place," Moore would say, "and concluded that she was going there to give her husband and their gang information as to our [the Moores' and the Home Guards'] whereabouts. Seeing her up there, I expected an attack from Blalock and his gang that same night, and, accordingly, we were on the watch for them at my brother's place all night long."[13]

Waiting at the farmhouse were seven guards and five of the Moores. "A hundred or so Guards" prowled "the settlement within hearing of any gunfire near the farm," Jesse stated.[14]

Jesse Moore had guessed wrong about the time of the assault—but only by an hour or two.

"Our party reached the place about daybreak," Keith would state.[15] According to his report of the action, Keith "posted himself with a few of his men on a ridge above and near the house, and he sent the others around and below the house to open fire upon it and to rout out of it the squad of Home Guards that he was led to believe were quartered there for the night.[16]

"[He] knew that this firing would be heard for some distance along the valley and would set in motion any other squads of the rebels he supposed to be within earshot of it," he would report.[17]

A veteran of so many ambushes he had both launched and incurred, Keith was confident that he, Malinda, and their men could hit the Moores and any guards in the house, steal their horses, and vanish up the Grandfather or Blowing Rock before the rebels could arrive in force. He also would say that from the ridge, the "movements of any approaching Rebels could be seen from his point of observation," allowing him to break off the raid at any moment to guarantee his company's escape.[18]

To Joseph Webb, Keith Blalock's plan appeared sound, the tactics of a canny partisan leader. "We reached the immediate neighborhood of Mr. Moore's house about halfway between daylight and sunrise," Webb would write, "and there he [Keith] gave direction to Simeon Philyaw, a recruiting officer [one of Kirk's men serving with Hartley], to take one half of the party and to proceed down the road till they came opposite the house, while he [Keith] and the rest of the party would go around and come up to it from behind."[19]

Keith, eager to take on his old foes the Moores face-to-face rather than shoot at them from the ridge, had decided at the last moment to "come into their yard."[20] He told Malinda to remain at her perch on the high ground— "to cover him down there."[21]

Webb clambered down the ridge "with Blalock's division of the party."[22]

Suddenly something went wrong—"a Guard," Webb would write, "had discovered the approach of Philyaw's men as they came down the road."[23]

To Keith's fury, his plan disintegrated as "the Guard saw Philyaw's boys before they got fairly into position."[24]

"We were in too far to break off," Keith would recall.[25]

☙

As the guard who had spotted Philyaw's men shouted the alarm and ran for cover, Jesse Moore, one of Carroll Moore's sons, was walking across an orchard to his father's house. Named after his uncle, who was in the house grabbing for his Enfield, the seventeen-year-old youth was a Home Guard in Bingham's militia. Now, the gangly, lank-haired youth, having thought that it was safe to go out since Blalock had not attacked during the night, was carrying a few rabbits he had just killed and the rifle-gun he had used on them.

Moore, keenly aware that the Blalocks were on the loose again, had made certain to reload before emerging from the woods and heading into the orchard. Some fifty yards away, seven horses, Home Guards' mounts, lined the hitching rail in front of the main porch.

Young Moore froze at the guard's cry, turned, and gaped as "Blalock and his party came up at this juncture out of the woods and commenced firing at the house and the men inside it."[26] From the ridge Malinda and the others laid down heavy bursts from their Spencers.

As Keith and his squad burst into the orchard and straight at the youth, Moore dropped the rabbits and ran as hard as he could in the snow toward the house. "The Rebels who were in the house and about the barn broke and scattered in all directions," Keith would remember, "some of them running in the direction of the point at which I was stationed."[27] Two of the men—the boy's namesake and Patterson Moore—squeezed off rounds in hope of giving the fleeing teen some sort of aid.

According to the elder Jesse Moore, "When we discovered a party of a dozen men approaching the house from down the road, upon which I and the three boys and two other Guards went out the back way, I went first to the end of the farmhouse and fired my rifle at the party in the road and then fled into the orchard near at hand where we made a stand under cover of the trees."[28] Crouching behind a thick trunk against which bullets from the Union Spencers slammed, Moore tried to cover his nephew. So did Patterson Moore.

"The boys on coming out of the house ran towards a wood where they were encountered by Blalock and a gang of about a dozen men under him," Jesse Moore recounted, "and our boys then turned and ran down into the orchard, pursued by Blalock and his party, and as they approached, I raised my musket, loaded with an ounce ball and twelve bullets about the size of a buckshot and took down one of the ones wearing a Yankee uniform."[29]

As Moore took aim at the onrushing federals and guerrillas, several Spencer rounds whistled past his nephew; in front of the teen, bullets from the rebel Enfield poured from the farmhouse's windows and whined past him at Keith and his men. At the same time Malinda and the men around her continued to rake the house and fields.

Ignoring the fusillades, Keith stopped in the orchard, calmly aimed his Spencer at Patterson Moore, and fired. "I crippled him," Keith would say.[30]

"I saw Patterson's thigh broken by a shot from Blalock's rifle," said Jesse Moore.[31]

"We all opened up on the Guards at this point," Webb would write, "and Keith Blalock shot breaking the thigh of one of them, Patterson Moore."[32]

Moore cried out and tumbled backward, the bone cracked in two by the Spencer's copper-wrapped round.

With too much distance to the trees where his namesake and two other Home Guards still made their stand, and with Blalock and his men closing fast, young Jesse Moore turned and raised his rifle, loaded, as was his uncle's, with an ounce ball and twelve buckshot-sized bullets. To the boy's horror, Keith surged ahead of the other attackers and, holding the Spencer in his good arm, the right, leveled it at him.

"About a couple of hundred yards outside the house and in the orchard," Keith would state, "I was a little above him on a little hill."[33] Keith and Jesse Moore "both raised our guns and fired at each other at the same moment, Moore's gun a little the quickest."[34] Both men crumpled to the snow at virtually the same instant as Keith's bullet shattered Moore's left heel and ankle and the youth's shot crashed into Keith's face—Moore's desperate shot had not caught Keith head on, but at an angle that crushed his right cheekbone and obliterated the right eye.

Later, Keith would say that he remembered the agony of the "ball's entering sidewise and putting it [his eye] entirely out and remaining lodged on the inside of the skull just opposite and about an inch above the right ear."[35]

To a friend, Keith would later remark that "when he was shot in the right eye, he was in the act of taking aim with his gun, the right side of his face to the breech of the piece [a Spencer rifle] and the barrel resting on his left arm at the elbow, being unable to grasp it with his left hand on account of his previous wound."[36]

Several participants in the clash would soon assert that Keith was mistaken as to the identity of the man who had shot him. The elder Jesse Moore would claim that he was the one who really shot Keith. According to the teen's uncle, he had fired at Keith from a distance of approximately sixty yards behind the tree as soon as Keith approached the nephew, "and at the discharge of the piece, Blalock fell to the ground shot in the right eye with one of the [twelve-load] bullets."[37]

Running forward with Keith into the orchard, Joe Webb saw Keith fall. Webb would later back the older Moore's claim: "Jesse Moore fired at Blalock at a distance of fifty to sixty yards, the shot striking him in the inner corner of the right eye and ranging towards the nose. The piece fired was a musket."[38] Webb wrote that "the shot that hit him [Keith] was supposed to be a small one, but the damage was anything but small."[39]

Jesse Moore would claim that while "he was shot in the heel, it was not by Blalock," but his father flatly stated that "Blalock's shots hit my son in the heel and ankle and Patterson in the thigh."[40]

Joe Webb helped Keith wobble to his feet and half-dragged, half-carried him out of the orchard and into the woods. With Keith down, the assault faltered and then broke apart. Still on the ridge, Malinda and the dozen men with her pinned down the Moores and the guards for the moment, but the raiders knew it might be only a matter of a few minutes before Bingham's men poured up the road.

Finding a horse or a mule for their grievously wounded leader and fleeing the farm as quickly as possible confronted the unionists. "In the hurry to get him [Keith] mounted and carried out of further danger after receiving his wound of the eye," wrote Joe Webb, "we had some difficulty in finding an animal on which to place him."[41]

Although Carroll Moore's "horse and mules had been let out at the time of the first attack on his house," Moore noted that Webb quickly found a solution to the dilemma: "As soon as the firing had ceased, Webb threatened to kill one of my [Moore's] negroes if he didn't show him where my horses were hid. The guards' horses had broken loose during the fight.

"Thereupon, the negro showed him where they were concealed in a ravine near the house. Webb took the mules and a racking pony away with him."[42]

Jesse Moore also said that Webb stole the mules and the horse, but contended that he had stolen the expensive pony out of the family's stable. With the guns now silent, "Carroll Moore's eleven-year-old daughter to whom it [the pony] belonged ran into the stable and begged Webb not to take it, but he would not listen to her entreaties."[43]

Webb never denied any detail of Jesse Moore's version. Years later, Keith's friend told a war department investigator that "in a few minutes after Keith Blalock was shot, his wife and some of the men started immediately with him, carrying him on foot, back up the mountain to Estes's house.

"About the same time, Webb went to one of Mr. Carroll Moore's negroes and commanded him to show him where the horses were, telling him that he had orders to bring them and bring them he would; that the negro at first hesitated, but being threatened, he showed Webb a couple of mules and the pony already referred to, all belonging to Mr. Moore and his daughter, which Webb took to his comrades and Mrs. Blalock."[44]

To the investigator, Webb also testified that when he had reached Estes's house, he "had told Jim Hartley that Mr. Moore's daughter had begged to have the pony returned and that Webb had promised her that he would do so if Hartley would consent to it, but Hartley wouldn't listen to anything of the kind."[45]

Naturally, Keith had nothing but plaudits for Webb, "for as soon as [Keith] was wounded, Joe Webb was the one of the party who got me the racking pony that belonged to the Moores, and placed me across it and conveyed me out of the neighborhood."[46]

The story of the horse theft amused Keith anytime he spoke of it. "Webb clapped his gun to the head of one of Moore's negroes and told him that if he didn't instantly show him a horse, he would blow his daylights out," Keith said. "Upon which the negro took him in to the girl's pony."[47]

Slipping in and out of consciousness on the trek back up to the home of Madison Estes, Keith was vaguely aware of Malinda alongside and of "being supported by two men, one on either side of the pony."[48]

Just as Keith and his band had feared, the rebels who had converged upon the Moore farm twenty minutes or so after the raiders had fled chased them toward Estes's house. They would glimpse the "squads of Home Guards that started in pursuit of them that same afternoon," slowly but doggedly making their way up the trail.[49]

Malinda and Keith's companions stopped with him at Estes's house "shortly after sunrise, not very long after the raid on Moore's," according to Daniel Moore.[50] They only stayed long enough to clean Keith's shattered socket as best they could for the moment and to apprise Hartley of how the attack had gone awry.

Joined by Hartley and his men, Keith, Malinda, and the rest of their company set out for Lewis Banner's and then Tennessee. But with Keith weak from blood loss and shock, Hartley decided that their party was strong enough to risk cutting short the first day's journey, and they spent the evening of January 7, 1865, at the house of a unionist named Mrs. Emmaline Johnson, on the banks of the Watauga River.

꙳

As Keith continued to drift in and out of consciousness, Hartley sent several of his men to Shull's Mill to bring back a physician friendly with "Uncle Lewis" Banner. Back in the Globe Valley, the Moores, despite the wounds to Jesse and Patterson, were jubilant in their belief that no one, not even Keith Blalock, could survive such a blast to the face. "The rebels cheered the news that Keith was dead or close to it," said Murray Coffey.[51]

The belief would embolden the Home Guards for several weeks to come, but not enough to risk pursuing the Blalocks as far as Lewis Banner's turf, which teemed with Kirk's men and Stoneman's scouts coming into and returning from the mountains of the Tennessee–North Carolina border counties. By the morning of January 8, 1865, the rebels had given up the chase "in the foothills of the Blue Ridge," and, with Keith literally sprawled across the racking pony's back, the company made its way down to Lewis Banner's.[52] William Voncannon, about to slip into western North Carolina himself on a scout for George Kirk, saw "Blalock and four or five of his companions there, among them his wife, all on their way to Crab Orchard when he [Keith] was strong enough."[53]

"He looked horrible," Voncannon stated. "The ball of his right eye was destroyed when I saw him, and from his swelling from his ruined eye down to the ear, I supposed that the ball was lodged in the inside of his head and would have to stay there."[54]

Keith and Malinda did not stay long at Uncle Lewis's, riding out the next day and heading toward Crab Orchard to rest with Malinda's relatives. They journeyed alone along the familiar trails, for on that same morning, Joe Webb wrote, "Hartley met up with a party of Kirk's men between Mrs. Johnson's and Banner's that was going over into Wilkes County, North Carolina, and turned back with them."[55] The Blalocks' men, including Webb, offered their good-byes to the couple, wondering if Keith's wound would claim him. At the very least, Webb said, they figured that the war was over for Keith and Malinda.

Before either the Blalocks or Hartley's band had parted, one last bit of guerrilla business had been "transacted." Webb "kept the pony"—so much for his promise to return the horse to Moore's daughter—"and the Blalocks one of the mules and a man by the name of Carpenter, who was one of Hartley's men and took part in the attack on the guards, took the other one."[56]

Later, Carroll Moore would say, "I learned that Blalock took one of my mules into Crab Orchard and sold it. I never did learn what happened to my girl's racking pony."[57]

For the next three weeks, Keith grappled with pain and fever. Slowly, with what can only be deemed astonishing recuperative powers, he began to regain his strength and talked about getting back to the 10th and then back on scouts in North Carolina. Malinda tended him day and night, cleaning the swollen, empty eye socket as the doctor had shown her and applying poultices. Whenever Keith's pain increased, she used a venerable mountain remedy—corn whiskey—and lots of it.

Malinda believed that Jesse Moore had gotten lucky in his father's orchard, not because he had hit his target, as all mountain boys could shoot, but because Keith's crooked, still-painful left wrist had hindered his own aim. "His arm [the left one] was getting almost useless and forced him to handle a rifle one-armed," she said. "If Keith were whole, Moore would have been done before he ran two steps."[58]

Down in the Globe Valley, the Moores circulated stories that Keith and Malinda had raided the family not in any official capacity for the union, but as simple outlaws to whom no military laws applied. Jesse Moore wrote: "The loss of that eye he [Keith] received in a bushwhacker's raid even though he was in a federal uniform."[59]

A rebel cousin of Keith seconded the assumption: "The way he got his right eye shot out is that he came in [Caldwell] county leading a squad of soldiers and with his wife, and the squad got into a fight, and I can't swear that Blalock was in line of duty when he was wounded."[60]

From Home Guard headquarters at Camp Mast and at Lenoir, the men were again directed to execute the Blalocks or any of their men as bushwhackers.

It would not have mattered a bit to Keith's enemies, but Captain Minihan, of the 10th Michigan, officially noted that the Blalocks were "on scout duty in Caldwell County, N.C., when he [Keith] and his squad were in action with Rebel Scouts and he received a gunshot wound in the head, causing the loss of his right eye, near Lenore [*sic*]. The fight was with men of Captain Bingham's Company, N.C. Militia, Confederate Home Guard."[61]

CHAPTER TWENTY-ONE
He Did Not Deserve His Fate

❧

ON Sunday, February 5, 1865, a combined force of Major Bingham's Home Guards and a company of Avery's 17th Battalion galloped into Coffey Gap. Captain James Marlow, leading the regulars, was acting on intelligence that Austin Coffey was hiding several unionist guerrillas.

Marlow, a twenty-eight-year-old officer who had seen hard duty with Lee's army, loathed his current duties battling partisans and bushwhackers and was inclined to execute them almost on sight. Having narrowly survived an ambuscade two weeks earlier by a band of men alleged by some to be Kirk's, by others to be the Blalocks', Marlow was in an undeniably foul mood that February night.

The Home Guards and Marlow's company surrounded Austin Coffey's home. The captain and several of his men then stomped onto the porch and banged the thick door open with rifle butts.

Keith's mother stood in the entry hall with her arms folded, her eyes, the same pale blue as her son's, fixed on Marlow; the officer's men crashed through the house, overturning furniture, breaking dishes and mirrors, and tearing up rugs and curtains with their cavalry sabers. Several of the soldiers stormed into the basement and pounded back up the stone steps minutes later with Thomas Wright, "a known Unionist and outlier," now bound and bloody.[1]

Marlow and the rest took their captive out of the house just as John Boyd and five guardsmen with him rode up. Boyd yelled to Marlow that someone had seen Austin Coffey and several men enter his rebel brother McCaleb's house, which McCaleb had vacated after the Blalocks had killed William Coffey.

Marlow barked the order to ride to McCaleb's property, and the 150 men careered down the Morganton Road.

Keith Blalock's mother, meanwhile, "went a nigh-way and gave warning to the inmates of McCaleb's house before Marlow arrived by calling out in a loud voice that 'the Rebels' were coming."[2] One of Keith's scouts, Alex Johnson, raced out the back door just as the cavalry and guards crossed from the road to the front yard. Dozens of muzzles lit up the night, but Johnson reached the woods unharmed. Marlow sent half his men in pursuit, but they would return empty-handed, Johnson eluding them in the dark woods.

Boyd accompanied Marlow and several soldiers into McCaleb's house, pointed at a tall man with thick white hair, and identified him as Austin Coffey. Marlow's men escorted Keith's stepfather outside, tied his hands, and hoisted him onto a horse. Then, Marlow, who had been ordered by Avery to link up with another detachment of cavalry, led by Captain Nelson Miller, at Valle Crucis, sent Boyd and the Home Guards back to Camp Mast.

From the woods, Keith's mother watched as Marlow's command galloped toward Blowing Rock, her husband's white-haired visage rapidly fading from her sight. "She was somewhat reassured that it was regular soldiers and not the guards who took Austin off," a relative would note.[3]

❧

The cavalrymen rode several miles up the Blowing Rock "road," little more than a small, snowy trail. Halfway between Shull's Mill and Blowing Rock, they pulled up at the house of Tom Henley, a guard now riding with Bingham's men back to Camp Mast and brother of the man who had killed Keith's comrade Edmund Ivy.

Henley's house lay empty, and Marlow ordered his men to dismount, tie up the horses, and camp in and around the house for the rest of the night.

Once inside, Marlow and his men kindled a fire and cooked bacon and corn mush, which they shared with Coffey. Marlow reassured the elderly man that he would not be harmed, but said that he would be jailed for a time in Lenoir.

Sitting against the wall near the fireplace, Coffey, like many of the gray-clad men around him, began to doze. Marlow, however, paced back and forth in front of the blaze.

Watching the officer from a spot near the front door was John Walker, the man who, with Keith's and Levi Coffey's help, had duped Bingham by staging his own kidnapping by unionists and making himself subject to a fake parole. To Major Avery's 17th Battalion, which had been rounding up every available male from eighteen to fifty-five, the piece of paper meant nothing, and Walker now found himself wearing a gray wool uniform and carrying an Enfield.

Marlow suddenly wheeled over to the door and pointed at Walker. Walker snapped to attention.

To Walker's horror, the officer ordered him to walk up to the sleeping Coffey and execute him. Walker, at that moment displaying incredible nerve, would tell a Coffey relative: "Marlow detailed me to kill the old man, but I refused."[4]

For a long moment, Walker wondered whether Marlow would have him shot on the spot. Marlow then pointed at another soldier, whom Walker later described as "a base-born fellow named Robert Glass, who volunteered to do the act."[5]

Glass stole over to the fireplace, got down on one knee, put a pistol to the side of Coffey's head, and, in Walker's recollection, "blew out the old man's brains."[6]

Soldiers startled from sleep clambered to their feet and were greeted by Marlow's order to remove the body.

Once outside, the soldiers pitched Austin Coffey's corpse into a snow-cloaked laurel thicket.

A week later, several of Coffey's neighbors sent out by Keith's mother to search for her spouse spotted a stray dog wandering through the snow of the Blowing Rock road with a hand clamped between his jaws. A man recognized a silver ring on a nearly fleshless finger as one that Austin Coffey had always worn.

They tracked the dog to Tom Henley's house and into the thicket, where they found what animals had left of Austin Coffey.

Even many of the region's Confederates were dismayed by Coffey's execution. One local would state: "Austin Coffey did not deserve his fate. He had fed Confederates as well as Union men at his house . . . and had tried to prevent Keith and Malinda's raids on Lott Green's and Carroll Moore's houses."[7]

Jesse Moore opined: "Austin paid for Keith and Malinda. It was not right."[8]

Austin Coffey's sister-in-law Polly took a decidedly harsher stance toward his murder. "He was killed by the Confederate soldiers under Colonel Avery in February 1865 because all through the war, Austin, who knew all about Blalock and his wife depredating through the county, harbored Blalock. Austin shared the same obnoxious Unionism as Blalock."[9]

Langston Estes believed, as did most neighbors regardless of the degree of their Yankee or rebel loyalties, that three recent events had doomed "the old man" because they had enraged Confederate Major Avery: Coffey's and his wife's helping to hide Keith in the laurel thicket after he had been shot in the arm; their "sheltering and feeding" Keith, George Perkins, and Bill Blackwell just a few days before they murdered William Coffey; and "Blalocks' and his men's visit at his stepfather's house not long before the raid at Moore's."[10]

Locals knew that Austin Coffey had been horrified and saddened by his brother's murder, but that he had laid the deed squarely on George Perkins, refusing to believe that his stepson had given the order. But from the beginning of the war, "Old Austin" had made no secret of his unionist beliefs and of his willingness to provide all the help he could for "Blalock's operation."[11] Those facts, the neighbors realized, had delivered Coffey to Captain Marlow and Robert Glass on February 5, 1865, even though John Boyd had pointed Austin Coffey out that night to the Confederate soldiers.

Austin Coffey's widow decried the act as "outright, simple murder."[12]

"I knew what my son's intent would be," she would state, "and he was right to do it. His men would get the word to him. Austin was a Unionist, it was true, but he never lifted a hand against a Rebel and never resisted when the soldiers came looking for food and stock, and everyone around knew it."[13]

Throughout Watauga and Caldwell, people did not need to speculate on what Keith Blalock's response to the killing of his stepfather would be—he would "lift a hand" against Austin Coffey's killers unless, as was rumored, Keith was dead or hurt too gravely to do anything at all.[14]

CHAPTER TWENTY-TWO
Even If It Takes Forty Years

W HEN Keith Blalock was told that John B. Boyd had helped arrest Austin Coffey and that Coffey was dead," wrote a friend, "he swore that he would kill Boyd if it took forty years after the war to do so."[1] Also believing that Marlow had been acting on Avery's orders, Keith similarly pledged to kill the commander of the 17th Battalion.

The questions as to Keith's health and as to his ability to punish local rebels for the death of his stepfather evaporated within a week after Austin Coffey's body had been discovered. Although Keith could easily have received a medical discharge because of his loss of an eye, as Captain Minihan wrote, the Watauga scout donned a patch over the gaping socket and stayed on duty. Malinda, as always, was there at his side. Both had a good inkling from Kirk about what was coming in March 1865: a horde of Union cavalry with which Stoneman would storm into western North Carolina. The 10th Michigan would ride in the vanguard, and Malinda informed her cousin that "we [the Blalocks] could not have missed it."[2]

Just a few days after Austin Coffey's death, Scout Captain James Champion, a recruiting officer for a Tennessee cavalry regiment and described by a Banner's Elk man as "a stocky man, very becoming to his uniform and altogether worthy of his rank," arrived near Banner's Elk with roughly one hundred "Union men," some of them Stoneman's and Kirk's scouts, others from bands of local guerrillas.[3] "Most of [them] were armed after one fashion or another, but many had few weapons at all."[4]

Through the unionist network in Watauga and Caldwell Counties, Champion sent out word that he was going to launch a daring, long-shot raid against Camp Mast, where so many of the Blalocks' foes, family and otherwise, had served throughout the war. When Keith and Malinda heard of Champion's intent, they saddled up with ten of their men, Keith leaving the hideout for the first time since he had been wounded. Gaunt, bearded, with a black patch over the empty socket, he looked to a fellow scout like "some fiendish creation."[5] For enemies who thought never to see him again, the visage especially radiated menace.

The Blalocks joined Champion at Valle Crucis, where they shared dinner, "one of Henry Taylor's beeves," with the scout and with old friend William Voncannon.[6] He would recall, "Blalock and his wife joined us in Watauga County for the attack on the home guards under Major Harvey Bingham."[7] In a probable surprise to most who knew them, Keith and Malinda even seconded the Tennessee scout's warning to every man that anyone who had come looking only to loot the camp had better depart because he would shoot any such miscreants exceeding his orders to ambush the camp, capture the garrison, and destroy their arms and munitions. By midnight, the force shrank from 123 to 100.

Several hours before the dawn of February 15, 1865, they rode down a trail to Brushy Fork Creek, forded the waist-deep water, and climbed the ridge between that stream and ice-encrusted Cove Creek. Camp Mast lay stretched out before them just before dawn.

Amazingly, according to one of the soldiers, T. P. Adams, of Dog Skin Creek, they had reached their destination undetected: "It seemed . . . as we passed over the frozen ground, that the clang of the horses' shoes had aroused every dog in Christendom, and just before [our] reaching the camp a flock of sheep became frightened and fled helter-skelter down the ridge toward the camp, with bells jingling and sheep bleating, thus making a veritable pandemonium."[8]

The camp's guards, posted around watch fires, either dozed or shrugged off the animals' clatter as nothing unusual. In their wooden huts and tents, the rest of the guards still slept.

Champion now set his plan into motion. Dividing his men into three companies, led by scouts I. V. Reese, Aaron Voncannon, and Champion himself, he placed men at regular intervals on the ridgeline encircling the camp and instructed every other man to build a fire. In case a melee erupted, Champion had secured his own position with Keith and Malinda's heavily armed squad.

As the pallid, freezing dawn seeped across the clearing, reveille sounded across the camp, and the Home Guards, rubbing and blowing on their hands in the cold, stepped from their quarters to see "an apparent wall of smoke and fire" all around them.[9] The ridges appeared to be crawling with a sizable force, the rebels staring upwards in shock.

A local man fighting for neither side observed: "Back of the hill was a line of campfires long enough to warm a large army where the men in jeans concealed their clothing by showing only their heads."[10]

General Franklin, "General being his baptismal name and not a mere empty title of military rank," was sent in a federal officer's uniform down to the camp under a flag of truce and returned twenty minutes later with Guard Captain George McGuire, a wounded veteran of Lee's army and now one of Bingham's staff.[11] To Keith and Malinda's disappointment, McGuire had revealed to Franklin that their longtime nemesis Major Harvey Bingham was in Asheville for a meeting with other guard commanders.

Only one of the Watauga militia's two companies was in the camp, and McGuire stated that he had already taken a vote on whether to fight or not. Only eleven of his men wanted to take on the "federal" force.

By nine o'clock, the garrison surrendered. They stacked their arms, formed up in double-file, and waited for hundreds of Yankee cavalrymen to gallop into the clearing and march them off to east Tennessee. The rebels' collective jaws dropped as Champion's motley command appeared. "Two thirds of their [the Confederates'] captors were their rag-tag and bob-tailed neighbors who had heard lead whiz from the home-guard guns as they [unionists] ran for dear life to the nearest woods," Shepherd Dugger, a teen at the time, remembered.[12] The Blalocks could testify to the truth of Dugger's words.

Dozens of Watauga Confederates' surprise gave way to dread as Keith, Malinda, and their men, Spencers at the ready, "took charge of the prisoners."[13] With his one good eye, Keith glared down at every face as he cantered slowly up and down both lines. He did not find John Boyd, William and McCaleb Coffey, the Greens, or the Moores among them. If Keith had, Champion, who had known and liked Austin Coffey, would not likely have objected to Keith's taking those men for a brief walk in the woods.

The raiders wasted little time in marching the Home Guards off to parole for most; and to Camp Chase, in Ohio, for the eleven who had craved a fight. For Keith and Malinda, at the head of the column as it crossed the Watauga River Bridge near Lewis and Sam Banner's homes, the route turned into something of a triumphal procession: "On the road from Valle Crucis to Banner Elk," an observer wrote, "there was but one family of Confederates left, Daniel Strickland's, and for these people [the unionists] to see this long-dreaded militia marching as Champion's [and Blalock's] prisoners was a greater show for them than a road full of lions, tigers, and elephants would be now. They [the column] marched in pairs—two guards with guns, behind two prisoners, each with his blanket rolled and tied in a circle that passed over one shoulder and under one arm."[14]

Home Guard Captain George McGuire never returned home at the war's end, fueling local Confederates' charges that he had been a traitor in on Champion's plan and had betrayed the militia. He never rebutted allegations that he had, in effect, handed Camp Mast over the polyglot Yankee force.

The fall of Camp Mast signaled that the crumbling Confederate defenses in the mountains of East Tennessee and western North Carolina lay wide open to the Blalocks' personal brand of warfare and to Stoneman's "grand thrust into the Confederacy's back."[15]

CHAPTER TWENTY-THREE
Stripped Down for Fast Action

D URING the last week of February 1865, Keith and Malinda paid a visit in broad daylight to McCaleb Coffey's house. Mc-Caleb was nowhere to be found, but, to the grim satisfaction of Keith's mother just down the road, her son, her daughter-in-law, and "at least ten brazen men of their company" alledgedly burned to the ground the house, outside of which the widow had taken her final look at her doomed husband.[1]

According to rebel neighbors, the Blalocks went on an orgy of "ransacking farms and killing Home Guards" throughout March 1865.[2] With the Grandfather and Blowing Rock teeming with unionists suddenly more willing to fight now that the end of the Confederacy seemed at hand, the Blalocks raided—always referred to as "scouted" in Minihan's reports—in bands of fifty or more.

Keith sent back reports to the 10th Michigan of Confederate activity in Watauga and Caldwell Counties and in March, his and fellow scouts' information gathered throughout the Blue Ridge had taken on increasingly vital importance to Grant, Sherman, and Stoneman. Stoneman's much anticipated thrust into western North Carolina was imminent, with Grant slowly and bloodily battering Lee's men in the trenches fronting Richmond and Petersburg, Virginia, and with Sherman poised to unleash his bummers' doses of total war from South Carolina into North Carolina. Stoneman's crucial task was to storm through the mountains of the Blalocks' home counties, cross into Virginia, and destroy as much as possible of the east Tennessee and Virginia Railroad, one of Lee's scant two extant supply lines. The federal cavalry would plunge south into the Piedmont of North Carolina to tear apart Lee's only other supply route, the Greensboro-Danville Railway.

Stoneman's force was composed of over six thousand tough, aggressive cavalrymen, including the 10th Michigan, men whom the general fondly called his "Cossacks."[3] Many were mountain unionists, some recruited by and piloted to federal lines by Keith and Malinda. As these hardened men prepared to return to their homes counties, they would embrace the same savage credo that had been used by a rebel to describe the Blalocks: "Now that the tables were turned and [rebel] families were at their mercy, they repaid what they had suffered."[4]

Grant, impressed by the devastating work of Sherman's bummers, informed Stoneman that his primary mission was "to destroy" anything that Lee or Johnston could use.[5] The sooner the better suited Grant, who, on March 1, urged Stoneman to hurry up. Still rounding up every available horse for the mission (no easy task after four years of horse stealing by Union and rebel forces alike in the region), Stoneman replied: "You [Grant] cannot be more anxious to get me off than I am to go."[6] From their perches along Blowing Rock and the Grandfather, no one was more anxious for the federal columns to appear in Watauga's passes than the Blalocks, who, with Hartley, Church, and the other proven scouts from the Blue Ridge, would guide the Union cavalry into Watauga County.

Keith and Malinda were waiting at Sugar Grove at 5 A.M. on March 28, 1865, when Stoneman's vanguard, the 12th Kentucky, crossed into North Carolina. The moment the couple had so long anticipated emerged as file after file of blue-uniformed troopers, "stripped down for fast action," flooded into the Blalocks' county.[7] Keith and Malinda helped pilot Stoneman's horde just north of Banner Elk, a friendly territory where, of the fourteen men of the hamlet who had fought in the conflict, thirteen had enlisted in federal regiments, several having signed recruitment papers proffered by Keith.

Just before noon, Stoneman's column reached Boone, in the shadow of the Grandfather. Keith, Malinda, and Hartley rode into town with Major Keogh, an aide-de-camp to Stoneman, with a hundred men of the 12th Kentucky. An equal number of Home Guards had mustered in the center of town in front of the Boone Courthouse, not because they had any idea that federal troops had crossed the mountain, but simply to ride out against a gang of bushwhackers.

One of the rebels, Calvin Green, recognized the Blalocks, and believing that the Union cavalry comprised a band of raiders and not the first of six thousand soldiers, fired at them. Dozens of rebels joined in as others ran into a house and unloosed a volley that blew a Kentuckian from his saddle.

Keogh ordered a charge, and the cavalrymen pounded straight at the Home Guards, snapping off Spencer and pistol fire as they ran down the rebels. Keith may have downed Warren Green "with a heart shot" in the federals' first volley.[8]

Behind the Blalocks and the other riders of Keogh's advance detachment, waves of blue-uniformed cavalrymen surged into Boone, blasting away at windows, and, as Malinda recalled, "pretty near shot up the whole town."[9]

Stunned by the federal numbers, most of the guards fled in all directions. But several still mounted a fierce fight. Calvin Green, a cousin of Lott Green, blew off a Kentucky trooper's arm as several riders converged on him. Keith reportedly was one of those who put a bullet in him; so did several other riders, leaving Green for dead.

Fifteen-year-old Steel Frazier, who had just joined the guards, was chased by six cavalrymen through several backyards. Armed with a Colt revolver, he turned around an instant before reaching the forest at Boone's edge and killed two of his pursuers with two shots. Then he fled into the woods, where he knew the trails and the stunned cavalrymen had no chance to find the fleet youth. He was fortunate that the Blalocks, who knew the terrain as well as Frazier, were still hunting for any other Greens in the center of town. Sheriff A. J. McBride, who had known Keith and Malinda since childhood, was hit in the chest near the heart, "but the ball followed a rib and lodged near his spine."[10] A federal surgeon removed the lead without any sort of anesthetic, and McBride would recall: "The fight got real hot for a few minutes, and a lot of us [the Home Guards] took shots at both the Blalocks. I do not know how they came out alive."[11]

One of Keith's purported victims, Calvin Green, was found still alive in the street where Keith had left him, was carried into a makeshift hospital at the house of Guard Captain Jordan Councill, and eventually recovered. Like his uncle Robert Green, the younger Green would carry, for the rest of his life, the evidence of Keith's fury.

In Stoneman's report of the melee, he recorded that "a detachment of the 12th Cavalry went forward and surprised and routed the rebels, killing nine and capturing sixty-eight" according to a local historian.[12] The Union losses were three dead and three wounded.

Keith was dismayed to learn the fate of Jacob Councill, the rebel captain's uncle and a man, as Keith noted, "who never bore arms for the Confederates and always was a friend to everyone, but died because he owned one slave."[13] As the fighting in Boone had ignited, Councill was plowing his field on the town's outskirts with his slave. As a squad of Union cavalrymen appeared alongside the field, the slave bolted over to them and cried out for them to free him from "my rebel master."[14] The soldiers obliged by gunning Councill down as he stood behind his plow.

The Councill family narrowly escaped another tragedy that wild afternoon. Mrs. Jane Councill, who had once been a playmate of Malinda and was married to the guard captain, had stepped with her infant onto her front porch just as the first shots were fired. Carbine blasts ripped into both sides of the door frame inches from her head. She ducked safely back into the house.

Furious at the resistance put up by the rebels, General Alvin B. Gillem, one of Stoneman's staff and an unabashed proponent of Sherman's policy of hitting civilians hard, ordered the cavalry to burn down the courthouse. All of Watauga County's historical records were destroyed in the blaze.

When Stoneman arrived to find the building a smoldering ruin, he rebuked Gillem. The embers of the courthouse, however, were a precursor of things to come from Gillem's command.

Stoneman next summoned Watauga unionists and scouts to his temporary headquarters, in Mrs. Councill's house, and based upon what Keith Blalock and others told him, decided that not enough forage for six thousand men remained in Watauga.

Keith and Malinda rode out that same day with the 10th Michigan, part of Colonel William Palmer's brigade, and helped guide the column through Deep Gap, in the Blue Ridge, and to Wilkesboro, Stoneman riding with them. The other two brigades took the Flat Gap road.

The brigades met on March 29, and the following morning, the Blalocks forded the rapidly rising Yadkin River, where several men of the 10th Michigan, the 15th Pennsylvania, and the 12th Ohio drowned in the churning waters. By Keith and Malinda's "standards" for a raid on rebel farms, Colonel Trowbridge let civilians off lightly along the route. Farmer James Gwyn wrote that the Blalocks' regiment "took only cattle & horses & mules & did not even enter our houses, or do violence to our families, & destroyed nothing but a little corn and oats which was thrown out to their horses. I kept out of the way thinking I might be taken off . . . but I need not have . . . they would not have molested me."[15]

A week later, a mission more to Keith and Malinda's liking emerged as they forded the Yadkin River again and rode north into Virginia on a scout of the terrain and any potential opposition awaiting Stoneman around Christiansburg, a key depot on the Virginia and Tennessee Railroad. Encountering only light resistance, Keith and Malinda "raided up and down the line" and, when the 10th came up, helped tear up their share of over one hundred miles of track and wreck several trestles and bridges.[16] "Burning down those bridges was one of the finest times he [Keith] had during the war," a Coffey relation would say.[17]

Keith, Malinda, and the 10th's other scouts skirmished with Confederate cavalry numerous times, and on April 8, on the Virginia border, they nearly galloped into a column of several hundred rebel riders and infantry. As Confederate volleys swept the road, the Blalocks and their squad turned and raced back the way they had come. The rebel cavalry pursued them, and now the Virginia troopers repeated the Blalocks' near fatal encounter by thudding toward two hundred and fifty of the Michiganders who had been riding just a mile or two behind Keith and Malinda's band and had galloped toward the guns' din. A short, sharp action followed before the Michigan men retired in good order. "That scrap was one of the closest escapes we had with Stoneman," Keith would remember. "We leaned forward on our horses as far as we could and just ran and prayed."[18]

Two days later, on April 10, 1865, the Blalocks were scouting near Salem, North Carolina, as the regiment, several miles behind, rode with orders to destroy the bridge over Abbott's Creek and proceed toward High Point, the site of a North Carolina Railroad depot. The Blalocks and other scouting parties came back with word that they had found no Confederate forces near the bridge or High Point.

Half of the 10th stormed into the town and destroyed the depot and a staggering $300,000 worth of Confederate supplies. Two hundred and fifty cavalrymen, with whom the Blalocks went, spent a hard night in the saddle on the ride to the bridge, but destroyed it without opposition before daylight of April 11.

As the 10th began to reassemble, pickets rushed up to Trowbridge to warn that they had skirmished with "a large body of Confederate infantry and cavalry" a mile away.[19] His men exhausted and, if the pickets' reports were accurate, faced with a rebel force four times the 10th's strength, Trowbridge had no choice but to push on toward Salisbury to rejoin Stoneman's main body. Posting a rearguard of two companies to delay the rebels, he "commenced to withdraw by alternate squadrons."[20] The Confederates, however, hit the 10th from behind and on the flanks. For six miles, they fought without letup; Keith and Malinda returned fire with their Spencers the entire route, taking down "not just a few" among the heavy Confederate casualties.[21]

Finally, aware that Stoneman's near-entire force loomed up the road, the rebels broke off the attack. The 10th reached the main body late on April 11 and bivouacked twelve miles north of the prize Stoneman had wanted all along—Salisbury, with its huge stockpiles of Confederate supplies and its infamous prison camp.

Along with the rest of the 10th, the Blalocks slept on the rain-soaked road beneath their horse blankets.

The citizens of Salisbury were terrified at the prospect of Stoneman's raiders seeking retribution for the horrors of the prison. Although all except the sickest Union captives had been evacuated in March 1865, thoughts of vengeance did fill many of Stoneman's men. From the escaped prisoners Keith and Malinda had helped pilot across the Blue Ridge, the couple had heard all about Salisbury's conditions: over ten thousand federal soldiers jammed into a cotton factory set on a mere six acres; the starvation and disease; the "dead house" where corpses rotted for days before burial;[22] and the infamous "cornfield" burial ground.[23] But as Stoneman's army finally took Salisbury on April 12, leveled the prison, and destroyed the enormous cache of supplies, the Blalocks had been sent with the 10th back to High Point to guard against any rebel assaults from that direction. The closest the couple got to Salisbury were their glimpses of the orange-yellow glow of the fires set by Stoneman's cavalry.

General Gillem gleefully ticked off the items incinerated by the flames: "10,000 stands of arms, 1,000,000 rounds of ammunition (small), 10,000 rounds of ammunition (artillery), 6,000 pounds of powder, 3 magazines, 6 depots, 10,000 bushels of corn, 75,000 suits of uniform clothing, 250,000 blankets (English manufacture), 20,000 pounds of leather, 6,000 pounds of bacon, 100,000 pounds of salt, 20,000 pounds of salt peter, 50,000 bushels of wheat, 80 barrels of turpentine, $15,000,000 Confederate money, a lot of medical [supplies] . . . worth over $100,000 gold."[24] Keith and Malinda, scouting at High Point instead of burning those massive stores at Salisbury, were "hugely disappointed to miss the party."[25]

A joyful development for the Blalocks and every man in Stoneman's army arrived with the news that Robert E. Lee had surrendered the Army of Northern Virginia at Appomattox Courthouse, Virginia, on April 10, 1865. Although General Joseph Johnston was still in the field with his army in central North Carolina, he, too, was beaten, by Sherman's men.

For Keith, Malinda, and the rest of Stoneman's raiders, the end of the campaign and the reality of victory were at hand.

On April 13, Stoneman ordered his troops west toward Tennessee. Keith and Malinda rode with the main body, which reached Taylorsville and filed into Caldwell County with nine hundred Confederate prisoners on April 15, 1865.

Keith and Malinda arrived near sunset in Lenoir, the very town in which they had enlisted in the 26th North Carolina so long ago. Now, they came back among "the Yanks [who] rushed in on us," according to Lenoir resident Mrs. George W. F. Harper.[26]

April 16, Easter Sunday, dawned sunny and clear, but Mrs. Harper lamented: "Oh! How unlike the Holy Sabbath, excitement, confusion, and hurry all day. Our poor prisoners seemed almost starved."[27]

Among those prisoners, "weary, ragged, many of them barefoot, sick, and almost dead of exhaustion" and jammed into a church and its grounds, was a man Keith Blalock had vowed to kill.[28] Major A. C. Avery, commander of the 17th Battalion and the rebel Keith held equally culpable as John Boyd in Austin Coffey's death, had been captured at Salisbury. Having glimpsed the Blalocks gallop by on the road to Lenoir, Avery was terrified that he would be recognized.

With many Caldwell rebels now prisoners, Stoneman allowed townspeople to begin "cooking, feeding them, and rounding up clothing for the wretched men."[29] One of them, Sidney Deal, a soldier in the 17th, "disguised him [Avery] with the help of other people."[30] Deal grabbed "P. A. Healon, a young boy running about," and sent him to fetch clothing from Mrs. J. C. Norwood, a relative of Avery.[31]

"Major Avery's beard was soon shaved," a Lenoir woman wrote, "and when he donned the clothing which the boy brought and appeared wearing only a mustache, even his own men failed to recognize him."[32]

Keith and Malinda waded into the prisoners that clotted the churchyard that Sunday, but failed to find anyone upon whom they were hoping to take revenge. Keith was told by a man who had served in the 26th that James Marlow had been killed near Salisbury.

On Monday morning, April 16, 1865, Stoneman sent a third of his army to Blowing Rock to escort the prisoners to east Tennessee, where other troops would march them off to Camp Chase in Ohio. Avery likely worried that he would never make it to Ohio when he saw that that the Blalocks were riding just a few feet away. His fear must have soared when Keith struck up a conversation with Sidney Deal, trudging next to Avery. Then Keith began talking to Avery, too. Deal would never forget the episode: "At Blowing Rock, Keith Blaylock [*sic*] befriended me and Avery, preventing our being harmed by other Union guards, all the while vowing that he would kill Avery the moment he laid eyes on him, not suspecting that he was at his side."[33]

Keith would never learn that he had talked for hours with the man who had sent Marlow and his men to arrest or kill Austin Coffey. Avery would go on to live a long life, raising a large family and running a successful law practice. He would always deny that he had authorized Marlow to execute Keith's stepfather.

Chapter Twenty-Four
Unfitting Him for Military Duty

WITH General Joseph Johnston's surrender to Sherman at Bennett's Farm, North Carolina, on April 26, 1865, the Civil War officially ended. Keith, however, could not return home until officially discharged; Malinda, who, despite her capacity as a scout for the 10th, could simply inform Captain Minihan that she was leaving, turning in her horse, uniform—her cap and tunic—her Spencer, and *"additional accoutrements;"* the items' total value listed at $400. But with "bands of lawless men, both Yankees and rebels, still killing in Watauga and Caldwell Counties," she and Keith decided that it was best that she accompany him first to Knoxville and then to Memphis, Tennessee, where the 10th would be garrisoned until the men were mustered out, issued their back pay, and sent home.[1]

In east Tennessee, Malinda and Keith parted for several weeks when she visited her relatives in Carter County to rest, start to grow her hair back, don skirts again, and, most importantly, resume—begin, in effect—her duties as mother to her son, Columbus, now two years old. "[Malinda] used to tell me that she met me at two," he told J. P. Arthur in 1910. "I was too young to think anything of it. She was the only mother I recalled."[2]

Before Malinda had departed the 10th with the blessing and thanks of Minihan, he told "Sam" that he "should file for a veteran's pension as soon as possible, as scouts were to be considered the same as regular soldiers."[3] Malinda did not ask if a husband and wife could both make pension claims. "She said that she had best let it drop," a relative would remember.[4]

In late July 1865, Malinda sent Keith a brief letter telling him that she and their son would soon arrive in Memphis, where she would stay with relatives on a farm just outside the city. When she met Keith a few weeks later, for the first time since 1861 she looked like "the girl he had courted and married, in petticoats, a blouse with a cameo on a chain, and a ribbon in her shoulder-length hair."[5] Keith, too, reacquainted himself with his son.

The man Malinda greeted in Memphis was ailing. Dogged by severe headaches and, Minihan wrote, "by the wound in the left wrist now totally disabling his arm," Keith spent most of his time in the infirmary or on his barracks cot.[6] Malinda, worried about him, would write, "I have to watch him very closely and he needs help to put on and take off his clothes on account of his bad arm."[7]

As Keith's injuries made it ever more difficult for him to perform the most mundane tasks of camp life, Minihan's concern for the mountaineer increased. He could not lead squads on scouting runs against bands of discharged federals and returning rebels stealing from local farmers.

In mid-October 1865, Minihan sent Keith to Assistant Surgeon Thomas Shaw to see if the Watauga soldier might qualify for an immediate disability discharge. The physician's report confirmed Minihan's view. "I [Dr. Shaw] certify that I have carefully examined the said William Blalock . . . and find him incapable of performing the duties of a soldier because of gunshot wound in the left wrist, also in right eye resulting in complete blindness in that member, all rendering him unfit for the Veteran reserve Corps or any other Military Service.

"I submit his case as being disabled to the degree of 3/4."[8]

Shaw and Minihan then filled out a Certificate of Disability for Discharge on October 18, 1865, and submitted it on Keith's behalf to Major H. W. Sears, now commanding the 10th Michigan. Minihan added that Keith's wounds were so severe that they were "disabling him to the extent of unfitting him for Military Duty."[9]

On October 21, 1865, Keith and Malinda received the welcome news that Sears had approved the medical discharge. "We were coming home for good," Malinda wrote.[10]

⚜

Before the couple and their son boarded a train bound from Memphis to Knoxville, Keith filed and signed a Declaration for Invalid Pension on October 28, 1865, listing his occupation as "a farmer" and requesting that, for the next three months, his mail be forwarded to "the Post Office address of Johnson's Depot, Carter County, East Tennessee," where he and Malinda planned to spend part of the upcoming winter with her relatives.[11] The claim completed, Keith drew $200 in pay from the quartermaster and turned in his Spencer and side arms.

As part of his claim, Keith stated: "I have never belonged to any organization in the Rebel service nor never did any Service therein."[12] He was already concerned that any reference to his stint in the 26th North Carolina might result in a denial or a reduction of his pension. His attempt to cover up his time in a Confederate uniform had commenced.

As the claimant's wife, Malinda was also required to provide the war department her personal assessment of her husband's condition: "About one half of the time," she wrote, "William Blalock is compelled on account of his injuries to remain in bed, at which times I have to wait on him continuously, and he is not able to do much of any thing for himself.

"I am the wife of William Blalock."[13]

"Minihan thanked me for my efforts," Keith later recorded, "and sent me home and told me to wish Sam Blalock well when I saw him."[14]

As the train steamed to Knoxville, Keith and Malinda's war had officially ended, both bearing the wounds of almost three years' worth of raiding and scouting for the union. But for Keith, wartime scores remained to be settled. One, in particular, obsessed him, and no matter the legal consequences, he was determined to take revenge for the death of Austin Coffey.

Shortly after the Blalocks arrived in Carter County, Keith strode into a general store and paid $50 for a Sharp's rifle and bullets.

CHAPTER TWENTY-FIVE
Is That You, Boyd?

E ARLY in February 1865, Keith and Malinda returned to Watauga County. Keith, despite his eye patch and his misshapen left wrist and forearm, "looked robust enough," according to James Green.[1] The Greens, the Moores, and the Blalocks' many other enemies in the region wondered if he intended to live peaceably or if he had other ideas. Meanwhile, he and Malinda temporarily moved in with his mother at Austin Coffey's home. For the first time, she and Malinda's parents met their grandson Columbus F. Blalock.

While Keith and other returning unionists warily eyed their neighbors, most people in the Blue Ridge tried to rebuild their lives. Virtually every family had seen husbands, fathers, and sons march or ride off with one side or the other, only to find death on distant battlefields or closer to home. Keith, James Moore, and even Malinda bore scars or crippled or missing limbs as graphic testimony to all that they had suffered.

In the months immediately following the war's end, a neighbor of the Blalocks wrote: "The great Civil War was over at last, and the harassed and impoverished people of Watauga and Caldwell Counties hoped for a cessation of hostilities and the burial of all animosities, feuds, and misunderstandings. Most men and women took heart of hope and began all over again. Ploughshare and reaping hook took the place of sword and rifle."[2]

Keith's "animosities and feuds" did not cool. And he and Malinda could not help but notice that much of the "law and order" below the Grandfather was applied by ex-Home Guards and returning Confederate soldiers at the request of the federal government. Whenever he left his mother's house, Keith always carried his Sharp's rifle. "There was no peace for Keith," a local wrote.[3]

On February 8, 1865, only a few days after the Blalocks' return, Keith and his former guerrilla comrade Thomas Wright set out on foot on a cold, clear afternoon toward the Globe Valley, Keith carrying his Sharp's rifle. They turned off a narrow path at the "head of the Globe," hid in a thicket, and waited.[4]

Earlier that day, John Boyd and twenty-two-year-old William Thomas Blair, a tough, broad-shouldered young man who had recently become engaged to Boyd's daughter Mary Elizabeth, set out for Blowing Rock to repair an old family cabin for the couple, who planned to move in after their wedding, on April 15, 1866. Blair, a year younger than Malinda Blalock and an old schoolmate of her and Keith, had been born and raised on his father's Watauga County farm.

Like Keith, Blair had seen hard service during the war. He had enlisted in Company E with fellow Watauga men and others from Ashe County and had soon found himself assigned to the 37th North Carolina Regiment. He was captured in action at Hanover Court House, Virginia, on May 27, 1862, and had been shipped north to the prison at Fort Columbus, New York, his war seemingly over. But along with several other Watauga men, he was paroled and exchanged at Aiken's Landing, Virginia, on August 5, 1862.

A rabid supporter of the Southern cause, Blair wasted little time in rejoining his regiment and fought in Stonewall Jackson's Second Corps. A Yankee Minie ball had plowed into his knee at the Second Battle of Manassas, on August 29, 1862, and he was sent back to Watauga to recuperate on his father's farm. Once home, he saw the able-bodied Keith Blalock strutting around the Grandfather as if there were no war on, and the wounded soldier of Jackson's famed Foot Cavalry added his voice to the many local rebels "suggesting" that Keith return to the rebel ranks.

Too seriously injured to ride with Bingham's men once Keith and Malinda unleashed raids throughout the mountains and the Globe Valley, Blair, helping his father as much as possible in their fields and orchards, carried his Enfield with him. The Confederate veteran was ready to take his shot at the Blalocks if they ever materialized on his family's land.

Keith and Malinda had reportedly shown up at the Blair farm in late 1864, but William Blair had returned to duty with the 37th, first as a teamster, then, though saddled with a permanent limp, as a soldier in the blood-soaked trenches of Petersburg, Virginia, in November and December 1864. Finally, with Lee's valiant Army of Northern Virginia battered and the war's end near, Blair's company commander sent him home, the rebel having done his fair share for the Confederacy. Reluctantly, Blair left the 37th.

Back in the Blue Ridge, Blair soon began spending time with Mary Elizabeth Boyd and almost as much time with her father once, to the shock of most people in the county, Keith and Malinda returned home to the terrain they had ravaged for three long years. Blair, who had experienced the war on some of its most sanguine fields, had seen and endured too much to be intimidated by Keith Blalock anymore; whenever John Boyd rode or walked the local trails, his prospective son-in-law, armed with a pistol and often a hunting rifle, usually accompanied him. He was prepared to use them against Keith if he attempted to bushwhack Boyd.

Keith Blalock and Thomas Wright heard voices drifting up the trail just after twilight and recognized them. John Boyd and William Blair appeared in a few moments, Boyd limping along with the aid of a cane, courtesy of a bullet lodged in his hip during a skirmish in April 1865 against Kirk's 3rd North Carolina Mounted.

The two men started and stopped at a sudden rustle in the thicket ahead and to their left. Before either could reach for the pistols concealed inside their heavy coats, Keith Blalock leaped from the bushes and pointed the Sharp's yawning bore at them.

Keith stepped forward to less than a foot from the pair, and Wright, also aiming his rifle at them, stepped onto the path. Keith asked, "Is that you, Boyd?"[5]

"Yes!" Boyd shouted.[6] He swung his cane at Keith's head, but Keith deflected the blow with his left wrist. Neighbors would later remark that Keith still seemed capable of using his "crippled" left arm when he had to.

Knocked backwards a few steps by the cane's force, Keith quickly regained his balance and pulled the trigger. The rifle roared and "knocked John Boyd first upwards and then backwards."[7]

Boyd fell on his back, groaning, rolled onto his side, and then lay still. "Blalock blew an enormous hole in Boyd's chest," Blair would testify.[8]

Keith ordered Blair to turn over his friend's body and watched for any hint of life. Satisfied that he had paid back Boyd for Austin Coffey, Keith and Wright strolled away, leaving Blair with Boyd's corpse.

Keith and his companion stopped at the first home they came to on the path home. Noah White, an old neutralist, let them in and was told by Keith that "I just settled with John Boyd and am going home. Tell the provost marshall that I'm responsible and that Wright never did a thing."[9] Then Keith hiked back to Austin Coffey's home and waited for the authorities.

The following morning, February 9, 1865, federal Major Frank Walcott entered Coffey's home with a squad of soldiers and Marshal A. C. Tyler, arrested Keith, and escorted him to a cell in the Morganton jail. "It looked for a while that Malinda would be getting a Union widow's pension," Keith related.[10]

Though Keith's enemies were enraged by Boyd's murder, they relished the prospect of watching Keith tried and hanged. There seemed no way that he could escape death this time, unlike his many brushes with it during the war. After all, even unionists who thought Keith entitled to have taken revenge on Boyd realized that William Blair had witnessed the killing. Some people wondered why Keith had not killed both men. That way, while suspicion would still have fallen on him, no one could have proved it. Keith himself answered the question, posed years later by a local historian: "My business was with Boyd only."[11]

The provost marshal at Morganton sent the case to the district court at Statesville, where any jury would be drawn from a populace whose ex-Confederates far outnumbered local unionists. Judge Emory Mitchell set the trial date for early March, but allowed Keith to remain incarcerated in Morganton, where Malinda, his mother, and his friends could visit more easily.

On the surface, prosecutor William P. Bynum had the quintessential "open-and-shut case." Blair's testimony before the grand jury in Statesville was devastating: "Keith Blalock bushwhacked us and shot down John Boyd, who was unarmed. Blalock had been hiding in the bushes."[12]

In an interview with Keith in his cell, Major Walcott heard about Austin Coffey's death and about Keith's service with George Kirk. Part of Walcott's duties as a military commissioner was to investigate "alleged persecution of Union men in Watauga County," and his superior, the federal Commander of the District of Western North Carolina, was none other than Kirk.[13]

Walcott soon informed Kirk that one of his ex-scouts and pilots was facing a noose in Statesville for "killing an infernal rebel and murderer in self-defense."[14] Claiming that Keith Blalock had fired only after Boyd tried to "kill him first with a heavy cane" and that Boyd had "weapons on his person," Walcott contended that "a clearer case of self-defense than Blalock's killing of John Boyd could not be made out."[15]

The Union officer further stretched credulity with his assertion that "Blalock is a Union man being pursued with malicious persecution."[16]

When challenged by a telegram from Kirk to explain the charge against Keith, Bynum countered that "Blalock killed Boyd since the war, but not in the discharge of any military duty or order."[17] Besides, Bynum wrote back, "the Grand Jury found true bills against him [Blalock]."[18] In effect, Bynum told Kirk that the federal Army had no say in Keith Blalock's case.

Kirk thought otherwise. Presenting the "facts" of Boyd's murder to Governor W. W. Holden, who had earned everlasting contempt from North Carolina Confederates for his antiwar stance—treason, in their eyes—Kirk wrangled a full pardon for his erstwhile scout.

Kirk went a step farther. At the officer's urging, Holden asked Bynum to open an investigation of the killing of Austin Coffey. But as passions ebbed, Bynum "failed to make out a case."[19]

In March 1865, Keith strode a free man from the Morganton jail. He and Malinda would "finally settle down."[20] The cycle of killing and retaliation had ebbed, but the old feuds would simmer in new ways for decades to come under the Grandfather.

PART FIVE

Hospitable and Highly Regarded
or
The Terror of This Town

CHAPTER TWENTY-SIX
A War of Words

🖋

THE notes of a skilled fiddler sent couples dancing across the main hall of a rambling but well-built log and stone house. In the flickering light of the wood fire banked in "the big stone fireplace," the couples, young and old, were bathed in "a suitable glow for love's wooings."[1] Outside, on the "long, lighted piazza," men and women sipped punch or corn whiskey, laughter rising up toward the Grandfather on the crisp clear April evening in 1879.[2]

One of the guests, law student Shepherd M. Dugger, lauded the hosts as "a very wholesome family, generous and hospitable and highly regarded."[3] The "mistress of the domicile," nearing forty and the mother of four boys, was still trim and pretty, something of an achievement in a region where many women of thirty looked twice their age from work, worry, and childbearing.[4] Her husband, tall and gray about the temples, had a commanding aspect to him.

Shepherd Dugger's hosts were Keith and Malinda Blalock, and to all appearances from the young man's idyllic words, the turmoil of the Civil War had lifted from that household some fifteen years since the last shots. The image belied the truth. While a convivial occasion, the guests carried such names as Banner, Wright, and Kirk, unionists and their children, not a Moore or a Green among them.

Keith and Malinda had indeed settled down in comparison to their past deeds and misdeeds. He was a farmer and a store owner and had bought a considerable amount of acreage in Watauga, Mitchell, and Caldwell Counties. Prominent in Republican politics, the logical party of choice for any of the region's ex-Union soldiers, he had run for a seat as Mitchell County's candidate for the state legislature in the summer of 1874. In the newspapers from Raleigh to nearby Bakersville, he had been heralded as the election's winner: the August 20, 1874, *Raleigh Era* proclaimed that "Blalock, Republican, is elected for Mitchell County over both of his competitors."[5] However, the ballots from the county's northeast district, "a hotbed of unrepentant and fiercely Confederate voters," had not yet been counted, and when they were, Keith lost by a mere fifteen votes to Democrat Moses Young.[6]

Keith remained, nonetheless, a strong Republican voice in the Blue Ridge, penning bluntly worded opinion pieces to the local newspapers.

The Moores, Greens, and Boyds had not only seen Keith get away with literal murder, but now they had also seen him just miss out on a seat in Raleigh—on "representing" some of them. Although neither they nor the Blalocks had resorted to gunplay to resolve their feuds, many locals' memories of the Blalocks' raiding in their blue uniforms remained as vivid as ever. That would never change, but the couple's enemies had begun fighting them with another weapon: words.

Nothing about the Blalocks rankled Confederate neighbors more than the wounded veteran's pension Keith had been drawing since February 26, 1865; Malinda had cashed the first installment of $60 less than three weeks after Keith had gunned down John Boyd.

The Blalocks had used much of the disability money to buy land and to build their home and, because of the stipend, were in far better financial shape than most of their neighbors. By 1873, when Keith's allotment rose to $140 a month, Ben and Lott Green and Jesse Moore began sending the war department letters that contested Keith's disability on two fronts. The first, raising Keith's earlier concerns, apprised the pension bureau that both Blalocks had served in the 26th North Carolina, the couple's ex-Confederate neighbors hoping that the fact would result in all or some of the Blalocks' money sliced.

The second printed campaign centered around the "nature of Blalock's wounds."[7] His old enemies asserted that Keith had suffered his shattered wrist and lost eye not in his official military duties, but in bushwhacker's raids.

In October 1874, Keith received a war department letter stating that he must refile his disability claim "as several men have questioned its authenticity."[8] Keith, to his doubtless fury, was compelled to swear out an affidavit in the Mitchell County Superior Courthouse in front of the clerk, John H. Greene. Brazenly, Keith testified: "I was late of Company D, 10th Michigan Cavalry and was never in the Rebel army."[9] He stated that all of his wounds were "in the U.S. Service."[10]

Keith caught a huge break for the moment when a clerical error maintained that he had reputedly fought in Company I of the 29th North Carolina, but when the company's former captain was queried about Blalock, the officer said that "never to my certain knowledge was [Blalock] a member or belonged to my company and regiment."[11]

Shortly after the documents were filed, Keith's pension was reapproved. The war of words, however, had just begun.

Confederates of the region launched their next attack on the Blalock pension in February 1875. John M. Stafford, one of the few locals who had gone off with Company F of the 26th and had survived to tell of it, moved to Bakersville, in Mitchell County, in 1874 and eagerly lent his voice to the campaign against Keith: "I know that William Blalock and his wife both joined the Confederate service. He was a volunteer and stayed in the service for quite some time."[12]

Stafford also swore that he had been on leave in Caldwell County, his former home, and had seen "them [the Blalocks] raiding or scouting in the mountains there. I cannot imagine what military authority he was under when he was wounded there in a fight taking horses from Carroll Moore's house and he was shot by the Citizen Jesse Moore."[13] Stafford conveniently neglected to mention that "Citizen Jesse Moore" and his father had been Home Guards. As scouts for the 10th, Keith and Malinda had been authorized by Captain Minihan to harass the guards whenever they found them.

Right behind Stafford at the Mitchell County Courthouse on February 13, 1875, stepped Samuel M. Blalock, who identified himself as "a cousin of William Blalock."[14]

"At the commencement of the war in 1861," he said, "William Blalock entered the Confederate Service. He belonged to the 26th North Carolina Regent, and his wife also enlisted in the Confederate army dressed in men's clothes, and she assumed my name."[15]

The third man to testify against Blalock's pension that day was Carroll Moore, who swore that "the Blalocks were not in the line of duty when Keith Blalock was shot in the wrist and later the eye."[16]

Having heard the three statements, Mitchell County Judge Moses E. Jenks, a friend of the Greens, submitted to the Pension Office "my report in the Case of William Blalock, Co. D., 10th Michigan Cavalry," but did so without speaking to Keith.[17] The Blalocks, he wrote, had left their house near Bakersville six weeks earlier to spend time in a lodge they owned "about twenty miles in the mountains."[18] Rather than wait for them to give him their account, he wrote—correctly—that they "had served in the Rebel Army" and added—incorrectly—that Keith "received his wound while stealing horses."[19]

Jenks continued: "As to the circumstances under which he was wounded, it appears he was foraging, but whether he was acting with authority or leading his Company of the 10th on his own unofficial business will have to be seen.

"I [am] of the opinion that no evidence that is completely reliable can be obtained in this state that will prove that the prisoner was in the line of duty when wounded."[20]

The war department continued to issue Keith his pension, and, every year, received letters and affidavits contesting it. Showing that his experience in politics had taught Keith some verbal adroitness, he "qualified" his earlier testimony that he had "never served in the Rebel army" to he had "never served voluntarily."[21] He alleged that he had been "coerced to join, being threatened to be handcuffed and sent to the front."[22] Never did he mention at the courthouse how Malinda ended up in the 26th. The war department accepted "impressment" as a legitimate reason for a soldier or a sailor wearing an enemy uniform, gutting for good any claims that Keith's time in the 26th was grounds for revocation or reduction of his pension.

In January 1879, when the annual batch of letters and affidavits about Keith arrived at the war department, this time downplaying his Confederate service and focusing on whether his wounds occurred on official military duty, Keith was ready. He had written to Captain Minihan and Lieutenant Fields, and both former officers of the 10th Michigan sent the Pension Office sworn, notarized documents stating in unequivocal terms that Keith had been engaged in official "scouts" for the regiment when wounded.[23]

Keith could not claim that he had been "on a scout" when he had gunned down John Boyd in February 1866, but would always maintain that the act was "just." But in 1882, the Blalocks learned the identity of the man who had actually pulled the trigger on Austin Coffey—Robert Glass. J. Filmore Coffey, a relative of Keith from Foscoe, had stopped to spend a night at the cabin of John Walker, the man who had staged his own "capture" by unionist "partisans" to avoid further service with the Watauga Home Guard and the man who had refused Captain James Marlow's order to execute Austin Coffey. While sitting in front of the fireplace with J. Filmore Coffey, Walker revealed the actual events of that brutal February 1865 night in Tom Henley's cabin. Coffey, knowing full well what Keith Blalock's reaction would likely be when he learned the actual name of the man who had murdered Keith's stepfather, asked Walker if Glass was still in the region. The host replied that "Glass, after suffering much mental torture, died long before 1882 in Rutherford County," North Carolina.[24]

To John P. Arthur, J. Filmore Coffey "acquit[ted] both John Boyd and Major A. C. Avery of all complicity" in Austin Coffey's murder.[25] Keith, predictably, always maintained that John Boyd's identification of Coffey on February 5, 1865, and Avery's order—never proven—made the pair equally culpable as Glass in "the murder of the respected old man."[26] Keith's relatives speculated that if Glass had still been alive, Keith would have "settled accounts" with the man.

The Blalocks' chief battle remained with their neighbors fighting to close accounts on Keith's pension. Keith and Malinda may have thought they had finally fended off all of the challenges to the disability chit until 1888. When the pension of fifty-year-old Keith increased to $150 a month, the Greens and the Moores, who regularly saw Keith riding, hunting, fishing, and hiking through the Blue Ridge—always armed—devised another way to contest his government allowance. They queried how a man so eminently able to lead a vigorous life could be so disabled as he claimed. At the least, they argued, his pension should be reduced from "3/4 to 1/4 disabled."[27]

This time, forty-six-year-old Malinda went on the offensive. On April 27, 1888, she wrote a letter to the war department: "About half of the time, my husband, William Blalock, is compelled on account of his constant head pains to remain in bed, at which times I have to wait on him, at which times I have to wait on him continuously, and he is not able to do anything for himself at such times. Also, his crippled arm and wrist are at times filled of paralysis.

"I am the wife of William Blalock."[28]

Malinda responded to their neighbors' ongoing protest in similar fashion four years later, writing that "he [Keith] does need my regular attention, and, when the arm is especially bad, needs to be fed by me or one of our sons at meals and his clothes have to be put on him & taken off by me or the boys. Often, he cannot use his left arm at all on account of a Gun Shot wound in the Army.

"The above are facts which I know."[29]

The Blalocks, now living in a large two-story house near Montezuma, North Carolina, were winning the long-running pension battle, a fact that spurred Keith's enemies to petition the pension office with words that boiled with anger, frustration, and enmity:

Montezuma, N.C.
July 31st, 1894
To the Commissioner of Pensions
Washington, D.C.
My Dear Sir,
    Many citizens of this town think that certain things here are an imposition on the federal government and should be investigated. We wish to inform you in regard to the general character of William Blalock (known in this county as Keith Blalock), a pensioner, and family.
    We understand that his is drawing $172 per month pension. We also understand that his is represented to you as very much disabled and [illegible].
    Now we wish to inform you that Mr. Blalock is apparently as healthy and robust a man as any in our county of his age, 56 years, and has even been seen herding hogs eight miles from home and most of the time has been alone since spring, on account of his wife visiting relatives in Tennessee, and also spends much time in fishing day and night by himself, and that he has no mark of disability except the loss of an eye, which he received in a 'bushwhacker's' raid in time of the war, in Globe, N. C.
    For the veracity of the above we refer to Mr. James Moore, Post

Master, and Mr. M.L. Moore, Globe, N.C. These gentlemen will also inform you that he and his wife both served in the Confederate army until things got 'too hot.'

Mr. Blalock and wife now have a family of themselves and four sons who are a terror in this town. One son has already been prosecuted for carrying concealed weapons, shooting a man.

Another son is now bound to our next court for assaulting with weapons a hack [carriage] in the public highway, and also for carrying concealed weapons and misbehavior in the streets of town.

We also refer you to W.W. Clay, Justice of the Peace, who will inform you that he convicted Mrs. Blalock for carrying concealed weapons and assaulting, with weapons, a gentleman in this town on the 23rd just. Also write to Mr. Baumgarner, Mayor of Montezuma, who will inform you that he convicted the said Mrs. Blalock for disorderly conduct on the streets on the 21st Just.

Now we wish you to know that we are ready and willing to support the deserving pensioners, but we think it an outrage to give such rabble such an enormous sum, inabling [sic] them to violate the laws with impunity, to drink and shoot at night terrifying the laboring citizens and sleep during the day, all at the expense of the Government, while more deserving soldiers are drawing only $8 a month.

I remain yours in confidence,
Hiram H. Crisp[30]

The idea that the Moores and Hiram Crisp, except for Crisp having served in the Confederate army or the Home Guard, "supported deserving [federal] pensions" was laughable, and each of the Blalocks' "crimes" Crisp cited were overturned or dropped. "Carrying concealed weapons" in the Blue Ridge was a statute rarely enforced, as most men carried them everywhere. And Malinda was hardly the town's only woman who did so.

The man she allegedly assaulted was "one of the Greens" who had accosted Keith in the street at a moment "when his left arm was useless."[31] Malinda had pulled a pistol on the antagonist to scare him off.

In the case of Columbus Blalock and the hack that he had reportedly assaulted, the charges fell apart when witnesses testified that the driver had intentionally attempted to run over Blalock.

In Montezuma, where ex-rebels were the majority, their neighbors constantly challenged the Blalocks verbally and sometimes physically. The years had softened neither Keith nor Malinda, and they refused to back down or be run out of the town. Predictably, their sons knew how to brawl and shoot and had also been taught to stand up to any antagonist.

Although the pension office gave no credence to Crisp's litany of the

Blalocks' alleged crimes, the agency decided that another investigation of Keith's disability disbursement was warranted. To the excitement of all the Blalocks' local enemies, the couple received a summons to appear before Special Examiner of the Pension Office Nathaniel B. Miller on August 8, 1895, at the Mitchell County Court House, in Montezuma. Also summoned were Hiram Crisp and a host of the Blalocks' neighbors.

On August 8, Keith was called first in front of Miller. Keith was "duly sworn to answer truly all interrogations propounded to him during this Special Examination of aforesaid pension claim."

"I am fifty-six years old," Keith began, "and I have no occupation but fishing. I am the identical William Blalock who is pensioner under Certificate Number 5-8976."[32]

Staring across a desk at Blalock, whose hair was now "mostly gray and whose wound to the eye immediately ascertained," Miller asked: "What disabilities are you pensioned for?"

Keith replied, "A gunshot wound of my left forearm and a gunshot wound of my head causing the loss of my right eye, and resulting paralysis. I draw a pension of $172 per month."

"Please, Mr. Blalock, state all the military service you ever rendered, giving names of the organizations in which you served and the dates of enlistments and discharge from each one."

Keith's foes, who had carped for nearly thirty years about his stint in the 26th North Carolina and still maintained that his scouting for the union was invalid, eagerly awaited his reply.

He chose his words carefully: "I first signed an enlistment paper with Company D, 10th Michigan Volunteer Cavalry. I joined in the Spring of 1864, and my discharge certificate shows that I enlisted the first day of June that same year and was discharged on October 21, 1865, by reason of disability."

"Were you ever in the Secessionist Army, Mr. Blalock?"[33]

Obviously unwilling to risk a full-fledged lie, Keith offered something between a half-truth and a lie, trusting that it would all come down to his word against that of his foes and that as "an ex-Union man," Miller might be inclined to see things Keith's way. "No, I was never actually in the service of the Confederate army," Keith said, "but, yes, I was conscripted by the rebel army."

Keith knew full well that Company F's early muster rolls, which would have proven that he had volunteered—no matter how unwillingly—for the 26th, had been destroyed when Stoneman's raiders burned the Boone courthouse in March 1865.

"I went to Kinston, North Carolina, and reported to Zeb Vance, who commanded the regiment," Keith continued. "I did not want to go in and did not intend to if I could help it. I eventually pretended that I was not able for duty.

"I was not sick at that time, but had a breaking out at that time pretty much all over me."

"Were you examined by a Confederate doctor?" Miller asked.

"Yes, I think so, by some Doctor there, and I think that he told me to go home and rest up awhile. Don't know his name, but guess that he was a regiment doctor," Keith said. Hiram Crisp would later say that "Blalock knew full well who the doctor was, but was not about to give a name in case the man [the physician] might be still around somewhere."

"Did you ever swear the loyalty oath for the Confederacy?" Miller queried.

"Don't recall taking any oath—except the Union oath," answered Keith.

He added: "This was all that I had to do with the rebel army—except when they had me a prisoner three or four times after leaving them at Kinston and before I enlisted in the 10th Michigan Cavalry."

"How long was it after leaving the rebel army at Kinston, North Carolina, before you enlisted in the 10th Michigan Cavalry?" the special examiner pressed.

"I think it was something like a year," stated Keith.

Then, seemingly intent upon proving his disdain for the Confederacy and to better cover his term in the 26th, Keith went on: "I think it was something like a year. I don't remember the date I went to Kinston." Again, Keith knew all of the dates, but also knew that "his papers in the Confederate service" had been burned in 1865.

"I was captured by the rebel Home Guards," Keith volunteered, "but was only kept a prisoner for a few days each time because I'd always make my escape. At the time I was a prisoner, they threatened me with 'Castle Thunder,' which I understood to be a rebel prison in Richmond, Virginia, and one from which I'd never come home, as they said."

Miller would recall that at this point, "Mr. Blalock grinned and said to me, 'I told the rebels that they would have to get me there to the prison first.'"

Miller tersely continued: "Please state, Mr. Blalock, when and under what circumstances you incurred your gunshot wounds."

Keith was ready for this part of the examination, confident in his facts. "In August 1864, I was in Caldwell County, North Carolina, recruiting away as I was returning to my command, then stationed at Strawberry Plains, Tennessee. When I was passing near my old house, eight miles from here, on the new road leading to Blowing Rock, Watauga County, North Carolina, I was shot in the left forearm by rebel bushwhackers, and I ran and made my escape."

Now, Keith added a half-truth: "No one was with me at the time." A family member would later claim that what "Old Keith meant was that he was hiding all by himself in the laurel near his mother's house."

"I then scouted and finally returned to Tennessee and stayed at the house of Mrs. Lurene Stouts, on Shell Creek, in Carter County, Tennessee, and remained scouting and recruiting for the Union there for a month or more."

Miller asked: "And then, Mr. Blalock?"

Keith answered, "I think that I returned to Caldwell County, and there I met up with Captain Jim Hartley, of the 3rd North Carolina Mounted Infantry. He may have been a lieutenant then, not yet a captain, and he wanted me to take some federal soldiers and go and find out the location and strength of the rebel Home Guard supposed to be at or near Globe, in Caldwell County."

"Did you take this to be an order, Mr. Blalock?" Miller inquired.

"Yes, I was a Union soldier, and Jim Hartley outranked me. I took twenty or twenty-five men and went and did find the Home Guards at and all around the home and barns of Carroll Moore, himself a rebel."

"Is this where you were wounded again?" asked Miller.

"Yes, at Moore's we got into a fight, and my eye was shot out by one of the rebels."

Appealing again to Miller's "Yankee stripes," Keith said, "Some of my men that morning were recruits that I was going to carry through to our lines. They had taken the enlistment papers I had and would join the Union Army. You can ask two of them, Taylor Gragg and Joseph Milton Webb, who were with me. They're both of Caldwell County."

Miller now steered his questions from how Keith had suffered his wounds to how much he still suffered from their effects.

Once more, Keith was ready with his answers, and no matter how much his enemies in the neighborhood still contested the lingering effects of his arm wound, Miller would find Keith's report on the ravages of the "head shot" compelling as he looked at the eyelid folded limply across the ruined and sightless socket.

"At times," Keith offered, "the ball, which still remains lodged inside my skull, shoots pains all through my face, head, and mouth. They are so fierce that I am forced to bed until they abate. Whenever I catch cold, I can feel the ball pressing even more, and am completely blind with the pain at these times.

"While at relatives in Gillam County, North Carolina, I had a stroke of paralysis, and Doctor Bacon treated me and said that the bullet caused it and that because of my arm's near-useless condition since my gunshot wound there, the paralysis made the arm even worse."

"What are the other effects of your paralysis?" Miller prodded.

"Well," Keith replied, "ever since I had that first stroke of paralysis, since then I can't recollect some things, and I sometimes forget what I am talking about and can't even think of what I want to say."

"Does your condition prevent you from working much?" Miller queried.

"I cannot work any, not like I could," stated Keith. "I sometimes fish a little."

For the first time, Miller turned genial, "interested in Old Keith's fishing," Columbus Blalock would say. Keith responded as one avid mountain fisherman to another, not realizing that Miller's line of questioning went to just how badly affected Keith's old arm wound was.

"How do you fish, with a net or a pole and hooks?" Miller asked, "smiling all the time now."

"I fish with a fly-hook and catch mountain trout," said Keith.

"Yesterday was a good one—did you go fishing? If so, what luck did you have?"

"Yes, I was fishing," Keith replied. "I had tolerably good luck and caught about ten, I think."

"Where do you fish mostly, and how far from your home?"

"My favorite spot these days is the Linville River, up about one mile from my house," Keith stated. Obviously understanding where Miller's questions were headed, Keith added: "I always take one of my sons' boys or else one of my nephews with me when I go a' fishing. If someone's with me and can watch over me, it's fine for me to go lots of days and even overnight once in a while."

"Does your paralysis also affect your coming and going in town so that you must be always accompanied?" the examiner asked.

"Well, it has been about a year since my last serious stroke of paralysis," Keith said. "I go about town unattended only when I'm able and only because I'm well-acquainted with it."

"At this point," Miller wrote, "I shook William Blalock's good hand and concluded the interview."[34]

Miller compared Keith's answers and his own impressions about the interview to those of a meeting between the pair shortly after the special examiner had read "the complaint letter of H. H. Crisp."[35] On August 7, 1895, Miller "went to the little town of Montezuma, North Carolina, and found that the pensioner [Keith] had gone fishing."

"Late in the afternoon," Miller would write, "Blalock came home with a string of fish, and I spoke with him a short while. He consented to come to the courthouse on the appointed date, August 28, 1895. He was friendly in manner, but guarded.

"I also spoke to his wife, who said she acts as his guardian, and she seemed anxious to discuss H. H. Crisp's letter and also agreed to come to the courthouse for an interview. I learned that she has a military record.

"At first look, the pensioner seemed to be enjoying good physical health, and I was surprised to find him drawing such a large pension."

The government agent added: "She [Malinda] is a sharp, shrewd woman and knows what it takes to get a pension."[36]

On the same day, Miller had visited with Hiram Crisp at his home, in Caldwell County. "Mr. Crisp's reputation for truth is only fair," Miller wrote. "But in this case I decided to explore further. He is also prejudiced against the pensioner's wife and family."[37]

❧

After concluding his courthouse interview of Keith, Miller "next called in Mrs. Sarah Malinda Blalock."[38]

Malinda began: "I am fifty-two years old, a housewife in Montezuma, in Mitchell County, North Carolina, and I am the wife of William Blalock and am also his guardian."

Blurring the true circumstances of Keith's enlistment in the 26th and the true length and nature of his and her own service in the Confederate army, Malinda testified that "my husband was conscripted, and I went with him to Kingston [*sic*], North Carolina, and think we stayed there for a bit—I can't recall how long—and my husband was sick in his tent and was rejected on account of disability and sent home. I then joined him on the way back."

Malinda did reveal to Miller that she had cut her hair, enlisted as "Little Sammy Blalock," and had revealed her gender to Zeb Vance.

"Were you conscripted, too?" the examiner asked.

"No, sir," Malinda answered.

"What is your husband's mental condition?" asked Miller in an abrupt change of inquiry.

"A lot of times," she replied, "he don't know nothing, and then again he knows right smart. He takes it by spells."

Miller would note that "she was indeed a smart woman and had her answers prepared."

"Who of your neighbors would know of his mental condition for the last three or four months?" he asked.

She quickly responded: "James Loving, the postmaster, and Luther Matery, a merchant [a general-store owner]."

"Are they your friends?" the agent countered.

"Yes, they are our friends so far as I know."

"Mrs. Blalock, have you any enemies or evil wishers?"

If Miller had ever asked the same question around the Globe Valley, he would have found a long list of "evil wishers."

"I don't know of any," Malinda claimed, "except the Crisps. Joseph D. Crisp and his son Hiram H. Crisp have been threatening to stop our pension."

Miller paused for a moment and offered Malinda a glass of water, "which she declined." Then he resumed the interrogation.

"Is your husband's medical condition such that he requires the constant attention and watching of another person, or does he just require such attention periodically?"

Malinda knew exactly what was at stake, and her answer reflected the fact: "He does require watching all the time, sir, or at least he should be watched all the time. I have a boy hired to watch him when I can't be around. Adolphus Pritchard is his name, and he's my nephew.

"I have hired and kept him going on two years."

In Miller's final question of the interview, he abruptly shifted his verbal direction again. "What was your unit in the Confederate army?"

Unflappable, Malinda replied, "I don't recall exactly, but think we were with Company F, the 26th North Carolina. I think our captain was Ballew or Rankin."[39]

She knew full well that both men could never testify against her and Keith. The former Confederate officers had passed away since the war.

❧

As Malinda left the office and joined Keith outside, she saw Jesse Moore heading in the direction of the courthouse. For Moore's family and the Blalocks, the Civil War and the feud had not ended.

Moore's turn to testify would come later that day. Following Malinda into Miller's office for interviews in the agent's investigation of the Blalocks' pension were two of the couple's friends, James Loving and Luther Matery.

Loving, a congenial thirty-five-year-old merchant and the local postmaster, told Miller that "I [Loving] have known the pensioner for about four years."[40]

Loving went on, "My store and his dwelling are near each other at present. I have seen and conversed with him frequently, most every day or so, for the last two or three years. He frequents my store and post office."

"Do you know anything of his service in the C.S.A. [Confederate Army]?"

The storekeeper answered, "I do not know anything of his service in the C.S.A. except what I have heard others say."

Those "others," men such as Jesse Moore and Crisp, who had seen Keith and Loving as the pair talked about "every subject," firmly believed that Keith had told Loving every aspect of the Blalocks' days with Company F.

"Is Mr. Blalock a man of sound or unsound health and mind?" the examiner asked.

"His mind is sound so far as I know—if his mind is unsound, I have never noticed it," said Loving. "I have frequently talked with him about the West [he and his wife visited her relatives in California and Oregon a few years back], and he would tell me about the country and the blue mountains out there. He likes to talk about how he hunted along the streams out there and how clear and bright the sky was and how still and cold it was out there. Anyhow, hearing him speak and describe the country out there shows me that his recollection is good.

"In fact, I have heard him speak and express his opinion on various topics, and he has always impressed me as a man of good judgement on all matters."

Then Loving provided testimony that would have had the Blalocks' enemies, one of their fiercest awaiting his turn with Miller, shaking their heads. "Mr. Blalock is a peaceable, law-abiding citizen."

Still, Loving did admit that the Blalocks' "boys" had proven "rowdy and unruly" on occasion: "He has some sons who have not always acted as they should, but I don't think our people are prejudiced against him on that account."

The presence of Jesse Moore and, later, Hiram H. Crisp, both men pacing in the courthouse hallways, belied Loving's latter statement.

"Is Mr. Blalock's physical and mental condition such as to require the aid and attention of another person?" inquired Miller.

With words that would have received Keith's and Malinda's wholehearted approval, the storekeeper answered, "I believe that they ought to send someone with him when he goes about the town, when he goes away on fishing trips, and when he goes into the woods.

"Though I have seen him away from home two miles distant alone and unattended, I thought it would be better if he had help on account of his wounds."

In response to the question concerning Keith's "mental condition," his friend asserted that "[Keith's] physical condition is the problem, not his faculties, which are good."

Miller, pressing Loving about Keith's physical woes, posed a hypothetical question: "If Mr. Blalock were to stay at his house all day, would his condition require the assistance and attention of another person?"

Inadvertently, Loving stepped a little into the verbal trap. "No, sir," he insisted. "I think not. At least I see no evidence that he would require constant assistance inside his house. Except for the pain of his eye wound and the limits of his arm, he appears to be in very good health."

If Keith and Malinda had known what Loving would say next, thinking he was praising Keith, they would have undoubtedly been upset by their friend's well-intentioned but puzzling words in regard to Keith's "near total disability." Loving said, "Mr. Blalock walks about anywhere he pleases, often unattended. He walks and goes hunting squirrels, and I have seen him coming back from the woods with guns and dead squirrels within the last year, and never saw anyone with him. I have seen him out fishing by himself."

So had Special Examiner Miller.

Loving concluded: "I am not related to the Blalocks, nor an interested party to the pension, nor prejudiced."[41]

Loving's fellow merchant Martin L. Matery faced Miller's scrutiny next. After describing himself as "a forty-two-year-old general shopkeeper and personally acquainted with William Blalock for two-and-a-half years in Montezuma," Matery said, "I have seen Blalock almost twice daily in my store, where he trades with me, and have frequently conversed with him.

"I know nothing of his service with the Confederate army and know he got his wounds serving the Union forces.

"All I know of him doing since I have known him is to hunt and fish frequently."

Miller asked if the merchant thought that Keith's wounds were affecting his mental ability to take care of himself. "Sometimes," Matery opined, "I think that pain doesn't make the old man's mind always right. I have noticed in talking to him that his mind is occasionally wavy, first on one thing and then another. At times, his mind is exceedingly good, and at other times, when he says he is in pain, he appears off the track."

Questioned next about Keith's physical capacities, the shopkeeper said that, in his own opinion, Keith "needed attention all of the time."

"Very often," Matery added, "here in town I see him going about by himself unattended though in great pain. But when he goes out fishing or hunting, I think that Mrs. Blalock has a boy that she sends with him most of the time.

"I think that his physical pain is pronounced. His wounds do incapacitate him a great deal. He has bad spells sometimes with his head, where he still has a Confederate bullet."

Miller inquired, "How long since he had a bad spell?"

"About six months ago. He has spells of falling and epilepsy and at such times he needs a person around him at all hours."[42]

Wanting to talk to someone "with no prejudice of friendship or spite toward the pensioner," Miller called J. L. Carpenter, a farmer and "hotel man well acquainted with Blalock, having known him for thirty years and still seeing him daily."[43]

Carpenter contended that Keith had "got his eye shot out by the rebel bushwhacker Jesse Moore" and that "I believe Blalock's mental condition to be good."

"What do you mean by good?" asked the agent.

"Well," replied Carpenter, "Blalock talks with as good sense on most any subject as any man I ever talked with, and his judgement is good and ideas are correct, and if he has any mental derangement, I haven't discovered it."

Then, proving that he was no friend of the Blalocks, Carpenter volunteered that "it is the general opinion of people that he should get something for his war wounds, but many feel that he gets too much, too big a pension for a man who goes where he pleases and when he pleases.

"To me, he seems perfectly capable of taking care of himself and does not need the constant attention of others. Can't tell you how many times I've seen him hunting and fishing all by himself."[44]

Having solicited so much medical testimony from laypeople, Miller next summoned Dr. Walter C. Goss, a Montezuma "physician" all of twenty-four years old. "I'm not even sure the pup needed to shave yet," Keith would say.[45]

In an introductory statement to Miller, Goss said, "I am not a graduate of any medical college, but have attended two courses of lectures at the Tennessee Medical College of Knoxville and have been engaged in the practice of my profession about eighteen months.

"I am acquainted with Mr. Blalock and have known him about twelve months," Goss continued. "He and his family see me for their ailments, and I frequently converse with him. I have had to treat him some for the constant effects of his gunshot wound of the eye, cheek, and head."

When asked by the examiner about Blalock's soundness of mind, Goss said that "he is very much his own man and lives by his own rules. He is well-informed about politics and the law. As a matter of fact, I recall what Mr. Blalock said to me about a law that the Legislature passed against fishing wherever a stream runs through someone's property in the mountains.

"Mr. Blalock remarked that he had made a law of his own that allowed him to fish wherever God put them in the water. I have gone fishing and hunting with Mr. Blalock myself, and he is certainly a good hand at both. Though he really has the use of only his right arm, I have seen him take down partridges with a rifle at quite a ways off.

"He does need help because of his wounds, and I often see someone go with him when he fishes over at the Linville and Fox Rivers. But he does not have any regular attendant to go with him all the time. A little boy [Adolphus Pritchard] does accompany him some of the time."

Dr. Goss ended his testimony by saying that while Keith should have someone with him in the woods or at the rivers, he did not require full-time attention at home. "Mr Blalock is disabled, but not completely enough to stop him from doing what he likes to do."[46]

✒

As soon as Dr. Goss left the courthouse, Special Examiner Miller walked into the hall and informed Hiram Crisp that "his testimony would not be required."

Miller noted that Crisp "left quite angry, as I had decided that his testimony would be so prejudiced as to make it useless to my investigation of the pensioner's degree of physical and mental disability."[47]

If Keith and Malinda thought Miller would also dismiss Jesse Moore without a hearing, they guessed incorrectly. Their sixty-eight-year-old, lifelong foe brushed past them and into Miller's office; the door was closed moments later.

"I am a farmer in the Globe Valley, over in Caldwell County," Moore stated. "I used to know Keith Blalock and all of his family, who lived near me during the war years.

"I was a member of the Confederate Army Home Guards, under both Major Harvey Bingham and Colonel J. Walton."

Miller asked, "Mr. Moore, do you have any knowledge as to how William Blalock came by his wounds?"

Jesse Moore had waited decades for a chance to pay back the Blalocks and to put a legal stamp on his claim that it was he who had shot Keith Blalock. Now, with what Miller described as "extreme deliberation," Moore set out to do all he could to gut his old enemy's war disability pension.

"On the seventh or eighth day of January 1865," Moore stated, "I was near at the house of Carroll Moore with some five or six other Home Guards, mostly boys, and there was a party of a hundred or more Guards and some regular cavalry searching the roads for bushwhackers we knew to be operating around the Grandfather Mountain."

"Did you see Mr. Blalock that day?" asked Miller.

"I surely did—and his wife, the woman outside this room with him now. The Blalocks were at the head of about twenty-five other men, mostly deserters, bushwhackers, murderers, and robbers. Blalock had on a federal uniform, but I have never believed that he ever enlisted with them, though I do recollect that he and his wife often rode and bushwhacked with Kirk and his men during the war."

Miller replied, "I have records showing that Mr. Blalock was a member of the 10th Michigan Cavalry and a scout for Colonel George Kirk."

Perhaps surprised, Moore said, "That may well be, but Blalock might have found some way to get his name on a paper without anyone knowing of it."

The agent did not respond to Moore's rejoinder and instead inquired about the action at Carroll Moore's and the manner in which Keith had been wounded.

"They tried to bushwhack us, but we had a pretty good notion they were coming, as I had spied Malinda Blalock heading up to a unionist hideout the night before. She was armed with a Spencer rifle and could use it.

"Near daylight, they attacked us from all sides, and I worked my way out into the yard, and the Blalocks and their band began firing at me. I had a rifle-gun and a musket, and I shot the rifle at them first and then the musket. We were outnumbered and trying to hold them until the Home Guards and some of Avery's men [the 17th North Carolina Battalion] could get to us.

"Blalock came rushing into Moore's orchard, and I shot my musket at him. I saw him fall to the ground with his gun, which he had drawn on me at the same time that I fired. My musket was loaded with Ball Buck [shot]. One of my shots took effect in his eye, which I have since learned resulted in the loss of the eye's sight. Don't think I have seen him since that day. Patterson Moore was shot by Blalock just before I got him, the ball cracking Patterson's leg in two.

"As soon as the bushwhackers saw I shot Blalock, all the rest fled."

Miller wrote of the "great interest with which I [Miller] listened to Mr. Moore's account," and then asked a question that Moore had certainly hoped he would get a chance to address.

"Did you consider Mr. Blalock a soldier in the service of the Union army at that time?"

Moore ripped into the subject. "Blalock and his wife were bushwhackers, he being a deserter, too. For him, the war was an excuse to plunder up and down the valleys and say he was a' doing it all for the Union army. The same with his men. They had most all been in the rebel army and had left it and had banded themselves together for the purpose of plunder and robbery. They had before that morning at Carroll Moore's place raided all over the mountains and robbed from good rebel people and some who had no side in the war. They [the Blalocks] robbed the rebel citizens, and that was the bushwhackers' object that day, same as always during almost the entire war."[48]

Concluding his screed against the Blalocks, but still surprised that there was documentary proof of Keith's Union service, Moore said: "It does not really matter whether Blalock signed the enlistment paper or not. Soldier or not, Blalock was a bad man during the war, and in place of staying at the front with the men he grew up with and who fought for the rebels, he chose to stay around here with his band of robbers and to plunder us people, good Confederates.

"There was a pension man here once," Moore added, "and he inquired into all this business. Don't know his name, but he said that he had the authority from Washington to reduce or take away Blalock's pension. It was some twelve or fifteen years ago, but it was dropped, on account, I figure, that the pension man was a Union man."[49]

In a case of classic understatement, Moore turned and said, "My feelings toward Blalock are not very kind."[50]

Miller, in his report back to Washington, stressed the matter of "insanity" and Blalock's pension case. When using the word, he was not referring to "Bedlam-style mental disability," but to a war department proviso that recognized erratic behavior brought on by chronic pain from battlefield wounds.[51] When Miller, in his interrogations for the case, had constantly queried the parties on Keith's mental state—"insanity" the era's all-inclusive term for any strange or erratic behavior—he was simply trying to assess whether insanity brought on by Keith's wounds was strong enough to qualify him as "mentally disabled by wounds."[52] Of course, Keith was in pain much of the time, his wounds all too real. But Miller surmised that some of it might have been an act to maintain three-quarters disability status. On August 30, 1895, Miller sent his recommendation in Keith Blalock's pension case to Washington, D.C.

Inv. Certificate. No. 5-8.976.
William Blalock.
(By Guardian)
Private Co. D.   10th Mich. Cav.
P.O. Montezuma, Mitchell Co. N.C.
Asheville, N.C. Aug. 30, 1895.
Sirs:

I have the honor to return here with the Complaint letter of H. H. Crisp dated July 31, 1894, and Bureaucrative of instruction dated Aug. 11, 1895, in the above entitled claim and my preliminary report therein.

Went to the little town of Montezuma N.C. the home of Complainant and pensioner on the 7th inst. And found that complainant was in Caldwell county teaching school. I also found the pensioner had gone fishing. Late in the afternoon pensioner came home with a string of fish and as I could not learn, of any one, the service nor certificate. No. of claims, I thought it advisable to call upon pensioner for the desired information, which I did on the next morning. I also took a statement from his wife, who is his guardian, as she *seemed anxious to make one, and learned that she has both a Rebel and Federal military record. I was surprised to find the pensioner drawing $172 per month and enjoying good physical health and what I call a high intellect.*

I also called up four other persons who live within 150 yards of pensioner, and took a deposition from each. All these witnesses bear good reputations, but Martin L. Matery was very much biased in pensioners' favor. Pensioner trades at his store and he has a financial interest indirectly in the pension.

Later on while in Caldwell County I found complainant Crisp and his deposition appears herewith. His reputation for truth is only fair, but in this case he is entitled to some credence. He is also prejudiced against the entire family of the pensioner.

There was but one Doctor living near pensioner, Dr. Goss, whose deposition appears herewithin.

Other evidence of the same character could be had and no doubt but what the Guardian could go out and procure evidence showing that her husband is a "raving maniac." She is an intelligent and resourceful woman who knows all about a military and disability pension. Notwithstanding she could probably get such evidence, the facts in this case are different.

His alleged insanity or mental incapacity is simply a fraud, a pretense, a scheme, a hoax, and a great imposition on this Government.

A man who is an expert fisherman and squirrel-hunter and talks with the sense pensioner does, certainly does not require the regular and constant attention and aid of another person.

I do not believe that he requires frequent and periodical attention.

It certainly is not the purpose nor spirit of the board to furnish a pensioner an attendant while he goes out on a hunting or fishing excursion.

I am of the opinion that this pension should be reduced to $130 per month. I am quite sure it should be reduced to $150 if not to $130.

If it should become necessary to order this pensioner examined by a Board of Surgeons he should not be sent before the Board at Boone, N.C. for the President of that Board has a very great desire that the consent not be maintained. (I learned this indirectly.) I believe pensioner feigned insanity when before the last Board.

So far as his being declared insane by any County Court, it does not preclude the Government.

It is an easy matter to have any person adjudged insane in N.C. if that person and his wife and four sons all favor it.

Nothing is so easy and so cheap as manufacturing evidence. I learned of another pensioner in the same county who was going to have the Court declare him insane, and his object is apparent to even a one-eyed man. I shall keep my eye on him and will see how he succeeds.

I recommended that action be taken to reduce this pension to at least $150 if not $130.

I think the question as to incurrence of wounds in service and line of duty has once been settled by Special Examination. The pensioner did suffer his wounds in the service of the U.S. Army in the late war. Very respectfully

> N. B. Miller
> Special Examiner[53]

The pension office reduced Keith's pension, but only to $150. Moore, Crisp, and the Blalocks' other rebel neighbors had won a small victory, but it did not last long. By 1900, Keith's pension was raised back to three-quarter disability status, $175 per month.

The 1895 investigation was the last attempt by former Confederates to contest Keith Blalock's pension. He would draw it for the rest of his life.

In 1895, slowly, arguably for the first time in three decades since the couple rode with the 10th, the Civil War was finally ending for Keith and Malinda. Their neighbors began to leave them alone, and the Blalocks granted them the same hard-won courtesy.

EPILOGUE

O N March 19, 1903, sixty-one-year-old Malinda Blalock died peacefully in her sleep of natural causes. "Keith was with her when she passed," a friend wrote.[1]

She was buried in the Montezuma Community Cemetery.

Devastated by her death, Keith moved from Montezuma to nearby Hickory to live with his son Columbus and his family. Within weeks of Malinda's death, Keith began acting erratically, leading Columbus to seek legal guardian status over his father. To the pension office, Columbus wrote: "We have to watch him wherever he goes at all times because he has become so confused about all things. I have to watch him very carefully and help him put on and take off his clothes when nature calls. He has always loved to fish, but now he seems to have a mania for fishing and having gone [local vernacular for wandering with no purpose], and though one of us is usually with him, he, when we tell him we must go home, insists that the opposite direction from his home is the proper road leading home.

"He sometimes tries to slip off from me, and I have to watch him even more closely.

"Sometimes I am unable to induce him to come home until after dark and am much worn and tired persuading and pulling him home.

"The statements contained in this affidavit were with him in my presence."[2]

On May 22, 1903, less than two months after Malinda's death, Commissioner of Pensions Wilder appointed Columbus Blalock the guardian for Keith, "the pensioner having been adjudged of unsound mind and want of understanding entirely incompatible to managing his own affairs."[3]

Keith recovered within a year, and neighbors remarked how strong he was despite "the arm and head pains that he suffered."[4] Now, he no longer needed his family watching his every step and indulged his solitary passions, fishing and hiking. "Just Old Keith Blalock and his rifle and pole," the *Bakersville Observer* would note in a 1908 piece on colorful characters of the region.[5]

Keith took up another pursuit that even his rough-and-tumble family found startling, given his advancing years and his old wounds. Early in the morning, he would pilot a small railroad handcar that he had purchased and would dash along miles of mountain tracks, pumping the vehicle furiously with his one good arm on hairpin turns and dips and rises on the rails. Although his hair had gone completely gray, he still possessed the muscular build and stamina, when his wounds were not afflicting him, of a man half his age.

Keith walked the several miles to the Montezuma Cemetery nearly every day to visit Malinda's grave, and at least once a year from 1903 to 1913, he traveled up the Grandfather and camped for several days, walking the trails and visiting the haunts of his and Malinda's youth. The Globe, scene of so much death and depredation more than half a century ago, stretched tranquilly below him, most of his old rebel foes there now in their graves, like Malinda.

On the morning of April 11, 1913, seventy-seven-year-old Keith Blalock rolled his handcar onto the tracks in Hickory and churned off as usual. As he negotiated a tricky mountain curve several miles outside town, he picked up too much speed, overshot the bend, and careened off the tracks into a gorge. The handcar landed in a tangled heap on top of Keith, crushing him to death if the fall had not already killed him.

Keith's violent death somehow seemed fitting to those who had loved or hated him most. And, after his lifetime of feuds throughout the Blue Ridge, many locals found it hard to believe that Keith Blalock had died in a simple, though brutal, accident. For years, some neighbors would claim that several men of John Boyd's family had been seen at the site of Keith's plunge a few hours before he veered off the tracks. Other people said it was the Moores. Both families vehemently denied the rumors, and nothing came of them. That no one from these two clans or that of the Greens mourned him was never denied.

Keith Blalock was buried alongside Malinda on April 14, 1913. For his sons, one final task for their late father remained. They informed the pension office that "the Old Man W. M. Blalock of this place died on the 11th of August 1913."[6]

Today, depending on which descendants of the Blalocks, the Coffeys, and the other Blue Ridge clans one speaks with, the mention of Keith and Malinda elicits praise or denunciation. Soldiers in blue and gray, bushwhackers, loyal unionists, Confederate traitors—all of these labels have described the Blalocks. Another term fits them best: a devoted couple.

The epitaph on Keith Blalock's gravestone would have enraged him:

SOLDIER
26TH NORTH CAROLINA INFANTRY
C.S.A.

Placed on Keith's gravestone by the North Carolina Confederate Veterans Burial Index Project several years ago, the words are technically true. From David Moore, however, came a more fitting epitaph for William McKesson "Keith" Blalock: "He was a Union man from the beginning to the close of the war."[7]

ENDNOTES

CHAPTER 1

1. John C. Inscoe, "Mountain Masters: Slaveholding in Western North Carolina," *North Carolina Historical Review*, April 1984, pp. 145–146.

2. John C. Campbell, *Southern Highlander*, p. 90.

3. Emma Bell Miles, *The Spirit of the Mountains*, p. 140.

4. Miles, pp. 18–19.

5. Cecil J. Sharp, *English Folk Songs from the Southern Appalachians*, p. 98.

6. Robert Coles, *Migrants, Sharecroppers, Mountaineers*, p. 241.

7. Sharp, p. 124.

8. Ibid.

9. Miles, p. 150

10. Ibid.

11. Ibid.

12. Campbell, p. 183.

13. Miles, p. 98.

14. Campbell, p. 179.

15. Miles, pp. 98–102; Phillip Shaw Paludan, *Victims: A True Story of the Civil War*, p. 19; Campbell, *Southern Highlanders*, pp. 176–180.

16. Ibid.

17. Ibid.

18. Ibid.

19. Miles, p. 58.

20. Ibid.

21. Campbell, p. 111–112.

22. Paludan, p. 25.

23. Ibid.

24. A. S. Merrimon, *Journal, 1853–1854*, pp. 310–311.

25. Ibid., pp. 325–326.

26. *Official Records of the Civil War*, Series 2, Volume 1, p. 386; *New York Tribune*, August 10, 1871, p. 2.

27. John P. Arthur, *Western North Carolina*, p. 333..

28. Ted Blalock, Jr., "Keith and 'Sam' Blalock," Avery County Heritage, 1901, p. 8.

29. Ibid.

30. "Malinda Blalock to John P. Arthur," (undated, c. 1900), William Eury Collection.

31. Coles, pp. 203–204.

32 Miles, pp. 17–18.

33. Coles, pp. 23–24.

34. Miles, p. 65.

35. Miles, pp. 64–69.

36. Ibid.

37. "Jesse Moore to John Benton," October 24, 1878, Record Group 15, National Archives, Washington, D.C.

38. Miles, p. 66.

39. Ibid.

40. Ibid., p. 64–69.

41. Ibid.

42. Paludan, p. 15.

43. Ibid.

44. Miles, p. 16.

45. "Sarah Robertson to John P. Arthur," 1899, William Eury Collection.

46. Ibid.

47. "Keith Blalock to John P. Arthur," 1910, William Eury Collection.

48. "Keith Blalock to J. H. Greene," July 8, 1876, Record Group 15, National Archives, Washington, D.C.
49. C. Dowd, *Life of Zebulon B. Vance*, p. 86.
50. Author's interview with Murray Coffey, April 11, 1998.
51. Ibid.

CHAPTER 2

1. Emma Miles, *The Spirit of the Mountains*, p. 18.
2. John P. Arthur, *Western North Carolina*, p. 333.
3. Ted Blalock Jr., "Keith and 'Sam' Blalock," p. 1.
4. Ibid.
5. A commonly used nineteenth-century Blue Ridge term for "hen-pecked."
6. "Keith Blalock to J. H. Greene," November 3, 1874, Record Group 15, National Archives, Washington, D.C.
7. Robert Paul Ambrose, "A Critical Year (April 1860-April 1861)," p. 15.
8. "Keith Blalock to J. H. Greene," November 3, 1874, Record Group 15, Natonal Archives, Washington, D.C.
9. "Affidavit of Thomas O. Pritchard to J. H. Greene," December 15, 1874, Record Group 15, National Archives, Washington, D.C.
10. A commonly used term in the mountains during the Civil War to describe supporters of the Union.
11. William R. Trotter, *Bushwhackers*, p. 34.
12. Ibid., p. 35.
13. John P. Arthur, *A History of Watauga County*, p. 160.
14. Ted Blalock, Jr., p. 1.
15. Ambrose, p. 33.
16. Ibid., p. 37.
17. "Keith Blalock to J. H. Greene," November 3, 1874, Record Group 15, National Archives, Washington, D.C.

18. Ambrose, p. 22; C. Dowd, *Life of Zebulon B. Vance*, pp. 441-442.
19. "Vance's Speech," *The Asheville Spectator*, April 14, 1862, p. 1.
20. Ambrose, p. 22; Dowd, pp. 441-442.
21. Ibid.
22. Ted Blalock, Jr., p. 1.
23. "Keith Blalock to J. H. Greene," December 15, 1874, Record Group 15, National Archives, Washington, D.C.
24. Ambrose, p. 42.
25. A term used derisively by mountain unionists to describe secession.
26. Muriel E. Sheppard, *Cabins in the Laurel*, p. 65.
27. John G. Barrett, *The Civil War in North Carolina*, p. 10.
28. Ibid.
29. Nancy Alexander, *Here Will I Dwell: The Story of Caldwell County*, p. 127.
30. A term used derisively by mountain rebels to describe any unionist political candidate.
31. Alexander Jones, *Knocking at the Door*, p. 7.
32. Ibid., p. 8.
33. Ibid., p. 8.
34. Ibid., p. 10.
35. William Brownlow, *Sketches of Secession*, p. 17.
36. Sidney Andrews, *The South Since the War*, pp. 111-112.
37. "Keith Blalock to J. H. Greene," November 3, 1874, Record Group 15, National Archives, Washington, D.C.
38. Frederick Law Olmsted, *A Journey in the Back Country*, p. 226.
39. Ambrose, p. 42.
40. Alexander, p. 132.
41. Ibid. p. 129.
42. Ibid.
43. Ibid.
44. Ibid.
45. Ted Blalock, Jr., p. 2.
46. "Affidavit of Thomas O. Pritchard to J. H. Greene," December 15, 1874, Record

Group 15, National Archives, Washington, D.C.

47. "Keith Blalock to J. H. Greene," November 3, 1874, Record Group 15, National Archives, Washington, D.C.

48. Bud Altmayer, *A Family History of Watauga County* ("Keith and Malinda Blalock and Family"), p. 25.

49. Alexander, p. 135.

50. John P. Arthur, *A History of Watauga County*, p. 129.

51. Alexander, p. 129.

52. "Keith Blalock to J. H. Greene," November 3, 1874, Record Group 15, National Archives, Washington, D.C.

53. Interview of Levi Coffey by John P. Arthur, June 1912, William Eury Collection.

54. Author's Interview of Murray Coffey, April 11, 1998.

55. "Keith Blalock to J. H. Greene," November 3, 1874, Record Group 15, National Archives, Washington, D.C.

56. Interview of Murray Coffey, April 11, 1998.

57. "Keith Blalock to J. H. Greene," October 27, 1874, Record Group 15, National Archives, Washington, D.C.

58. Arthur, *A History of Watauga County*, p. 161; William R. Trotter, *Bushwhackers*, p. 150.

59. Ibid.

CHAPTER 3

1. Expression meaning only to give lip service to an oath.

2. *Official Records of the Civil War*, Series 2, Volume 10, pp. 841–849.

3. Nancy Alexander, *Here Will I Dwell: The Story of Caldwell County*, p. 132.

4. "Sarah Robertson to John P. Arthur," 1895, William Eury Collection.

5. "Affidavit of Malinda Blalock to N. B. Miller, August 30, 1895," Record Group 15, William M. Blalock, Pension File, National Archives, Washington, D.C.

6. "Jesse Moore to John Benton," October 24, 1878, Record Group 15, National Archives, Washington, D.C.

7. "Malinda Blalock to N. B. Miller," August 8, 1895, Record Group 15, National Archives, Washington, D.C.

8. Ibid.

9. Ibid.

10. Ibid.

11. "James Moore to John Benton," October 24, 1878, Record Group 15, National Archives, Washington, D.C.

12. *Confederate Veteran*, October 1898, p. 10.

13. *Roll of Honor*, Company F, 26th North Carolina Infantry, State Archives of North Carolina, Raleigh, "Private S. M. Blaylock [sic]," 1863.

14. David McGee, "The 26th Regiment of North Carolina Troops," p. 1.

15. "James Moore to John Benton," October 24, 1878.

16. *Diary of T. W. Setser*, August 1, 1861, Entry, State Archives of North Carolina.

17. *Roll of Honor*, Company F, 26th North Carolina, "Private S. M. Blaylock [sic]."

18. "James Moore to John Benton," October 24, 1878.

19. *Roll of Honor*, 1863.

20. "James Moore to John Benton," October 24, 1878; Jeff Weaver, "Hoopskirt for a Shell Jacket," p. 2.

21. "Malinda Blalock to N. B. Miller," August 8, 1895.

22. John P. Arthur, *A History of Watauga County*, p. 160; William R. Trotter, *Bushwhackers*, p. 148.

23. T. W. Setser, *Diary*, December 21, 1861, entry.

CHAPTER 4

1. "Affidavit of Malinda Blalock to N. B. Miller," August 8, 1895, Record Group 15, National Archives, Washington, D.C.

2. "Keith Blalock to Austin Coffey," April 25, 1862, William Eury Collection.

3. T. W. Setzer, *Diary,* February 1, 1862, entry.

4. "Letter of Keith Blalock to N. B. Miller," August 9, 1895, Record Group 15, National Archives, Washington, D.C.

5. Ibid.; "Letter of Keith Blalock to J. H. Greene," November 3, 1874, Record Group 15, National Archives, Washington, D.C.

6. Ibid; "Letter of Keith Blalock to John Benton," October 27, 1878, Record Group 15, National Archives, Washington, D.C.

7. "Keith Blalock to J. H. Greene," November 3, 1874, Record Group 15, National Archives, Washington, D.C.

8. Ibid; "Keith Blalock to John Benton," October 27, 1878, Record Group 15, National Archives, Washington, D.C.; "Keith Blalock to N. B. Miller," August 8, 1895, Record Group 15, National Archives, Washington, D.C.

9. Ibid.

10. Ibid.

11. Ibid.

12. Ibid.

13. *Roll of Honor,* Company F, 26th North Carolina Infantry, 1863, State Archives of North Carolina, Raleigh.

14. "The Story of 'Joe,'" *Confederate Veteran,* October 1898, p. 10.

15. John P. Arthur, *Western North Carolina: A History from 1730–1913,* p. 333.

16. *Roll of Honor,* Company F, 26th North Carolina Infantry, 1863.

17. Ibid.

18. "The Story of 'Joe,'" *Confederate Veteran,* October 1898, p. 10.

19. "Malinda Blalock to N. B. Miller," August 9, 1895, Record Group 15, National Archives, Washington, D.C.

20. Ibid.

21. "Letter of Carroll Moore to the U.S. War Department," October 24, 1878, Record Group 15, National Archives, Washington, D.C.

22. *Roll of Honor,* Company F, 26th North Carolina Infantry, 1863; "Malinda Blalock to N. B. Miller," August 9, 1895, Record Group 15, National Archives, Washington, D.C.

23. "Malinda Blalock to N. B. Miller," August 8, 1895, Record Group 15, National Archives, Washington, D.C.

CHAPTER 5

1. "Keith Blalock to J. H. Greene," November 3, 1874, Record Group 15, National Archives, Washington, D.C.

2. "Affidavit of Adolphus Pritchard to J. H. Greene," December 19, 1874, Record Group 15, National Archives, Washington, D.C.

3. "Malinda Blalock to N. B. Miller," August 8, 1895, Record Group 15, National Archives, Washington, D.C.

4. John P. Arthur, *A History of Watauga County,* p. 228.

5. Ted Blalock, Jr., "Keith and 'Sam' Blalock," p. 2.

6. Arthur, p. 228.

7. Ibid., p. 229.

8. Ibid.

9. Jeff Weaver, "Hoopskirt for a Shell Jacket," p. 1.

10. "Keith Blalock to J. H. Greene," November 3, 1874, Record Group 15, National Archives, Washington, D.C.

11. "Malinda Blalock to N. B. Miller," August 8, 1895, Record Group 15, National Archives, Washington, D.C.

12. John P. Arthur, *Western North Carolina,* p. 90.

13. Ibid.

14. "Keith Blalock to J. H. Greene," November 3, 1874, Record Group 15, National Archives, Washington, D.C.

15. John P. Arthur, *A History of Watauga County,* p. 186.

16. Ibid.

17. "Affidavit of David Moore to John

Benton," October 23, 1878, Record Group 15, National Archives, Washington, D.C.

18. William R. Trotter, *Bushwhackers*, p. 149.

19. "Letter of Carroll Moore to the U.S. War Department," October 24, 1878, Record Group 15, National Archives, Washington, D.C.

20. Ibid.

21. "Affidavit of Jesse Moore to John Benton," October 24, 1878, Record Group 15, National Archives, Washington, D.C.

22. "Letter of Carroll Moore to the U.S. War Department," October 24, 1878, Record Group 15, National Archives, Washington, D.C.

23. Georgia L. Tatum, *Disloyalty in the Confederacy*, p. 114.

24. John G. Barrett, *The Civil War in North Carolina*, pp. 183-184.

25. Ibid.

26. "Keith Blalock to J. H. Greene," November 3, 1874, Record Group 15, National Archives, Washington, D.C.

27. "Letter of Captain Henry McCoy to Zebulon B. Vance," May 27, 1863.

28. "Keith Blalock to J. H. Greene," November 3, 1874, Record Group 15, National Archives, Washington, D.C.

29. "Letter of James A. Seddon to Zebulon B. Vance," May 21, 1862, Zebulon B. Vance Papers, North Carolina State Archives.

30. *Official Records of the War of the Rebellion*, Volume 18, p. 998.

31. "Keith Blalock to J. H. Greene," November 3, 1874, Record Group 15, National Archives, Washington, D.C.

32. Many North Carolina newspapers labeled William Johnson "Jefferson Davis's man."

33. Several North Carolina newspapers branded Vance the "Northern or Federal candidate."

34. C. Dowd, *Life of Zebulon B. Vance*, p. 87.

35. Ibid, p. 276.

36. Ibid.

37. "Letter of J. S. Brooks to His Sister," April 26, 1862, J. S. Brooks Papers, Southern Historical Collections, University of North Carolina, Chapel Hill.

38. "Keith Blalock to N. B. Miller," August 8, 1895, Record Group 15, National Archives, Washington, D.C.

39. Jeff Weaver, "Hoopskirt for a Shell Jacket," p. 2.

40. "Affidavit of Mrs. Mary Coffey to John Benton," October 25, 1878, Record Group 15, National Archives, Washington, D.C.

41. John P. Arthur, *A History of Watauga County*, p. 167.

42. Common expression of the era.

43. Interview with Murray Coffey, April 11, 1998.

44. "Keith Blalock to J. H. Greene," November 3, 1874, Record Group 15, National Archives, Washington, D.C.

45. David Dodge, "The Cave-Dwellers of the Confederacy," p. 519, National Archives, Washington, D.C.

46. "Keith Blalock to N. B. Miller," August 8, 1895, Record Group 15, National Archives, Washington, D.C.

47. David Dodge, "The Cave-Dwellers of the Confederacy," p. 519.

48. Ibid.

49. Ibid.

50. Jeff Weaver, "Hoopskirt for a Shell Jacket," p. 2.

51. J. V. Hadley, *Seven Months a Prisoner*, p. 246.

52. David Dodge, "The Cave-Dwellers of the Confederacy," p. 518.

53. "Malinda Blalock to N. B. Miller," August 8, 1895, Record Group 15, National Archives, Washington, D.C.

54. David Dodge, pp. 518-519.

55. Ibid., p. 518.

56. Ibid., pp. 518-519.

57. Ted Blalock, Jr., "Keith and 'Sam' Blalock," p. 2

58. David Dodge, "The Cave-Dwellers of the Confederacy," p. 518-519.

59. Common military slang of the era.

60. Common military term of the era.

61. William R. Trotter, *Bushwhackers*, p. 161.

62. "Affidavit of Adolphus Pritchard to J. H. Greene," December 19, 1874, National Archives, Washington, D.C.

63. "Keith Blalock to J. H. Greene," November 3, 1874, Record Group 15, National Archives, Washington, D.C.

64. "Malinda Blalock to N. B. Miller," August 8, 1895, Record Group 15, National Archives, Washington, D.C.

65. "Affidavit of McCaleb Coffey to John

Benton," October 24, 1878, Record Group 15, National Archives, Washington, D.C.

66. "Malinda Blalock to N. B. Miller," August 8, 1895, Record Group 15, National Archives, Washington, D.C.

67. "Affidavit of George Perkins to J. H. Greene," December 18, 1874, Record Group 15, National Archives, Washington, D.C.

68. "Affidavit of McCaleb Coffey to John Benton," October 24, 1878, Record Group 15, National Archives, Washington, D.C.

69. Ibid.

70. List of Deserters from Confederate Army, Watauga and Caldwell Counties, William Eury Collection.

CHAPTER 6

1. John P. Arthur, *A History of Watauga County*, p. 338.

2. "Keith Blalock to John Benton," October 27, 1878, Record Group 15, National Archives, Washington, D.C.

3. John P. Arthur, *Western North Carolina: A History from 1730 to 1913*, p. 171.

4. "Affidavit of David Moore to John Benton," October 23, 1878, Record Group 15, National Archives, Washington, D.C.

5. "Affidavit of Jesse Moore to John Benton," October 24, 1878, Record Group 15, National Archives, Washington, D.C.

6. A term commonly used in the North Carolina mountains during the Civil War.

7. "Affidavit of Joseph M. Webb to John Benton," October 23, 1878, Record Group 15, National Archives, Washington, D.C.

8. David Dodge, "The Cave-Dwellers of the Confederacy," *Atlantic Monthly*, LXVIII, October 1891, p. 519.

9. A common expression during the nineteenth century in the Blue Ridge Mountains.

10. John P. Arthur, *A History of Watauga County*, p. 166.

11. "Jesse Moore to John Benton," October 24, 1878, Record Group 15, National Archives, Washington, D.C.

12. Arthur, *A History of Watauga County*, p. 162, 169.

13. "Affidavit of Langston L. Estes to John Benton," October 24, 1878, Record Group 15, National Archives, Washington, D.C.

14. A phrase coined by Zebulon Vance in reference to North Carolina's hated Conscription Act of 1862.

15. The derisive term that North Carolinians applied to one of the Conscription Act's exemption clauses.

16. William R. Trotter, *Bushwhackers*, p. 40.

17. "Devices Practiced To Avoid Going in the Army," *The Historical Magazine and Notes and Queries Concerning the Antiques, History, and Biography of America*, IX, June 1871, pp. 400-401.

18. Ibid.

19. "Letter of Keith Blalock to J. H. Greene," November 3, 1874, Record Group 15, National Archives, Washington, D.C.

20. Ibid.

21. Ibid

22. Ibid.

23. Ibid.

24. "Letter of Carroll Moore to the U.S. War Department," October 24, 1878, Record Group 15, National Archives, Washington, D.C.

25. "Keith Blalock to J. H. Greene," November 3, 1874.

26. "Malinda Blalock to N. B. Miller," August 9, 1895, Record Group 15, National Archives, Washington, D.C.

27. "Keith Blalock to J. H. Greene," November 3, 1874; "Keith Blalock to J. H. Greene," April 13, 1876, Record Group 15, National Archives, Washington, D.C.; "Keith Blalock to J. H. Greene," July 8, 1876, Record Group 15, National Archives, Washington, D.C.

28. Ibid.

29. "Affidavit of Mrs. Martha Coffey to John Benton," October 25, 1878, Record

Group 15, National Archives, Washington, D.C.

30. "Keith Blalock to J. H. Greene," November 3, 1874, Record Group 15, National Archives, Washington, D.C.

31. A common military expression of the Civil War era.

32. David Dodge, "The Cave-Dwellers of the Confederacy," p. 516.

33. Ibid.

34. Ibid.

35. Ibid., p. 517.

36. Ibid.

37. Ibid.

38. Ibid.

39. Ibid., p. 516.

40. Ibid., p. 517.

41. John P. Arthur, *Western North Carolina*, p. 333.

42. "Malinda Blalock to N. B. Miller," August 9, 1895.

43. Ibid.

44. "Keith Blalock to J. H. Greene," November 3, 1874, Record Group 15, National Archives, Washington, D.C.

CHAPTER 7

1. "Malinda Blalock to N. B. Miller," August 9, 1895, Record Group 15, National Archives, Washington, D.C.

2. "Affidavit of Jesse Moore to John Benton," October 24, 1878, Record Group 15, National Archives, Washington, D.C.

3. "Affidavit of Joseph Webb to John Benton," October 24, 1878, Record Group 15, National Archives, Washington, D.C.

4. "Keith Blalock to J. H. Greene," November 3, 1874, Record Group 15, National Archives, Washington, D.C.

5 John P. Arthur, *A History of Watauga County*, p. 176.

6. Ibid.

7. Ibid., p. 161.

8. Ibid.

9. "Keith Blalock to J. H. Greene," No-

vember 3, 1874, Record Group 15, National Archives, Washington, D.C.

10. "Affidavit of Mrs. Martha Coffey to John Benton," October 25, 1878, Record Group 15, National Archives, Washington, D.C.

11. Ibid.

CHAPTER 8

1. "Keith Blalock to J.H. Greene," November 3, 1874, Record Group 15, National Archives, Washington, D.C.

2. Ibid; "Affidavit of Joseph M. Webb to John Benton," October 23, 1878, Record Group 15, National Archives, Washington, D.C.

3. Daniel Ellis, *Thrilling Adventures of Daniel Ellis, Scout*, p. 110.

4. Ibid., p. 73.

5. The term was used to describe the mountain escape routes for unionists (civilians) and Union prisoners-of-war.

6. John P. Arthur, *A History of Watauga County*, p. 227.

7. "Affidavit of William Voncannon to John Benton," October 25, 1878, Record Group 15, National Archives, Washington, D.C.

8. John P. Arthur, *Western North Carolina*, p. 614.

9. "Keith Blalock to J. H. Greene," November 3, 1874, Record Group 15, National Archives, Washington, D.C.; Arthur, *Watauga County*, p. 227.

10. "Keith Blalock to J. H. Greene," November 3, 1874, Record Group 15, National Archives, Washington, D.C.

11. "Letter of Malinda Blalock to Adolphus Pritchard," August 25, 1897, Record Group 15, National Archives, Washington, D.C.

12. "Keith Blalock to J. H. Greene," November 3, 1874, Record Group 15, National Archives, Washington, D.C.

13. Ellis, *Thrilling Adventures*, p. 86.

14. "Malinda Blalock to N. B. Miller," August 30, 1895, Record Group 15, National Archives, Washington, D.C.

15. Ellis, p. 90.

16. Ibid., p. 95.

17. Daniel Dodge, "The Cave-Dwellers of the Confederacy," p. 516.

18. Ellis, p. 101.

19. Common term of the region.

20. Ellis, p. 101.

21. "Keith Blalock to N. B. Miller," August 8, 1895, Record Group 15, National Archives, Washington, D.C.

22. Ibid.; "Certificate of Disability Compile by Captain James Minihan," October 21, 1865, Record Group 15, National Archives, Washington, D.C.; "Letter of James Minihan to the U.S. Sanitary Commission Army and Navy Claim Agency," November 10, 1865, Washington, D.C.

23. "Affidavit of Mrs. Mary Coffey to N. B. Miller," October 25, 1878, Record Group 15, National Archives, Washington, D.C.

24. "Letter of General Robert Vance to Governor Zebulon Vance," December 10, 1864, North Carolina State Archives.

25. Compiled Military Service Record of George W. Kirk, Union Army, Record Group 94, National Archives, Washington, D.C.

26. Ibid.

27. "Letter of Keith Blalock to J. H. Greene," November 3, 1874, Record Group 15, National Archives, Washington, D.C.

28. "Letter of George W. Kirk, 2nd North Carolina Mounted Infantry File," March 16, 1818, Record Group 15, National Archives, Washington, D.C.

29. William R. Trotter, *Bushwhackers*, p. 116.

30. *Instructions for the Government of Armies of the United States in the Field* (1863), Article LXXXII, General Orders 100.

31. "Letter of Carroll Moore to the U.S. War Department," October 24, 1878, Record Group 15, National Archives, Washington, D.C.

32. "Affidavit of Joseph M. Webb to John Benton," October 23, 1878, Record Group 15, National Archives, Washington, D.C.

CHAPTER 9

1. "Affidavit of Joseph M. Webb to John Benton," October 23, 1878, Record Group 15, National Archives, Washington, D.C.

2. *Official Records of the War of Rebellion*, Volume 10, Part 2, p. 320.

3. Ibid.

4. Philip Shaw Paludan, *Victims: A True Story of the Civil War*, pp. 62-63.

5. "Affidavit of David Moore to John Benton," October 23, 1878, Record Group 15, National Archives, Washington, D.C.

6. John G. Barrett, *The Civil War in North Carolina*, pp. 183-184.

7. Proclamation of Governor Zebulon Vance, May 11, 1863, Governors' Papers, North Carolina State Archives.

8. "Letter of J. Blanton to Zebulon Vance," May 11, 1863, Zebulon Vance Papers, North Carolina State Archives.

9. "Letter of T. W. Atkins to James A. Seddon," July 29, 1863, Zebulon Vance Papers, North Carolina State Archives.

10. "Keith Blalock to J. H. Greene," November 3, 1874, Record Group 15, National Archives, Washington, D.C.

11. John P. Arthur, *Western North Carolina*, p. 227.

12. "Malinda Blalock to N. B. Miller," August 8, 1895, Record Group 15, National Archives, Washington, D.C.

13. Home Guard Act of July 1863 (Guards for Home Defense), Records of the North Carolina General Assembly, North Carolina State Archives.

14. "Affidavit of Joseph M. Webb to John Benton," October 23, 1878, Record

Group 15, National Archives, Washington, D.C.

15. Shepherd M. Dugger, *The War Trails of the Blue Ridge*, p. 110.

16. Ibid.

17. Ibid.

18. "Keith Blalock to John P. Arthur," 1910, William Eury Collection.

19. John P. Arthur, *A History of Watauga County*, p. 161.

20. "Keith Blalock to J. H. Greene," November 3, 1874, Record Group 15, National Archives, Washington, D.C.

21. Author's Interview of Murray Coffey, April 11, 1998.

22. *Official Records of the War of Rebellion*, Volume 53, pp. 326-327.

23. Ibid.

24. "Affidavit of James Moore to John Benton," October 24, 1878, Record Group 15, National Archives, Washington, D.C.

25. "Affidavit of Jesse Moore to John Benton," October 24, 1878, Record Group 15, National Archives, Washington, D.C.

26. "Letter of Carroll Moore to the U.S. War Department," October 24, 1878, Record Group 15, National Archives, Washington, D.C.

27. "Affidavit of Langston L. Estes," October 24, 1878, Record Group 15, National Archives, Washington, D.C.

28. Ibid.

29. Ibid.

30. "Affidavit of Mrs. Martha Coffey to John Benton," October 25, 1878, Record Group 15, National Archives, Washington, D.C.

31. Ibid.

CHAPTER 10

1. Author's Interview of Murray Coffey, April 11, 1998.

2. "Malinda Blalock to N. B. Miller," August 8, 1895, Record Group 15, National Archives, Washington, D.C.

3. "Keith Blalock to J. H. Greene," November 3, 1874, Record Group 15, National Archives, Washington, D.C.

4. "Affidavit of Jesse Moore to John Benton," October 24, 1878, National Archives, Washington, D.C.

5. David McGee, "The 26th Regiment of North Carolina Troops – Unparalleled Loss," p. 3.

6. Ibid.

7. "Affidavit of Jesse Moore to John Benton," October 24, 1878, Record Group 15, National Archives, Washington, D.C.

8. McGee, p. 4.

9. Ibid.

10. Ibid.

11. Ibid., p. 5.

12. Ibid.

13. Ibid.

14. Ibid., p. 6.

15. Nancy Alexander, *Here Will I Dwell: The Story of Caldwell County*, p. 133.

16. "Affidavit of Jesse Moore to John Benton," October 24, 1878, Record Group 15, National Archives, Washington, D.C.

17. Ibid.

18. *The Journal of David Schenck*, July 1863, Southern Historical Collection, University of North Carolina, Chapel Hill.

19. Compiled Military Service Records of George W. Kirk, Union Army, 3rd North Carolina Mounted Infantry File, Record Group 94, National Archives, Washington, D.C.

20. "Letter of M. Nelson to Zebulon B.Vance," June 11, 1863, Vance Papers, North Carolina State Archives.

21. Frank Wilkeson, *Recollections of a Private Soldier*, p. 234.

22. John P. Arthur, *A History of Watauga County*, pp. 172-173.

23. Ibid.

24. John G. Barrett, *The Civil War in North Carolina*, p. 188.

25. "Letter of R. L. Abernathy to Zebu-

lon Vance," February 23, 1863, Vance Papers, North Carolina State Archives.

26. "Keith Blalock to N. B. Miller," August 8, 1895, Record Group 15, National Archives, Washington, D.C.

27. Ibid.

28. "R. L. Abernathy to Zebulon Vance," February 23, 1863, Vance Papers, North Carolina State Archives.

29. Barrett, p. 188.

30. Ibid.

31. Ibid., p. 189

32. "Letter of Zebulon Vance to James A. Seddon," December 1863, North Carolina State Archives.

33. "Keith Blalock to J. H. Greene," November 3, 1874, Record Group 15, National Archives, Washington, D.C..

34. "Affidavit of Langston L. Estes to John Benton," October 24, 1878, Record Group 15, National Archives, Washington, D.C.

35. "Affidavit of Adolphus Pritchard to J. H. Greene," December 14, 1874, Record Group 15, National Archives, Washington, D.C.

36. "Letter of Helen MacTier," North Carolina State Archive, January 1903.

37. "Affidavit of Jesse Moore to John Benton," October 24, 1878, Record Group 15, National Archives, Washington, D.C.

38. James Madison Drake, *Fast and Loose in Dixie*, pp. 176-177.

39. Albert Castel, "The Guerrilla War," p. 34.

40. Author's interview of Murray Coffey, April 11, 1998.

41. Ted Blalock, Jr., "Keith and 'Sam' Blalock," *Avery County Heritage*, p. 2.

42. Wilma Dykeman, *The French Broad*, p. 98.

CHAPTER 11

1. "Letter of Carroll Moore to the U.S. War Department," October 24, 1878,

Record Group 15, National Archives, Washington, D.C.

2. "Affidavit of Jesse Moore to John Benton," October 24, 1878, Record Group 15, National Archives, Washington, D.C.

3. Ibid.

4. "Keith Blalock to N. B. Miller," August 8, 1895, Record Group 15, National Archives, Washington, D.C.

5. "Keith Blalock to J. H. Greene," November 3, 1874, Record Group 15, National Archives, Washington, D.C.

6. "Letter of Carroll Moore to the U.S. War Department," October 24, 1878, Record Group 15, National Archives, Washington, D.C.

7. "Affidavit of Jesse Moore to John Benton," October 24, 1878, Record Group 15, National Archives, Washington, D.C.

CHAPTER 12

1. J. V. Hadley, *Seven Months a Prisoner*, p. 246.

2. "Keith Blalock to N. B. Miller," August 8, 1895, Record Group 15, National Archives, Washington, D.C.

3. Author's interview of Murray Coffey, April 11, 1998.

4. Common term of the era for reconnaissance.

5. "Bloody Madison" was the term given to the region by Confederate troops stationed there.

6. Common epithets of the region during the Civil War.

7. "Keith Blalock to J. H. Greene," November 3, 1874, Record Group 15, National Archives, Washington, D.C.

8. Charles E. Kirk, *History of the 15th Pennsylvania Cavalry*, pp. 332–333.

9. "Letter of M.B. Moore to Zebulon B. Vance," November 10, 1863, Governors' Papers, North Carolina State Archives.

10. "Keith Blalock to N. B. Miller," No-

vember 3, 1874, Record Group 15, National Archives, Washington, D.C.

11. William R. Trotter, *Bushwhackers*, p. 98.

12. *The Raleigh Weekly North Carolina Standard*, November 14, 1863, p. 2.

13. "Affidavit of Mrs. Martha Coffey to John Benton," October 25, 1878, Record Group 15, National Archives, Washington, D.C.

CHAPTER 13

1. "Letter of Malinda Blalock to Adolphus Pritchard," April 10, 1875, Record Group 15, National Archives, Washington, D.C.

2. "Affidavit of Mrs. Martha Coffey to John Benton,"October 25, 1878, Record Group 15, National Archives, Washington, D.C.

3. "Keith Blalock to J. H. Greene," November 3, 1875, Record Group 15, National Archives, Washington, D.C.; "Keith Blalock to N.B. Miller," August 8, 1895, Record Group 15, National Archives, Washington, D.C.

4. "Lieutenant Frederick Field to Keith Blalock," December 10, 1863, Record Group 15, National Archives, Washington, D.C.

5. A term commonly used by Union soldiers in Tennessee and in North Carolina.

6. Charles E. Kirk (editor), *History of the Fifteenth Cavalry*, p. 507.

7. *Official Records of the War of Rebellion*, Volume 23, p. 518.

8. Ibid.

9. "Keith Blalock to N. B. Miller," August 8, 1895, Record Group 15, National Archives, Washington, D.C.

10. Ibid.

11. Ibid.

12. Author's Interview with Murray Coffey, April 11, 1998.

13. Ibid.

14. "Affidavit of Jesse Moore to N.B. Miller," August 8, 1895, Record Group 15, National Archives, Washington, D.C.

15. Ibid.

16. "Letter of Carroll Moore to the U.S. War Department," October 24, 1878, Record Group 15, National Archives, Washington, D.C.

17. Albert D. Richardson, *The Secret Service—The Field, the Dungeon, and the Escape*, pp. 465-466.

18. Ibid.

19. Ibid.

20. J. V. Hadley, *Seven Months a Prisoner*, pp. 180-181.

21. Ibid.

22. "Keith Blalock to N. B. Miller," August 8, 1895, Record Group 15, National Archives, Washington, D.C.

23. Ibid.

24. "Joseph M. Webb to John Benton," October 23, 1878, Record Group 15, National Archives, Washington, D.C.

25. Ibid.

26. J. V. Hadley, *Seven Months a Prisoner*, pp. 211-213.

27. "Affidavit of David Moore to John Benton," October 23, 1878, Record Group 15, National Archives, Washington, D.C.

28. Muriel H. Sheppard, *Cabins in the Laurel*, p. 64.

29. William R. Trotter, *Bushwhackers*, p. 103.

30. Author's Interview with Murray Coffey, April 11, 1998.

31. Charles E. Kirk (editor), *History of the 15th Pennsylvania*, p. 353.

32. Ibid.

33. "Keith Blalock to N. B. Miller," August 8, 1895, Record Group 15, National Archives, Washington, D.C.

34. Daniel Ellis, *Thrilling Adventures of Daniel Ellis, Scout*, p. 145.

35. Ibid., p. 146.

36. Ibid.

37. Ibid., p. 147.

38. Ibid., p. 148.

39. Ibid., p. 150.

40. "Affidavit of Mrs. Martha Coffey to John Benton," October 25, 1878, Record Group 15, National Archives, Washington, D.C.

CHAPTER 14

1. "Malinda Blalock to N. B. Miller," August 8, 1895, Record Group 15, National Archives, Washington, D.C.

2. "Keith Blalock to N. B. Miller," August 8, 1895, Record Group 15, National Archives, Washington, D.C.

3. Nancy Alexander, *Here Will I Dwell: The Story of Caldwell County*, p. 136.

4. "Affidavit of Burton Johnson to John Benton," October 25, 1878, Record Group 15, National Archives, Washington, D.C.

5. "Letter of Rufus Patterson to the *Raleigh Weekly Era*," December 3, 1863, North Carolina State Archives.

6. "Joseph M. Webb to John Benton," October 23, 1878, Record Group 15, National Archives, Washington, D.C.

7. Ibid.

8. "Letter of Hiram H. Crisp to the Commissioner of Pensions," July 31, 1894, Record Group 15, National Archives, Washington, D.C.

9. "Keith Blalock to J. H. Greene," November 3, 1874, Record Group 15, National Archives, Washington, D.C.

10. "Keith Blalock to N. B. Miller," August 8, 1895, Record Group 15, National Archives, Washington, D.C.

11. *Official Records of the War of Rebellion*, Volume 53, p. 324.

12. "Keith Blalock to N. B. Miller," August 8, 1895, Record Group 15, National Archives, Washington, D.C.

13. "Keith Blalock to John Benton," November 3, 1874, Record Group 15, National Archives, Washington, D.C.

14. Ibid.

15. "Letter of Todd R. Caldwell to Zebulon B. Vance," April 4, 1864, Governors' Papers, North Carolina State Archives.

16. "Letter of Lieutenant J. C. Wills to Zebulon B. Vance," April 29, 1864, Zebulon B. Vance Papers, North Carolina State Archives.

17. Ibid.

18. "Affidavit of James Moore to John Benton," October 24, 1878, Record Group 15, National Archives, Washington, D.C.

19. "Letter of Harvey Bingham to General John W. McElroy," April 14, 1864, William Eury Collection.

20. *Official Records of the War of Rebellion*, Volume 53, pp. 326-327.

21. "Letter of Zebulon B. Vance to James A. Seddon," April 11, 1864, Zebulon B. Vance Papers, North Carolina State Archives.

22. Ella Lonn, *Desertion During the Civil War*, pp. 12-13.

23. *The North Carolina Weekly Standard*, March 11, 1864, p. 1.

24. *The Raleigh Weekly Register*, November 15, 1864, p. 1.

25. Phillip S. Paludan, *Victims: A True Story of the Civil War*, p. 83.

26. "Affidavit of David Moore to John Benton," October 23, 1878, Record Group 15, National Archives, Washington, D.C.

27. "Letter of Harvey Bingham to General John W. McElroy," April 14, 1864, William Eury Collection.

28. "Affidavit of Jesse Moore to John Benton," October 24, 1878, Record Group 15, National Archives, Washington, D.C.

29. "Keith Blalock to N. B. Miller," August 8, 1895, Record Group 15, National Archives, Washington, D.C.

30. Ibid.

31. Ibid.

32. "Letter of M. E. Paul to Moses E. Jenks," February 13, 1875, Record Group 15, National Archives, Washington, D.C.

33. "Keith Blalock to J. H. Greene," No-

vember 3, 1874, Record Group 15, National Archives, Washington, D.C.

34. "Affidavit of Adolphus Pritchard to J. H. Greene," December 19, 1874, Record Group 15, National Archives, Washington, D.C.

CHAPTER 15

1. "Keith Blalock to N. B. Miller," August 8, 1895, Record Group 15, National Archives, Washington D.C.

2. Ibid.

3. Ibid.

4. "Affidavit of Adolphus Pritchard to J. H. Greene," December 19, 1874, Record Group 15, National Archives, Washington, D.C.

5. "Keith Blalock to N. B. Miller," August 8, 1895, Record Group 15, National Archives, Washington, D.C.

6. Volunteer Enlistment Paper, 10th Michigan Cavalry, of Keith Blalock, June 1, 1864, Record Group 94, National Archives, Washington, D.C.

7. Ibid.

8. Interview of Keith Blalock by John P. Arthur, 1909, William Eury Collection.

9. Enlistment Paper, 10th Michigan Cavalry, of Keith Blalock.

10. Ibid.

11. Ibid.

12. John P. Arthur, *A History of Watauga County*, p. 166.

13. "Keith Blalock to N. B. Miller," August 8, 1895, Record Group 15, National Archives, Washington, D.C.

14. The term commonly applied to General William T. Sherman's brand of warfare.

15. "Keith Blalock to N. B. Miller," August 8, 1895, Record Group 15, National Archives, Washington, D.C.

16. Ibid.

17. Ibid.

18. "Joseph M. Webb to John Benton,"

October 23, 1878, Record Group 15, National Archives, Washington, D.C.

19. Ibid.

20. "Affidavit of Jesse Moore to John Benton," October 24, 1878, Record Group 15, National Archives, Washington, D.C.; "Affidavit of Jesse Moore to N. B. Miller," August 28, 1895, Record Group 15, National Archives, Washington, D.C.

21. Ibid.

22. "Affidavit of Langston L. Estes to John Benton," October 23, 1878, Record Group 15, National Archives, Washington, D.C.

23. Ibid.

24. "Affidavit of Mrs. McCaleb Coffey to John Benton," October 24, 1878, Record Group 15, National Archives, Washington, D.C.

25. Ibid.

26. "Affidavit of Mrs. Mary Coffey to John Benton," October 25, 1878, Record Group 15, National Archives, Washington, D.C.

27. Official Records of the 10th Michigan Cavalry, June 1864, Michigan Historical Society.

28. John P. Arthur, *Western North Carolina*, p. 626.

CHAPTER 16

1. John P. Arthur, *Western North Carolina*, p. 629.

2. Ibid., p. 606.

3. A common term used by soldiers of the era to describe a brief rest on the march.

4. John P. Arthur, *Western North Carolina*, p. 606.

5. Ibid.

6. Dewey E. Williams, *Burke County's Camp Vance*, p. 11.

7. Ibid.

8. Arthur, p. 606.

9. Shepherd M. Dugger, *The War Trails of the Blue Ridge*, p. 128.

10. Nancy Alexander, *Here Will I Dwell: The Story of Caldwell County*, p. 138.

11. Ibid; Arthur, p. 606.

12. Arthur, p. 606.

13. "Letter of Joseph Frankling to John P. Arthur," March 2, 1912, Willaim Eury Collection.

14. "Keith Blalock to N. B. Miller," August 8, 1895, Record Group 15, National Archives, Washington, D.C.

15. Interview of Colonel George Anderson Loven by John P. Arthur, June 1910, William Eury Collection.

16. Ibid.

17. Interview of Keith Blalock by John P. Arthur, 1909, William Eury Collection.

18. Interview of Colonel George Anderson Loven by John P. Arthur, June 1910, William Eury Collection.

19. "Affidavit of Mrs. M. E. Paul to Moses E. Jenks," February 13, 1875, Record Group 15, Washington, D.C.

20. "Letter of Captain N. C. Allen to General Robert C. Vance," June 30, 1864, North Carolina State Archives.

21. Ibid.

CHAPTER 17

1. Official Records of the 10th Michigan Cavalry Regiment, July-August 1864, Michigan Historical Society.

2. "Keith Blalock to N. B. Miller," August 8, 1895, Record Group 15, National Archives, Washington, D.C.

3. "Joseph M. Webb to John Benton," October 24, 1878, Record Group 15, National Archives, Washington, D.C.

4. J. V. Hadley, *Seven Months a Prisoner*, pp. 466-467.

5. Ibid., p. 465.

6. Ibid.

7. Ibid.

8. "Joseph M. Webb to N. B. Miller," October 23, 1878, Record Group 15, National Archives, Washington, D.C.; "Affi-

davit of David Moore to N. B. Miller," October 23, 1878, Record Group 14, National Archives, Washington, D.C.

9. "Affidavit of Carroll Moore to Moses E. Jenks," February 13, 1875, Record Group 15, National Archives, Washington, D.C.

10. "Letter of L. L. Green to John P. Arthur," May 7, 1909, William Eury Collection.

11. "Affidavit of David Moore to John Benton," October 23, 1878, Record Group 15, National Archives, Washington, D.C.

12. "Letter of Carroll Moore to the U.S. War Department," October 24, 1878, Record Group 15, National Archives, Washington, D.C.

13. "L. L. Green to John P. Arthur," May 7, 1909, William Eury Collection.

14. Interview of Keith Blalock by John P. Arthur, 1910, William Eury Collection.

15. "Affidavit of David Moore to John Benton," October 23, 1878, Record Group 15, National Archives, Washington, D.C.

16. "Malinda Blalock to N. B. Miller," August 8, 1895, Record Group 15, National Archives, Washington, D.C.

17. "Affidavit of Jesse Moore to N. B. Miller," August 28, 1895, Record Group 15, National Archives, Washington, D.C.

18. Daniel Ellis, *Thrilling Adventures of Daniel Ellis, Scout*, pp. 185-188.

19. "Joseph Webb to John Benton," October 23, 1878, Record Group 15, National Archives, Washington, D.C.

20. Author's interview of Murray Coffey, April 11, 1998.

21. Ibid.

22. Albert D. Richardson, *The Secret Service—The Field, the Dungeon, and the Escape*, p. 465.

23. Ibid., p. 469

24. "Affidavit of Langston L. Estes to John Benton," October 24, 1878, Record Group 15, National Archives, Washington, D.C.

25. "Letter of L. L. Green to John P. Arthur," May 7, 1909, William Eury Collection.

26. "Letter of Lott Green to the Commissioner of Pensions," October 8, 1875, Record Group 15, National Archives, Washington, D.C.

27. Interview of Malinda Blalock by John P. Arthur, 1899, William Eury Collection.

28. Author's Interview of Murray Coffey, April 11, 1998.

29. "Letter of General William T. Sherman to T. C. Hindeman," October 17, 1862.

30. John P. Arthur, *A History of Watauga County*, p. 168.

31. Ibid.

32. Ibid.

33. Ibid.

34. "Keith Blalock to N. B. Miller," August 8, 1895, Record Group 15, National Archives, Washington, D.C.

35. "Letter of L. L. Green to John P. Arthur," May 7, 1909.

36. Ibid.

37. "Keith Blalock to N. B. Miller," August 8, 1895, Record Group 15, National Archives, Washington, D.C.

38. Ibid.

39. Ibid.

40. "Affidavit of William Voncannon to John Benton," October 25, 1878, Record Group 15, National Archives, Washington, D.C.

41. Ibid.

42. Ibid.

43. "Keith Blalock to N. B. Miller," August 8, 1895, Record Group 15, National Archives, Washington, D.C.

44. "Affidavit of David Moore to John Benton," October 23, 1878, Record Group 15, National Archives, Washington, D.C.

45. "Affidavit of Mrs. Martha Coffey to John Benton," October 25, 1878, Record Group 15, Washington, D.C.

46. Ibid.

47. Ibid.

48. Ibid.

49. "Affidavit of Mrs. Mary Coffey to John Benton," October 25, 1878, Record Group 15, National Archives, Washington, D.C.

50. "Keith Blalock to N. B. Miller," August 8, 1895, Record Group 15, National Archives, Washington, D.C.

51. "Joseph M. Webb to John Benton," October 23, 1878, Record Group 15, National Archives, Washington, D.C.

52. Ibid.

53. Ibid.

54. Ibid.

55. Ibid.

56. "Keith Blalock to N. B. Miller," August 8, 1895, Record Group 15, National Archives, Washington, D.C.

57. "Malinda Blalock to N. B. Miller," August 8, 1895, Record Group 15, National Archives, Washington, D.C.

58. "Affidavit of Jesse Moore to John Benton," October 24, 1878, Record Group 15, National Archives, Washington, D.C.

59. Ibid.

60. "Letter of Carroll Moore to the U.S. War Department," October 24, 1878, Record Group 15, National Archives, Washington, D.C.

61. "Affidavit of Mrs. McCaleb Coffey to John Benton," October 24, 1878, Record Group 15, National Archives, Washington, D.C.

62. "Certification of Keith Blalock's Wounds, written and signed by Captain James Minihan," October 1, 1865, Record Group 15, National Archives, Washington, D.C.; "Letter of Captain James Minihan to U.S. Sanitary Commission Army and Navy Claim Agency," November 10, 1865, Record Group 15, National Archives, Washington, D.C.

63. "Affidavit of Mrs. McCaleb Coffey to John Benton," October 24, 1878, Record

Group 15, National Archives, Washington, D.C.

CHAPTER 18

1. William Cotton, *Appalachian North Carolina*, p. 114.
2. Ibid.
3. John P. Arthur, *Western North Carolina*, p. 627.
4. "Affidavit of David Moore to John Benton," October 23, 1878, Record Group 15, National Archives, Washington, D.C.
5. The nickname used to describe General William T. Sherman's troops.
6. *Official Records of the War of Rebellion*, Volume 45, p. 1074.
7. Shelby Foote, *The Civil War: A Narrative, to Appomattox*, p. 595.
8. "Keith Blalock to N. B. Miller," August 8, 1895, Record Group 15, National Archives, Washington, D.C.

CHAPTER 19

1. Interview of Colonel George Anderson Loven by John P. Arthur, March 2, 1912, William Eury Collection.
2. "Keith Blalock to N. B. Miller," August 8, 1895, Record Group 15, National Archives, Washington, D.C.
3. "Affidavit of David Moore to John Benton," October 23, 1878, Record Group 15, National Archives, Washington, D.C.
4. Ibid.
5. Ibid.
6. Ibid.
7. Ibid.
8. Ibid.
9. Ibid.
10. Ibid.
11. Ibid.
12. "Joseph M. Webb to John Benton," October 23, 1878, Record Group 15, National Archives, Washington, D.C.
13. Ibid.
14. "Additional Affidavit of Joseph Webb to John Benton," October 24, 1878, Record Group 15, National Archives, Washington, D.C.
15. Ibid.
16. Ibid.
17. Ibid.
18. "Affidavit of Jesse Moore to John Benton," October 24, 1878, Record Group 15, National Archives, Washington, D.C.
19. "Letter of Carroll Moore to the U.S. War Department," October 24, 1878, Record Group 15, National Archives, Washington, D.C.
20. "Affidavit of Mrs. Mary Coffey," October 25, 1878, Record Group 15, National Archives, Washington, D.C.
21. "Affidavit of Mrs. McCaleb Coffey to John Benton," October 24, 1878, Record Group 15, National Archives, Washington, D.C.
22. Ibid.
23. "Affidavit of James Gragg to John Benton," October 23, 1878, Record Group 15, National Archives, Washington, D.C.
24. John P. Arthur, *Watauga County*, p. 166.
25. "James Gragg to John Benton," October 23, 1878, Record Group 15, National Archives, Washington, D.C.
26. Author's Interview of Murray Coffey, April 11, 1998.
27. "Affidavit of Jesse Moore to John Benton," October 24, 1878, Record Group 15, National Archives, Washington, D.C.
28. Ibid.
29. Ibid.
30. "Letter of Carroll Moore to the U.S. War Department," October 24, 1878, Record Group 15, National Archives, Washington, D.C.
31. "Joseph Webb to John Benton," October 23, 1878, Record Group 15, National Archives, Washington, D.C.
32. Ibid.
33. Ibid.

34. "Affidavit of Jesse Moore to John Benton," October 24, 1878, Record Group 15, National Archives, Washington, D.C.

CHAPTER 20

1. "Keith Blalock to N. B. Miller," August 8, 1895, Record Group 15, National Archives, Washington, D.C.

2. Ibid.

3. "Affidavit of David Moore to John Benton," October 23, 1878, Record Group 15, National Archives, Washington, D.C.

4. "Affidavit of Langston L. Estes to John Benton," October 24, 1878, Record Group 15, National Archives, Washington, D.C.

5. "Joseph M. Webb to John Benton," October 23, 1878, Record Group 15, National Archives, Washington, D.C.

6. Ibid.

7. Ibid.

8. Ibid.

9. "Affidavit of Langston L. Estes to John Benton," October 24, 1878, Record Group 15, National Archives, Washington, D.C.

10. "Affidavit of Mrs. McCaleb Coffey to John Benton," October 24, 1878, Record Group 15, National Archives, Washington, D.C.

11. "Joseph M. Webb to John Benton," October 23, 1878, Record Group 15, National Archives, Washington, D.C.

12. "Affidavit of Langston L. Estes to John Benton," October 24, 1878, Record Group 15, National Archives, Washington, D.C.

13. "Affidavit of Jesse Moore to John Benton," October 24, 1878, Record Group 15, National Archives, Washington, D.C.

14. Ibid.

15. "Keith Blalock to N. B. Miller," August 8, 1895, Record Group 15, National Archives, Washington, D.C.

16. Ibid.

17. Ibid.

18. "Keith Blalock to N.B. Miller," August 8, 1895, Record Group 15, National Archives, Washington, D.C.

19. "Joseph M. Webb to John Benton," October 23, 1878, Record Group 15, National Archives, Washington, D.C.

20. "Keith Blalock to N. B. Miller," August 8, 1895, Record Group 15, National Archives, Washington, D.C.

21. Ibid.

22. "Joseph M. Webb to John Benton," October 23, 1878, Record Group 15, National Archives, Washington, D.C.

23. Ibid.

24. Ibid.

25. "Keith Blalock to N. B. Miller," August 8, 1895, Record Group 15, National Archives, Washington, D.C.

26. "Affidavit of Jesse Moore to John Benton," October 24, 1878, Record Group 15, National Archives, Washington, D.C.

27. "Keith Blalock to N. B. Miller," August 8, 1895, Record Group 15, National Archives, Washington, D.C.

28. "Affidavit of Jesse Moore to John Benton," October 24, 1878, National Archives, Record Group 15, National Archives, Washington, D.C.

29. Ibid.

30. "Keith Blalock to N. B. Miller," August 8, 1895, Record Group 15, National Archives, Washington, D.C.

31. "Affidavit of Jesse Moore to John Benton," October 24, 1878, Record Group 15, National Archives, Washington, D.C.

32. "Joseph M. Webb to John Benton," October 23, 1878, Record Group 15, National Archives, Washington, D.C.

33. "Keith Blalock to N. B. Miller," August 8, 1895, Record Group 15, National Archives, Washington, D.C.

34. Ibid.

35. Ibid.

36. "Joseph M. Webb to John Benton," October 23, 1878, Record Group 15, National Archives, Washington, D.C.

37. "Affidavit of Jesse Moore to John

Benton," October 24, 1878, Record Group 15, National Archives, Washington, D.C.

38. "Joseph Webb to John Benton," October 23, 1878, Record Group 15, National Archives, Washington, D.C.

39. Ibid.

40. "Affidavit of Jesse Moore to John Benton," October 24, 1878, Record Group 15, National Archives, Washington, D.C.

41. "Joseph M. Webb to John Benton," October 23, 1878, Record Group 15, National Archives, Washington, D.C.

42. "Letter of Carroll Moore to the U.S. War Department," October 24, 1878, Record Group 14, National Archives, Washington, D.C.

43. "Affidavit of Jesse Moore to John Benton," October 24, 1878, Record Group 15, National Archives, Washington, D.C.

44. "Joseph M. Webb to John Benton," October 23, 1878, Record Group 15, National Archives, Washington, D.C.

45. Ibid.

46. "Keith Blalock to N. B. Miller," August 8, 1895, Record Group 15, National Archives, Washington, D.C.

47. Ibid.

48. Ibid.

49. "Joseph M. Webb to John Benton," October 23, 1878, Record Group 15, National Archives, Washington, D.C.

50. "Affidavit of David Moore to John Benton," October 23, 1878, Record Group 15, National Archives, Washington, D.C.

51. Author's interview with Murray Coffey, April 11, 1998.

52. "Affidavit of Jesse Moore to John Benton," October 24, 1878, Record Group 15, National Archives, Washington, D.C.

53. "Affidavit of William Voncannon to John Benton," October 25, 1878, Record Group 15, National Archives, Washington, D.C.

54. Ibid.

55. "Joseph M. Webb to John Benton,"

October 23, 1878, Record Group 15, National Archives, Washington, D.C.

56. Ibid.

57. "Letter of Carroll Moore to the U.S. War Department," October 24, 1878, Record Group 15, National Archives, Washington, D.C.

58. "Letter of Malinda Blalock to Adolphus Pritchard," April 10, 1875, Record Group 15, National Archives, Washington, D.C.

59. "Affidavit of James Moore to Moses E. Jenks," February 13, 1875, Record Group 15, National Archives, Washington, D.C.

60. "Affidavit of Samuel W. Blalock to Moses E. Jenks," February 13, 1875, Record Group 15, National Archives, Washington, D.C.

61. "Certification of Keith Blalock's Wounds, Written and Signed by Captain James Minihan," October 1, 1865, Record Group 15, National Archives, Washington, D.C.; "Letter of Captain James Minihan to U.S. Sanitary Commission Army and Navy Claim Agency," November 10, 1865, Record Group 15, National Archives, Washington, D.C.

CHAPTER 21

1. "Letter of Carroll Moore to the U.S. War Department," October 24, 1878, Record Group 15, National Archives, Washington, D.C.

2. John P. Arthur, *A History of Watauga County*, p. 168.

3. "Affidavit of Mrs. Martha Coffey to John Benton," October 25, 1878, Record Group 15, National Archives, Washington, D.C.

4. Interview of J. Filmore Coffey by John P. Arthur, June 1912, William Eury Collection.

5. John P. Arthur, *A History of Watauga County*, p. 167.

6. Ibid.

7. "Affidavit of David Moore to John Benton," October 23, 1878, Record Group 15, National Archives, Washington, D.C.

8. "Affidavit of Jesse Moore to John Benton," October 24, 1878, Record Group 15, National Archives, Washington, D.C.

9. "Affidavit of Mrs. McCaleb Coffey to John Benton," October 24, 1878, Record Group 15, National Archives, Washington, D.C.

10. "Affidavit of Langston L. Estes to John Benton," October 24, 1878, Record Group 15, National Archives, Washington, D.C.

11. Ibid.

12. "Affidavit of Mrs. Mary Coffey to John Benton," October 25, 1878, Record Group 15, National Archives, Washington, D.C.

13. Ibid.

14. Ibid.

CHAPTER 22

1. "Joseph Webb to John Benton," October 23, 1878, Record Group 15, National Archives, Washington, D.C.; John P. Arthur, *A History of Watauga County*, p. 184.

2. "Affidavit of Thomas Pritchard to M. E. Jenks," February 13, 1874, Record Group 15, National Archives, Washington, D.C.

3. Shepherd M. Dugger, *The War Trails of the Blue Ridge*, p. 118.

4. Ibid.

5. "Affidavit of William Voncannon to John Benton," October 25, 1878, Record Group 15, National Archives, Washington, D.C.

6. Ibid.

7. Ibid.

8. John P. Arthur, *A History of Watauga County*, p. 175.

9. Ibid.

10. Dugger, p. 119.

11. Arthur, p. 175.

12. Dugger, pp. 119–120.

13. Ibid., p. 120.

14. Ibid.

15. William R. Trotter, *Bushwhackers*, p. 250.

CHAPTER 23

1. "Affidavit of Mrs. McCaleb Coffey to John Benton," October 24, 1878, Record Group 15, National Archives, Washington, D.C.

2. "Letter of Carroll Moore to the U.S. War Department," October 24, 1878, Record Group 15, National Archives, Washington, D.C.

3. General George Stoneman's term for his cavalry in Tennessee and North Carolina.

4. Charles E. Kirk (editor), *History of the Fifteenth Pennsylvania Cavalry*, p. 507.

5. *Official Records of the War of the Rebellion*, Volume 45, p. 1074.

6. Ibid., Volume 49, p. 810.

7. Kirk, p. 493.

8. John P. Arthur, *A History of Watauga County*, p. 177.

9. "Malinda Blalock to N. B. Miller," August 8, 1895, Record Group 15, National Archives, Washington, D.C.

10. Arthur, p. 177.

11. Interview of A. J. McBride by John P. Arthur, June 1912, William Eury Collection.

12. Arthur, pp. 177–178.

13. "Keith Blalock to N. B. Miller," August 8, 1895, Record Group 15, National Archives, Washington, D.C.

14. Arthur, p. 178.

15. "Letter of James Gwyn to His Son," April 14, 1865, Southern Historical Collection, University of North Carolina, Chapel Hill.

16. "Keith Blalock to N. B. Miller," August 8, 1895, Record Group 15, National Archives, Washington, D.C.

17. Author's Interview of Murray Coffey, April 11, 1998.

18. Interview of Keith Blalock by John P. Arthur, 1910, William Eury Collection.

19. Records of the 10th Michigan Cavalry, April 1865.

20. Ibid.

21. "Keith Blalock to N. B. Miller," August 8, 1895, Record Group 15, National Archives, Washington, D.C.

22. The term used for Salisbury Prison's morgue.

23. The term used for Salisbury Prison's graveyard.

24. *Official Records of the War of the Rebellion*, Volume 49, p. 334.

25. "Keith Blalock to J. H. Greene," November 3, 1874, Record Group 15, National Archives, Washington, D.C.

26. Diary of Mrs. George W. F. Harper, April 15, 1865, Southern Historical Collection, University of North Carolina, Chapel Hill.

27. Ibid., April 16, 1865.

28. Nancy Alexander, *Here Will I Dwell: The Story of Caldwell County*, p. 141.

29. Ibid., p. 142.

30. Ibid.

31. Ibid.

32. Ibid.

33. Ibid.

CHAPTER 24

1. Nancy Alexander, *Here Will I Dwell: The Story of Caldwell County*, p. 143.

2. Interview of Columbus F. Blalock by John P. Arthur, June 1912, William Eury Collection.

3. Ibid.

4. "Affidavit of Adolphus Pritchard to J. H. Greene," December 19, 1874, Record Group 15, National Archives, Washington, D.C.

5. Ibid.

6. U.S. Army Certificate of Disability for Discharge, for Keith Blalock, October 21, 1865, Record Group 15, National Archives, Washington, D.C.

7. "Affidavit of Malinda Blalock to the U.S. War Department," November 10, 1865, Record Group 15, National Archives, Washington, D.C.

8. U.S. Army Certificate of Disability, for Keith Blalock, October 21, 1865, Record Group 15, National Archives, Washington, D.C.

9. Ibid.

10. "Affidavit of Adolphus Pritchard to J. H. Greene," December 19, 1874, Record Group 15, National Archives, Washington, D.C.

11. Keith Blalock's Declaration for Invalid Pension, October 28, 1865, Record Group 15, National Archives, Washington, D.C.

12. Ibid.

13. "Affidavit of Malinda Blalock to the War Department," November 10, 1865, Record Group 15, National Archives, Washington, D.C.

14. "Keith Blalock to N. B. Miller," August 8, 1895, Record Group 15, National Archives, Washington, D.C.

CHAPTER 25

1. "Affidavit of Jesse Moore to Moses E. Jenks," February 13, 1875, Record Group 15, National Archives, Washington, D.C.

2. John P. Arthur, *A History of Watauga County*, p. 182.

3. Ibid.

4. Ibid., p. 185.

5. Ibid.

6. Ibid.

7. Ibid.

8. Ibid.; *Correspondence of Jonathan Worth*, v.2, p. 725.

9. Ibid.

10. Interview of Keith Blalock by John P. Arthur, 1910, William Eury Collection.

11. Ibid.

12. Ibid.

13. "Keith Blalock to N. B. Miller," August 8, 1895, Record Group 15, National Archives, Washington, D.C.

14. John P. Arthur, *Western North Carolina*, p. 644.

15. Ibid.

16. Ibid.

17. Ibid.

18. Ibid.

19. Ibid.

20. Nancy Alexander, *Here Will I Dwell: The Story of Caldwell County*, p. 137.

CHAPTER 26

1. Shepherd M. Dugger, *The War Trails of the Blue Ridge*, p. 310.

2. Ibid.

3. Ibid., p. 305.

4. Ibid.

5. *The Raleigh Weekly Era*, August 13, 1874, p. 1.

6. Ibid.

7. "Letter of Moses E. Jenks to the Commissioner of Pensions," February 17, 1875, Record Group 15, National Archives, Washington, D.C.

8. Ibid.

9. "Keith Blalock to J. H. Greene," November 3, 1874, Record Group 15, National Archives, Washington, D.C.

10. Ibid.

11. "Letter of Moses E. Jenks to the Commissioner of Pensions," February 17, 1875, Record Group 15, National Archives, Washington, D.C.; "Keith Blalock to J. H. Greene," December 15, 1874, Record Group 15, National Archives, Washington, D.C.

12. "Affidavit of John M. Stafford to Moses E. Jenks," February 13, 1875, Record Group 15, National Archives, Washington, D.C.

13. Ibid.

14. "Affidavit of Samuel Blalock to Moses E. Jenks," February 13, 1875, Record Group 15, National Archives, Washington, D.C.

15. Ibid.

16. "Affidavit of Carroll Moore to Moses E. Jenks," February 13, 1875, Record Group 15, National Archives, Washington, D.C.

17. "Letter of Moses E. Jenks to the Commissioner of Pensions," February 17, 1875, Record Group 15, National Archives, Washington, D.C.

18. Ibid.

19. Ibid.

20. Ibid.

21. "Keith Blalock to J. H. Greene," November 3, 1874, Record Group 15, National Archives, Washington, D.C.; "Keith Blalock to J. H. Greene," December 15, 1874, Record Group 15, National Archives, Washington, D.C.

22. Ibid.

23. "Keith Blalock to J. H. Greene," November 3, 1874, Record Group 15, National Archives, Washington, D.C.

24. John P. Arthur, *A History of Watauga County*, p. 167.

25. Ibid.

26. Ibid., p. 166.

27. "Letter of Carroll Moore to War Department," February 13, 1888, Record Group 15, National Archives, Washington, D.C.

28. "Letter of Malinda Blalock to the U.S. War Department," April 27, 1888, Record Group 15, National Archives, Washington, D.C.

29. "Letter of Malinda Blalock to the U.S. War Department," August 12, 1892, Record Group 15, National Archives, Washington, D.C.

30. "Letter of Hiram H. Crisp to the Commissioner of Pensions," July 31, 1894, Record Group 15, National Archives, Washington, D.C.

31. "Affidavit of Malinda Blalock to N. B. Miller," August 8, 1895, Record Group 15, National Archives, Washington, D.C.

32. "N. B. Miller to the Commissioner of Pensions," August 8, 1895, Record Group 15, National Archives, Washington, D.C.; "Keith Blalock to N. B. Miller," August 8, 1895, Record Group 15, National Archives, Washington, D.C.

33. "Report of N. B. Miller to the Commissioner of Pensions," August 30, 1895, Record Group 15, National Archives, Washington, D.C.

34. Ibid.

35. Ibid.

36. Ibid.

37. Ibid.

38. Ibid.

39. "Malinda Blalock to N. B. Miller," August 8, 1895, Record Group 15, National Archives, Washington, D.C.

40. "Affidavit of James Loving to N. B. Miller," August 8, 1895, Record Group 15, National Archives, Washington, D.C.

41. Ibid.

42. "Affidavit of Martin Matery to N. B. Miller," August 8, 1895, Record Group 15, National Archives, Washington, D.C.

43. "Affidavit of J. L. Carpenter to N. B. Miller," August 8, 1895, Record Group 15, National Archives, Washington, D.C.

44. Ibid.

45. "Keith Blalock to N. B. Miller," August 8, 1895, Record Group 15, National Archives, Washington, D.C.

46. "Affidavit of Walter Goss to N. B. Miller," August 8, 1895, Record Group 15, National Archives, Washington, D.C.

47. "Report of N. B. Miller to the Commissioner of Pensions," August 30, 1895, Record Group 15, National Archives, Washington, D.C.

48. "Affidavit of Jesse Moore to N.B. Miller," August 28, 1895, Record Group 15, National Archives, Washington, D.C.

49. Ibid.

50. Ibid.

51. "Report of N. B. Miller to the Commissioner of Pensions," August 30, 1895, Record Group 15, National Archives, Washington, D.C.

52. Ibid.

53. Ibid.

EPILOGUE

1. Author interview of Murray Coffey, April 11, 1998.

2. "Letter of Columbus F. Blalock to the Commissioner of Pensions," May 3, 1903, Record Group 15, National Archives, Washington, D.C.

3. Guardianship Report on Keith Blalock, May 22, 1903, Record Group 15, National Archives, Washington, D.C.

4. "Letter of Columbus F. Blalock to the Commissioner of Pensions," May 3, 1903, Record Group 15, National Archives, Washington, D.C.

5. *The Bakersville Observer* (N.C.), September 7, 1908.

6. "Letter of William Holloway to the Commissioner of Pensions," September 16, 1913, Record Group 15, National Archives, Washington, D.C.

7. "Affidavit of David Moore to John Benton," October 23, 1878, Record Group 15, National Archives, Washington, D.C.

BIBLIOGRAPHY

ARCHIVAL SOURCES

Appalachian Collection: Western North Carolina; Papers, Manuscripts, and Letters by and about the Blalocks, the Greens, the Moores, the Coffeys, the Pritchards, and other families of Watauga and Caldwell Counties; interviews with Keith and Malinda Blalock and other Civil War figures of the Blue Ridge. Appalachian State University, Boone, North Carolina.

Avery County (North Carolina) Historical Society

Harriet Ellis Bradshaw Papers. "General Stoneman's Raid on Salisbury, North Carolina." Unpublished reminiscence. Southern Historical Collection, University of North Carolina at Chapel Hill

Caldwell County Public Library, Lenoir, North Carolina

Civil War Collection, North Carolina State Archives, Raleigh, North Carolina

William Eury Collection, Appalachian History, "Blalock File," Appalachian State University, Boone, North Carolina

Governors' Letter Books, North Carolina State Archives, Raleigh, North Carolina

Governors' Papers, North Carolina State Archives, Raleigh, North Carolina

William A. Graham Papers, North Carolina State Archives, Raleigh, North Carolina

Lenoir Family Papers, Southern Historical Collection, University of North Carolina at Chapel Hill

Library of Congress

Mitchell County Public Library, Bakersville, North Carolina

Frank Moore Papers, William R. Perkins Library, Duke University, Durham, North Carolina

North Carolina Collection, University of North Carolina at Chapel Hill

North Carolina State Archives, Civil War Collection

Record Group 15: Records of the Veterans Administration. William M. Blalock Pension File. Certificate #58976. National Archives, Washington, D.C.

Record Group 15: Letters and affidavits of William M. Blalock to the War Department. National Archives, Washington, D.C.

Record Group 15: Letters and affidavits of Sarah Malinda Blalock and Columbus F. Blalock to the War Department. National Archives, Washington, D.C.

Record Group 94: Records of the Adjutant General's Office. Administrative Precedent File. National Archives, Washington, D.C.

Record Group 94: Records of the Adjutant General's Office. AGO Document File Record Cards. National Archives, Washington, D.C.

Record Group 94: Compiled Medical Records, Mexican and Civil Wars. National Archives, Washington, D.C.

Record Group 94: Compiled Military Service Records (CMSR). Nation Archives, Washington, D.C.

Record Group 94: Records of the Adjutant General's Office. Hospital Registers, Civil War. National Archives, Washington, D.C.

Record Group 94: Records of the Adjutant General's Office. Records and Pension Office Document File. National Archives, Washington, D.C.

Record Group 94: Records and Pension Office Record Cards for William M. Blalock—#18460680; #18465947; #18466242; #9634–C-1888. National Archives, Washington, D.C.

Record Group 107: Records of the Office of the Secretary of War. Records Concerning the Conduct and Loyalty of Certain Union Army Officers, Civilian Employees of the War Department, and U.S. Citizens During the Civil War. National Archives, Washington, D.C.

Record Group 109: Letters Received by the Confederate Secretary of War, 1861–1865. National Archives, Washington, D.C.

Record Group 109: War Department Collection of Confederate Records, Bound Records. National Archives, Washington, D.C.

Record Group 109: War Department Collection of Confederate Records. Compiled Military Service Records (CMSR). National Archives, Washington, D.C.

Record Group 393: Special Orders, District of Upper East Tennessee. National Archives, Washington, D.C.

Report of the Committee on Pensions, No. 44, 43rd Congress, First Session, Social Set 1586. Library of Congress, Washington, D.C.

Society for the Historical Preservation of the 26th North Carolina Troops. Catawba, North Carolina.

Southern Historical Collection. University of North Carolina at Chapel Hill.

United Daughters of the Confederacy Papers. North Carolina State Archives, Raleigh, North Carolina

Unpublished Reminiscences of Confederate Veterans. University of North Carolina at Chapel Hill.

Zebulon B. Vance Papers. North Carolina State Archives, Raleigh, North Carolina.

Watauga County, North Carolina, North Carolina Records:

Court Records: Superior Court Minutes, 1873–1924

Civil Action Papers, 1873–1953

Criminal Actions Papers, 1873–1962

Election Records, 1878–1938

Estates Records: Record of Accounts 1873–1914; Appointment of Administrators, Executors, Guardians, and Masters, 1873–1916; Guardians' Records, 1873–1955; Guardians' Bonds, 1888–1910; Records of Settlements, 1873–1925

Land Records: Deeds, 1858–1976; Deeds of Trust, 1822–1976; Mortgage Deeds, 1877–1957; Cross-Index to Deeds, 1873–1949; Tax Levies on Land, 1874–1939; Miscellaneous Land Records, 1830–1962; Records of Probate, 1873–1885

Marriage, Divorce, and Vital Statistics: Marriage Licenses, 1850–1894; Marriage Registers, 1873–1954

PERIODICALS

The Atlantic Monthly, 1861–1900.

Bakersville Mountain Voice (North Carolina), 1865–1875.

Charlotte North Carolina Whig, 1861–1865.

Charlotte *Western Democrat,* 1861–1865.

The Confederate Veteran (Nashville, Tennessee), 1893–1932.

Daily Herald (Wilmington, North Carolina), 1860–1865.

Elizabeth City *Economist,* 1900.

The *Fayetteville Observer,* 1861–1865.

Frank Leslie's Illustrated Weekly.
The *Greensboro Patriot,* 1861–1866.
Harper's Monthly.
Harper's Weekly.
The *Hillsborough Recorder* (North Carolina), 1860–1865.
The *Knoxville Whig* (Tennessee), 1860–1865.
The Land We Love (Charlotte, North Carolina).
The Memphis Bulletin (Tennessee).
The *Milton Chronicle* (North Carolina), 1861–1865.
The *Nashville Dispatch* (Tennessee), 1860–1865.
The New Bern *North Carolina Times,* 1865.
The New York Times, 1860–1865.
The *North Carolina Presbyterian,* 1861–1863.
Our Living and Our Dead (New Bern and Raleigh, North Carolina), 1873–1876.
The *Raleigh Daily Conservative* (North Carolina), 1861–1865.
The *Raleigh Progress,* 1863–1865.
The *Raleigh Standard,* 1861–1865.
The *Raleigh State Journal,* 1862–1865.
The *Raleigh Weekly Era,* 1874.
The *Salisbury Daily Carolina Watchman,* (North Carolina) 1861–1865.
The *Southern Bivouac* (Louisville, Kentucky), 1882–1887.
Southern Historical Society Papers (Richmond, Virginia), 1876–Present.
The *Watauga Democrat* (North Carolina), 1887–Present.
The *Wilmington Journal* (North Carolina), 1861–1865.

ADDITIONAL SOURCES

Author's interviews with descendants of principals in the book: C. F. Blalock (grandson of Keith and Malinda Blalock); Murray Coffey (relative who knew Keith Blalock); Steven Sudderth (great-great-grandson of John Boyd); Jessie Blalock (great-great-granddaughter of Keith and Malinda Blalock); Paul Henley, Jr. (great-great-grandson of Henry Henley).

PRINTED SOURCES

Alexander, Nancy. *Here Will I Dwell: The Story of Caldwell County.* Raleigh, North Carolina: Rowan Printing Company, 1956.
Allen, W. C. *Annals of Haywood County.* Privately Printed, 1935.
Altmayer, Bud. *A Family History of Watauga County* ("Keith and Malinda Blalock and Family"). Boone, North Carolina: Appalachian State University Press, 1989.
Ambrose, Robert Paul. "A Critical Year (April 1860–April 1861): A Study of Unionist Sentiment in Western North Carolina During the Culminating Year of the Secession Movement." Doctoral Thesis: University of North Carolina, 1975.
Anderson, J. H. *North Carolina Women of the Confederacy.* Fayetteville, North Carolina: Rowan Publishing, 1926.
Anderson, Lucy London. "Confederate Clippings—'Sam Blalock.'" *Fayetteville* (North Carolina) *Observer,* October 9, 1923.
Andrews, Matthew Page. *The Women of the South in War Times.* Baltimore, Maryland: Norman, Remington, 1920.
Andrews, Sidney. *The South Since the War.* Boston: Ticknost & Fields, 1866.
Arthur, John Preston. *Western North Car-*

olina: A History from 1730–1913. Richmond, Virginia: Everett Waddey Company, 1915.

———. *A History of Watauga County, North Carolina, with Sketches of Prominent Families*. Richmond, Virginia: Everett Waddey Company, 1915.

Ashe, Samuel A. *A History of North Carolina*, 2 vols. Spartanburg, North Carolina: Reprint Press, 1971.

Avery County, North Carolina, Heritage: Biographies, Genealogies, and Church Histories, 2 vols. Compiled and edited by the Avery County Historical Society. Newland, North Carolina, 1976.

Bardolph, Richard. "Inconstant Rebels: Desertion of North Carolina Troops in the Civil War." *North Carolina Historical Review* 41 (1964): 163–89.

Barrett, John G. *The Civil War in North Carolina*. Chapel Hill, North Carolina: The University of North Carolina Press, 1963.

Barrett, John G., and Yearns, W. Buck. *North Carolina Civil War Documentary*. Chapel Hill, North Carolina: University of North Carolina Press, (rep.) 1983.

Beard, Mary R. *Women as Force in History*. New York: Macmillan, 1946.

Beymer, William Gilmore. *On Hazardous Service: Scouts and Spies of the North and South*. New York: Harper & Brothers, 1912.

Black, Robert C. *The Railroads of the Confederacy*. Chapel Hill: The University of North Carolina Press, 1952.

Blanton, DeAnne. "Women Soldiers of the Civil War." *Prologue Magazine* 24 (Spring 1993): 27–33.

Boatner, W.W. *The Civil War Dictionary*. New York: Facts on File (reprint of 1959 edition) 1992.

Botkin, B. A. *A Civil War Treasury of Tales, Legends, and Folklore*. New York: Random House, 1960.

Boyd, W. K. "Fiscal and Economic Conditions in North Carolina During the War." *North Carolina Booklet*, XIV, April 1915.

Brewer, Alberta. *Valley So Wild*. Knoxville, Tennessee: East Tennessee Historical Society, 1975.

Brockett, Linus P. *The Camp, the Battlefield, and the Hospital; or, Light and Shadows of the Great Rebellion*. Philadelphia: National Publishing, 1866.

Brockett, Linus P., and Vaughn, Mary C. *Women's Work in the Civil War: A Record of Heroism, Patriotism, and Patience*. Philadelphia: Zeigler, McCurdy, 1867.

Brooks, A. L., and Leftier, Hugh T., eds. *The Papers of Walter Clark*. Chapel Hill: The University of North Carolina Press, 1948.

Brown, Richard. *Strain of Violence*. New York: Oxford University Press, 1975.

Browne, Junius H. *Four Years in Secession: Adventures within and Beyond the Union Lines*. Hartford: O.D. Case and Co., 1865.

Brownlow, W. G. *Sketches of the Rise, Progress, and Decline of Secession*. Philadelphia: Philadelphia Historical Society, 1866.

Bryan, Charles Faulkner. "The Civil War in East Tennessee, a Social, Political, and Economic Study." Ph.D. Thesis, University of Tennessee, Knoxville, 1978.

Bullough, Vern L. and Bonnie. *Cross Dressing, Sex, and Gender*. Philadelphia: University of Pennsylvania Press, 1993.

Burson, William. *Race for Liberty*. Wellsville, Ohio: W.G. Foster, 1867.

Butler, Lindley S., and Watson, Alan D. *The North Carolina Experience—An Interpretive and Documentary History*. Chapel Hill, North Carolina: University of North Carolina Press, 1984.

Callahan, North. *Smoky Mountain Country*. New York: Duell, Sloan & Pearce, 1952.

Campbell, James B. "East Tennessee During

the Federal Occupation, 1863–1865."
Knoxville, Tennessee Historical Society,
No. 19, 1947.

Campbell, John C. *The Southern Highlander
and His Homeland.* New York: Russell
Sage, 1921.

Carpenter, Clarence A. *The Walton War
and Other Tales of the Great Smoky
Mountains.* Lakemont, Georgia: Copple
House Books, 1979.

Castel, Albert, ed. "The Guerrilla War."
Special Issue of *Civil War Times Illustrated,* October 1974.

Catton, Bruce. *The Civil War.* New York:
American Heritage Publishing Company,
Inc., 1960.

Clark, Walter, ed. *Histories of the Several
Regiments and Battalions from North
Carolina in the Great War, 1861–1865,*
4 vols. Goldsboro, North Carolina: Published by the State of North Carolina,
1901.

Clayton, Ellen C. *Female Warriors: Memori-
als of Female Valour and Heroism from
the Mythological Ages to the Present
Era,* 2 vols. London: Tinsley Brothers,
1879.

Clinton, Catherine, and Silber, Nina, eds.
*Divided Houses: Gender and the Civil
War.* New York: Oxford University
Press, 1992.

Coles, Robert. *Migrants, Sharecroppers,
Mountaineers.* Boston: Little, Brown,
1971.

Commager, Henry Steele, ed. *The Official
Atlas of the Civil War.* New York:
Thomas Yoseloff, Inc., 1958.

Connor, Robert D.W. *North Carolina: Re-
building an Ancient Commonwealth,
1584–1925,* 4 vols. Chicago and New
York: The American Historical Society,
Inc., 1929.

Cooper, Lieutenant Edward A. *In and Out
of Rebel Prisons.* Oswego, New York:
Oliphant, 1888.

Corbitt, D. L., ed. *Pictures of the Civil War*

Period in North Carolina. Raleigh,
North Carolina: North Carolina Department of Archives and History, 1958.

Correspondence of Jonathan Worth, vol. 2.
Raleigh, North Carolina: Edwards &
Broughton Printing Co., 1909.

Cotton, William D. "Appalachian North
Carolina: A Political Study, 1860–1889."
Ph.D. Thesis, University of North Car-
olina, Chapel Hill, 1954.

Craddock, Charles Egbert. *In the Tennessee
Mountains.* Boston: Houghton, Mifflin,
and Company, 1885.

Craig, D. I. *A History of the Development
of the Presbyterian Church in North
Carolina.* Richmond, Va.: Whittet &
Shepperson, 1907.

Crow, Vernon H., ed. "The Justness of Our
Cause: The Civil War Diaries of William
W. Stringfields." Knoxville, Tennessee:
Publications of the East Tennessee His-
torical Society, Nos. 56–57, 1980–1981.

Crow, Vernon H. *Storm in the Mountains.*
Cherokee, North Carolina: Museum of
the Cherokee, 1982.

Crute Jr., Joseph H. *Units of the Confederate States Army.* Midlothian, Virginia:
Derwent Books, 1987.

Davis, William C., ed. *The Image of War,
1861–1865,* volume one, *Shadows of the
Storm.* Garden City, New York: Double-
day, 1981.

Dodge, David. "Domestic Economy in the
Confederacy." *Atlantic Monthly* 58 (August 1886): 229–42.

———. "The Cave-Dwellers of the Confederacy." *Atlantic Monthly* 68 (1891):
524–21.

Dornbusch, C.E. *Military Bibliography of
the Civil War,* four volumes. New York:
New York Public Library, 1961–1972.

Dowd, C. *Life of Zebulon B. Vance.* Charlotte, North Carolina: Charlotte Publishing, 1897.

Drake, James Madison. *Fast and Loose in
Dixie.* New York: Author's Publishing
Company, 1887.

Dugger, Shepherd M. *War Trails of the Blue Ridge*. Banner Elk, North Carolina: Privately Published, 1932.

———. *The Balsam Groves of Grandfather Mountain*. Banner Elk, North Carolina: Privately Published, 1930.

Dykeman, Wilma. *The French Broad*. New York: Rinehart & Company, 1955.

Eaton, C., ed. "Diary of an Officer in Sherman's Army Marching Through the Carolinas." The Journal of Southern History, IX (May 1943).

Eller, Ronald. "Land and Family: An Historical View of Preindustrial Appalachia." *Appalachian Journal* 6 (Winter 1979).

Ellis, Daniel. *Thrilling Adventures of Daniel Ellis, The Great Union Guide of East Tennessee for a Period of Nearly Four Years During the Great Southern Rebellion. Written by Himself*. New York: Harper, 1876.

Eisenschiml, Otto, and Newman, Ralph. *The America Iliad: The Epic Story of the Civil War as Narrated by Eyewitnesses and Contemporaries*. Indianapolis: The Bobbs-Merrill Co., 1947.

Ewing, Elizabeth. *Women in Uniform Through the Centuries*. London: B.T. Batsford, 1975.

Fischer, Noel C. *War at Every Door: Partisan Politics & Guerrilla Violence in East Tennessee, 1860–1869*. Chapel Hill and London: University of North Carolina Press.

Garrison, Webb. "Southern Women Helped Soldiers in Gray." *Atlanta Constitution*, November 26, 1989.

Gaston, A. P. *Partisan Campaigns of Lawrence M. Allen*. Raleigh, North Carolina: Edwards Publishing, 1894.

Gilham, William. *Manual of Instruction for the Volunteers and Militia*. Richmond, Virginia: West and Johnson, 1861.

Ginsburg, Elaine K. *Passing and the Fictions of Identity*. Durham, North Carolina: Duke University Press, 1996.

Green, Colleen Blaylock. Blaylock Military Records. Knoxville, Tennessee: Privately Published, 1997.

Hadley, J. V. *Seven Months a Prisoner*, New York: Scribners & Sons, 1898.

Hall, Richard C. *Patriots in Disguise: Women Warriors of the Civil War*. New York: Paragon House, 1993.

Hamilton, J. G. deR. "Secession in North Carolina." *North Carolina in the War Between the States*, edited by D. H. Hill. Raleigh, North Carolina: State of North Carolina, 1926.

Hamilton, Joseph G. "Heroes of America." *Publications of the Southern Historical Association* 11 (January 1907): 10–19. "The North Carolina Courts and the Confederacy." *North Carolina Historical Review* 4 (October 1927): 366–403.

Hannum, Alberta Pierson. *Look Back in Love*. New York: Vanguard Press, 1969.

Hayes, Johnson J. *The Land of Wilkes*. Wilkesboro, North Carolina: Wilkes County Historical Society, 1962.

Hickerson, Thomas F. *Echoes of Happy Valley*. Chapel Hill, North Carolina: Privately Printed, 1962.

Hill, Daniel Harvey. *A History of North Carolina in the War Between the States*, 2 vols. Raleigh: Edwards and Broughton, 1926.

Hobsbawm, J. S. *Bandits*. London: Weidenfeld & Nicolson, 1969.

Holden, W. W. *Memoirs of W. W. Holden*. Edited by William K. Boyd. Durham: The Seeman Printery, 1911.

Holmes, Jeanne. *Women in the Military*. Novato, California: Presidio Press, 1982.

Humes, Thomas William. *The Loyal Mountaineers of Tennessee*. Knoxville, Tennessee: Ogden Brothers, 1888.

Hunt, John, and McIlwain, Bill. "The Battling Belles." *American Mercury 78*, March 1954.

Hyde, Mrs. Charles R. "The Women of the Confederacy." *Confederate Veteran* 32 (January 1924): 23.

Inscoe, John C. "Mountain Masters: Slave-holding in Western North Carolina." *North Carolina Historical Review,* April 1984.

Johnson, Guion Griffis. *Ante-Bellum North Carolina: A Social History.* Chapel Hill: University of North Carolina Press, 1937.

Johnson, Robert Underwood, and Buel, Clarence Clough, eds. *Battles and Leaders of the Civil War.* Commemorative Edition in Four Volumes. New York: Thomas Yoseloff, Inc., 1955.

Johnston, Frontis W., ed. *The Papers of Zebulon Baird Vance.* Raleigh State Department of Archives and History, 1963.

Johnston, Joseph E. *Narrative of Military Operations, Directed, During the Late War Between the States by Joseph E. Johnston, General CSA.* New York: D. Appleton and Co., 1874.

Jones, Alexander H. *Knocking at the Door.* Washington, D.C.: McGill & Witherow, 1866.

Jones, Virgil Carrington. *Gray Ghosts and Rebel Raiders.* New York: Holt, 1956.

Jordan, Weymouth T., ed. *North Carolina Troops, 1861–1865,* 10 vols. Raleigh, North Carolina: North Carolina Department of Archives and History, 1981.

Kaufman, Janet E. "'Under the Petticoat Flag': Women Soldiers in the Confederate Army." *Southern Studies* 23, 1984.

Kephart, Horace. *Our Southern Highlander.* Knoxville, Tennessee: University of Tennessee Press (reprint of 1922 edition), 1976.

Kerr, W. C. *Report of the Geological Survey of North Carolina.* Raleigh, North Carolina: State Printing Office, 1875.

Kirk, Charles E., ed. *History of the Fifteenth Pennsylvania Cavalry.* Philadelphia: J. B. Lippincott, 1906.

Laffin, John. *Women in Battle.* New York: Abelard-Schuman, 1967.

Lammers, Pat, and Boyce, Amey. "A Female in the Ranks." *Civil War Times Illustrated* 22, January 1984, pp. 24–30.

Larson, C. Kay. "Bonny Yank and Ginny Reb." *Minerva Magazine: Quarterly Report on Women and the Military* 8 (spring 1990), pp. 33–48.

Lefler, Hugh T., and Newsome, Albert R., eds. *North Carolina: The History of a Southern State.* Chapel Hill, North Carolina: University of North Carolina Press, 1975.

Leonard, Elizabeth D. *All the Daring of the Soldier: Women of the Civil War Armies.* New York: W. W. Norton & Company, 1999.

Linderman, Gerald F. *Embattled Courage: The Experience of Combat in the American Civil War.* New York: Free Press, 1987.

Livermore, T. L. *Numbers and Losses in the Civil War in America, 1861–1865.* Boston: Little, Brown, 1900.

Lonn, Ella. *Desertion During the Civil War.* New York: Century Co., 1928. *Salt as a Factory in the Confederacy.* University, Ala.: University of Alabama Press, 1963.

———. *Desertion During the Civil War.* New York: Century Publishing, 1928.

Lowery, Lawrence T. *Northern Opinion of Approaching Secession.* Northhampton, Mass.: Department of History of Smith College, 1918.

Lowry, Thomas P. *The Story the Soldiers Wouldn't Tell: Sex in the Civil War.* Mechanicsburg, Pennsylvania: Stackpole Books, 1994.

Madden, David. "Unionist Resistance to Confederate Occupation: The Bridge Burners of East Tennessee." Knoxville, Tennessee: Publications of the East Tennessee Historical Society, Nos. 52–53, 1980–1981.

Massey, Mary Elizabeth. "Southern Refugee Life During the Civil War." *North Carolina Historical Review,* XX (January-April 1943).

————. *Ersatz in the Confederacy.* New York: Columbia University Press, 1953.

————. *Bonnet Brigades.* New York: Alfred A. Knopf, 1966.

Mast, Greg. "'Sam' Blaylock [sic], 26th North Carolina Troops." *Military Images Magazine,* 11 (July-August 1989), p. 10.

McDonald, Forrest, and McWhiney, Grady. "The Antebellum Southern Herdsman: A Reinterpretation." *Journal of Southern History* 41 (May 1975), pp. 147–166.

McGee, R. G. *A History of Tennessee.* New York: American Book Company, 1900.

McKinney, Gordon B. *Southern Mountain Republicans, 1865–1900: Politics and the Appalachian Community.* Chapel Hill, North Carolina: University of North Carolina Press, 1978.

McLeod, John Angus. *From These Stones: The First Hundred Years of Mars Hill College.* Mars Hill, North Carolina: College Press, 1955.

McPherson, Edward, comp. *The Political History of the United States of America, During the Great Rebellion from November 6, 1880 to July 4, 1864.* Washington Government Printing Office, 1865.

McPherson, James M. *Ordeal by Fire: The Civil War and Reconstruction.* New York: Alfred A. Knopf, 1982.

————. *Battle Cry of Freedom.* New York: Oxford University Press, 1988.

McWhiney, Grady, and Jamieson, Perry. *Attack and Die—Civil War Tactics and the Southern Heritage.* Birmingham, Alabama: University of Alabama Press, 1982.

Medford, Clark. *The Early History of Haywood County.* Waynesville, North Carolina: Privately Published, 1961.

————. *Mountain Times, Mountain People.* Waynesville, North Carolina: Privately Published, 1963.

Miles, Emma Bell. *The Spirit of the Mountains.* Knoxville, Tennessee: University of Tennessee Press (reprint of 1905 edition), 1975.

Mitchell, Joseph R. *Military Leaders of the Civil War.* New York: G. P. Putnam's Sons, 1972.

Mitchell, Memory. *Legal Aspects of Conscription and Exemption in North Carolina, 1861–1865.* Chapel Hill, North Carolina: University of North Carolina Press, 1965.

Moore, Albert B. *Conscription and Conflict in the Confederacy.* New York: Macmillan, 1934.

Moore, Frank. *Women of the War: Their Heroism and Self-Sacrifice.* Hartford, Connecticut: S. S. Scranton, 1866.

Moore, Frank, ed. *The Rebellion Record: A Diary of American Events, with Documents, Narratives, Illustrative Incidents, Etc.* 12 vols. New York: G. P. Putnam & D. Van Nostrand, 1863–68.

Morley, Margaret W. *Carolina Mountains.* Boone, North Carolina: Privately Published, Rowan House, 1913.

"A Mountain Wedding," (1900) Manuscripts Collection, William Eury Collection.

Newsome, A. R. "The A. S. Merrimon Journal, 1853–1854." *North Carolina Historical Review* 8 (July 1931).

Noble, Marcus C. S. *A History of the Public Schools of North Carolina.* Chapel Hill: The University of North Carolina Press, 1930.

Noppen, Ina W. van. "The Significance of Stoneman's Last Raid." *North Carolina Historical Review,* January-October 1961.

————. *Stoneman's Last Raid.* Raleigh, North Carolina: North Carolina State University Press, 1966.

Noppen, Ina W. van, and John J. *Western North Carolina Since the Civil War.* Boone, North Carolina: Appalachian Consortium Press, 1973.

Nulton, Karen Sue. "The Social Civil War."

Ph.D. Dissertation, Rutgers University, New Brunswick, New Jersey, 1992.

Official Records of the War of Rebellion: A Compilation of the Official Records of the Union and Confederate Armies, 128 volumes. Washington D.C.: Library of Congress, 1880–1901.

Olmsted, Frederick Law. *A Journey in the Back Country.* New York: Mason Brothers, 1863.

Paludan, Phillip Shaw. *Victims: A True Story of the Civil War.* Knoxville, Tennessee: The University of Tennessee Press, 1981.

Phifer, Edward W. *Burke—The History of a North Carolina County, 1777–1920.* Morganton, North Carolina, 1977.

Phisterer, F. *Statistical Record of the Armies of the United States.* New York: Harper & Son, 1883.

Pittard, Pen L. *Prologue—A History of Alexander County.* Taylorsville, North Carolina: Privately Published, 1958.

Polk, L. L. *North Carolina Hand-Book.* Raleigh, North Carolina: Rowan Printing, 1879.

Raper, Horace W. "William W. Holden and the Peace Movement in North Carolina." *North Carolina Historical Review* 31 (October 1954): 493–516.

Richardson, Albert D. *The Secret Service: The Field, the Dungeon, and the Escape.* Hartford, Connecticut: American Publishing, 1865.

Robertson, John. *Michigan in the War.* Lansing, Michigan: W. S. George, State Printers, 1882.

Salmonson, Jessica Amanda. *The Encyclopedia of Amazons: Women Warriors from Antiquity to the Modern Era.* New York: Anchor Books, 1991.

Samuels, Shirley, ed. *The Culture of Sentimentality in Nineteenth-Century America.* New York: Oxford University Press, 1992.

Schwartzweller, Harry; Brown, James S;, and Mangalam, J. J. *Mountain Families in Transition.* University Park, Pennsylvania: Penn State University Press, 1971.

Shapiro, Henry D. *Appalachia on Our Mind: The Southern Mountains and Mountaineers in the American Consciousness, 1870–1920.* Chapel Hill, North Carolina: University of North Carolina Press, 1978.

Sheppard, Muriel E. *Cabins in the Laurel.* Chapel Hill, North Carolina: University of North Carolina Press, 1935.

Sherman, William T. *Memoirs of General T. Sherman,* 2 vols. New York: D. Appleton and Co., 1875.

Shultz, Jane Ellen. "Women at the Front: Gender and Genre in Literature of the American Civil War." Ph.D. Dissertation, University of Michigan, Ann Arbor, 1988.

Sifakis, Stewart. *Compendium of the Confederate Armies: North Carolina.* New York: Facts on File, 1992.

Siler, Leon M. "My Lai Controversy Recalls 1863 Tragedy on the Shelton Laurel." *The State Magazine.*

Simkins, Francis Butler, and Patton, James Welch. *The Women of the Confederacy.* New York: Garrett & Massie, 1936.

Sitterson, Joseph Carlyle. *The Secession Movement in North Carolina.* Chapel Hill, North Carolina: University of North Carolina Press, 1999.

Smalling, Curtis, ed. *The Heritage of Watauga County, North Carolina,* Volume I. Winston-Salem, North Carolina: The Southern Appalachian Historical Association, Hunter Publishing Company, 1984.

Smalling, Curtis, ed. *The Heritage of Watauga County, North Carolina,* Volume II. Winston-Salem, North Carolina: The Southern Appalachian Historical Association, Hunter Publishing Company, 1987.

Spencer, Cornelia Phillips. *The Last Ninety*

Days of the War in North Carolina. New York: Watchman Publishing Company, 1866.

Tatum, Georgia L. *Disloyalty in the Confederacy.* Chapel Hill, North Carolina: University of North Carolina Press, 1934.

"They Also Served." *Civil War Times Illustrated* 17 (August 1978), p. 41.

Thomas, Emory M. *The Confederacy as a Revolutionary Experience.* Englewood Cliffs, N.J.: Prentice Hall, Inc., 1971.

Trelease, Allen. "Who Were the Scalawags?" *Journal of Southern History* 29 (1963), pp. 445–468.

Trowbridge, Luther S. *A Brief History of the Tenth Michigan Cavalry.* Detroit: Friesman Brothers, 1905.

Tucker, Glenn. *Front Rank.* Raleigh, North Carolina: North Carolina Confederate Centennial Commission, 1962.

Underwood, George C. *History of the Twenty-Sixth Regiment of North Carolina Troops in the Great War, 1861–1865.* Wendell, North Carolina: Broadfoot Press, 1978.

Underwood, J. L. *The Women of the Confederacy.* New York: Neale Publishing, 1906.

Vandiver, Frank E. *Their Tattered Flags.* New York: Harper & Row, 1970.

Warner, E. J. *Generals in Gray.* Baton Rouge, Louisiana: Louisiana State University Press, 1959.

"A Week in the Great Smoky Mountains" (by "R"). *Southern Literary Messenger,* August 1860, pp. 119–130.

Weller, Jack E. *Yesterday's People: Life in Contemporary Appalachia.* Lexington, Kentucky: University of Kentucky Press, 1965.

Wellman, Manley Wade. *The Kingdom of Madison.* Chapel Hill, North Carolina: University of North Carolina Press, 1973.

Wharton, H.M., ed. *War Songs and Poems of the Southern Confederacy.* Philadelphia: J. B. Lippincott, 1904.

Wheeler, John H. *Historical Sketches of North Carolina.* Raleigh, North Carolina: Privately Published, 1851.

Wheelwright, Julie. *Amazons and Military Maids: Women Who Dressed as Men in the Pursuit of Life, Liberty, and Happiness.* London: Pandora Press, 1989.

Whitener, Daniel J. *History of Watauga County: Echoes of the Blue Ridge.* Boone, North Carolina: Watauga Centennial Commission, 1949.

Wiley, Bell Irvin. *Confederate Women.* Westport, Connecticut: Greenwood Press, 1975.

————. *The Life of Billy York: The Common Soldier of the Union.* Baton Rouge, Louisiana: Louisiana State University Press (reprint of 1952 edition), 1971.

————. *The Life of Johnny Reb: The Common Soldier of the Confederacy.* Baton Rouge, Louisiana: Louisiana State University Press (reprint of 1943 and 1970 editions), 1978.

Wilhelm Jr., Gene. "Appalachian Isolation: Fact or Fiction? *An Appalachian Symposium: Essays Written in Honor of Cratis D. Williams.* Boone, North Carolina: Applachian State University Press, 1977.

Wilkeson, Frank. *Recollections of a Private Soldier.* New York: G. P. Putnam and Sons, 1887.

Williams, Cratis D. "The Southern Mountaineer in Fact and Fiction." *Applachian Journal* 3 (1975).

Williams, Dewey E. *Burke County's Camp Vance.* Morganton, North Carolina: Privately Published, 1976.

Women's Edition of the Asheville Citizen. Asheville, North Carolina: Published by the Women of Asheville, November 1895.

Wooster, Ralph. *Politicians, Planters, and Plain Folk: Courthouse and State House in the Upper South, 1850–1860.* Knoxville: University of Tennessee Press, 1975.

Yates, R. E. *The Confederacy and Zeb Vance* (W.S. Hoole, ed.). Tuscaloosa, Alabama: Confederate Centennial Studies, N. 8, 19.

Yates, Richard E. *The Confederacy and Zeb Vance*. Tuscaloosa: University of Alabama Press, 1958.

———. "Governor Vance and the End of the War in North Carolina." *North Carolina Historical Review* 18 (October 1941): 315–38.

———. "Governor Vance and the Peace Movement." *North Carolina Historical Review* 17 (January and April 1940): 1–25, 89–113.

Yetman, Norman, R., ed. *Life Under the Peculiar Institution*. New York: Holt, Rinehart, and Winston.

Index

920 B10
BLA

21581

DATE DUE			
7-20-00			
9-12-00			
9-29-00			

NEWFOUNDLAND AREA PUBLIC LIBRARY
Newfoundland, Penna. 18445

DISCARDED

GAYLORD M2